Allen Brown's

ENGLISH CASTLES

Allen Brown's

ENGLISH CASTLES

R. Allen Brown

THE BOYDELL PRESS

First published 1954
Reprinted in paperback 1962

Revised edition 1977
B. T. Batsford Ltd

New edition 2004
The Boydell Press, Woodbridge

ISBN 1 84383 069 8

The Boydell Press is an imprint of Boydell & Brewer Ltd
PO Box 9, Woodbridge, Suffolk IP12 3DF, UK
and of Boydell & Brewer Inc.
668 Mt. Hope Avenue, Rochester, NY 14620, USA
website: www.boydellandbrewer.com

A CiP catalogue record for this book is available
from the British Library

Library of Congress Cataloging-in-Publication Data applied for

This publication is printed on acid-free paper

Typeset in Great Britain by
Data Standards Ltd, Frome, Somerset

Printed and bound in Great Britain by
Antony Rowe Ltd., Chippenham, Wiltshire

Contents

vi   List of Illustrations

viii   Acknowledgements

x   Introduction

xii   Preface to the 1976 edn

Chapter 1
1   Continental Origins

Chapter 2
21   The Norman Conquest of England

Chapter 3
34   The Norman and Angevin Period, 1066–1215

Chapter 4
64   Apogee

Chapter 5
89   Decline

Chapter 6
106 Castle-building

Chapter 7
123 The Castle in War

Chapter 8
150 The Castle in Peace

Chapter 9
161 The Castle in General

172 Notes

183 Guide to Further Reading

186 Index

List of Illustrations

Plates

Between pages 105 and 106

1 Dover
2 Langeais
3 Doué-la-Fontaine
4 Rennes, from the Bayeux Tapestry
5 Dinan, from the Bayeux Tapestry
6 Bayeux, from the Bayeux Tapestry
7 Hastings, from the Bayeux Tapestry
8 Farnham
9 Pleshey
10 Castle Acre
11 Ludlow
12 Framlingham
13 Colchester
14 Rochester
15 Castle Rising
16 Conisborough
17 Orford
18 Berkhamstead
19 Launceston
20 Château-Gaillard
21 Caernarvon
22 Conway
23 Harlech
24 Beaumaris
25 Kidwelly
26 Caerphilly
27 The Tower of London
28 Chepstow
29 Stokesay
30 Acton Burnell
31 Raglan
32 Nunney
33 Caister-by-Yarmouth
34 Tattershall
35 Bodiam
36 Windsor
37 Warwick

38 Carew
39 Rochester across the Medway
40 The earliest known illustration of a cannon, 1326

Line Drawings

I	Map of castles in England and Wales mentioned in text	ix
II	Richard's Castle, ground plan	26
III	Castle Tower, Penmaen, ground plan	28
IV	Hen Domen, Montgomery, ground plan	37
V	Pleshey, ground plan	39
VI	Lewes, ground plan	40
VII	Rochester, the keep, floor plans	48
VIII	Dover, plan of keep at 2nd-floor level	51
IX	Orford, the keep, floor plans	56
X	Comparative plans of twelfth-century keeps, a: Conisborough and Tickhill	57
XI	Comparative plans of twelfth-century keeps, b: Odiham and Chisham	58
XII	Châteaux-Gaillard, ground plan	63
XIII	Caernarvon, ground plan	66
XIV	Conway, ground plan	67
XV	Harlech, ground plan	73
XVI	Beaumaris, ground plan	74
XVII	Rhuddlan, ground plan	75
XVIII	Flint, ground plan	77
XIX	Kidwelly, ground plan	79
XX	Caerphilly, ground plan	80
XXI	The Tower of London, ground plan	82
XXII	Corfe, ground plan	84
XXIII	Chepstow, ground plan	85
XXIV	Queenborough, sixteenth-century ground plan	93
XXV	Bolton-in-Wensleydale, floor plans showing accommodation	100
XXVI	Bodiam, floor plans showing accommodation	101
XXVII	Map showing the impressment of labour for the king's works in Wales, 1282–83	116
XXVIII	Trebuchet, loaded	127
XXIX	Trebuchet, shooting	128
XXX	Crenellation	133
XXXI	Hoarding	134
XXXII	Machicolation	137

Acknowledgements

Mrs Vivien Brown and the Publishers are grateful to the following for their permission to reproduce the illustrations in this book:

Aerofilms Ltd, for plates 8, 27, 36; the late Professor Michel de Bouard, for plate 3; English Heritage (Department of the Environment Collection), for plate 1; Dr Robert Liddiard, for plates 10, 17, 18, 21, 24, 26, 35, 38, 39; Dr Tim Pestell, for plate 25.

Plates 4, 5, 6 and 7, detail of the Bayeux Tapestry (11th century), are reproduced by special permission of the City of Bayeux.

Plate 40 (Christ Church, Oxford, MS 92, f. 70v) is reproduced by kind permission of the Governing Body of Christ Church, Oxford.

Mrs Vivien Brown would like to express her thanks to Dr Richard Barber and the editorial staff of the publishers, and to Jonathan Coad and Robert Liddiard, for all their contributions towards the re-issue of this book.

Map of castles in England and Wales mentioned in the text

Allen Brown's English Castles

English Castles was first published in 1954 and rapidly established itself as the classic introduction to the subject. Firmly based on documentary and archaeological sources, as well as extensive field work by the author, *English Castles* surveyed the whole subject of the rise, heyday and decline of medieval castles in England and, despite its title, Wales with a breadth and lucidity that continue to command respect. When Allen Brown first wrote the book, there were few others working in the field. Much published work on castle history, despite earlier authors such as Allen's favourite Mrs E.S. Armitage, tended to owe more to sometimes over-romanticised myth and legend than to hard historic facts and field observation. There were of course exceptions to this general rule, such as the famous Ministry of Works 'blue guides' with their measured prose and carefully dated plans. These pioneered the scholarly, academic approach to the history, architecture and description of individual monuments in the care of the State. However, it has to be said that meticulous scholarship did not always equate with readability and many of the blue guides were early casualties of a later, less learned and more populist regime not so interested in rich text and dated plans. Allen's book introduced the subject to a public which wanted the wider picture and whose appetite had probably been whetted by visits to individual castles. The popularity of *English Castles* was such that a revised paperback edition followed in 1962 – I still possess my copy bought as an undergraduate for five shillings. In 1976, a new and quite extensively revised edition was published. It says much for Allen's original scholarship and research that the core of the book was still substantially his work of twenty years before. Nevertheless, in the intervening years there had been a remarkable growth in castle studies, as Allen acknowledged in his Preface to the new edition. He rightly drew attention to the publication of the medieval volumes of the *History of the King's Works*, but with characteristic modesty omitted to mention that he was one of the three authors of this seminal work. He also highlit new research, sponsored by the Royal Archaeological Institute, on the origins of castles. All this new information, which in many cases amplified and confirmed much of Allen's original text, was woven seamlessly into the new edition.

It might well be asked if a straight reprint of *English Castles* is justifiable now, nearly 50 years after its first publication and over 25 years after its last revision. Since 1976, there have been a great number of popular books on castles and the momentum of castle studies has greatly increased. Nearly all the authors of the popular general histories have tended to follow the path largely pioneered by *English Castles*, although some have included artillery defences as well. However, in most cases the authors have been writing without the deep knowledge and understanding of original documentary sources that enabled Allen to write with such authority and conviction. At the same time, in-depth archaeological and documentary investigation of individual sites, coupled with careful analysis of surviving fabric and the application of modern recording techniques, have transformed our knowledge of particular castles and their architectural development. For the most part, these investigations have enabled us to put flesh on bare bones, to amplify our knowledge and increase our insight. In a very few cases, archaeological excavations – as at Castle Acre – and detailed survey of surviving fabric – as at the White Tower and at Dover keep – are leading to reappraisals of generally held tenets on the early development of castles on the one hand and the architectural development of keeps on the other. Elsewhere, authors have looked at particular castle types, such as those entirely constructed of timber, and at the rise and subsequent decline of the medieval castle. Their social, political and economic aspects have also been the subject of research and publication, while spirited debate seeks to analyse the uses of their internal spaces in terms of the norms of everyday life rather than the rare periods when a castle was at war. In short, castle studies over the last quarter of a century have displayed a healthy and vibrant activity, not least in seeking to link British castle studies with research in the northern part of mainland Europe.

Yet despite all this continuing and welcome research activity, there is still a need for an authorititive and readable general introduction to the subject, a framework which clearly sets out the origins, architectural development, use and decline of the medieval castle. Allen's book does just this and has not been bettered since its original publication. For anyone new to the subject, as well as those needing a reference work, *English Castles* remains an essential item for their bookshelves.

Allen Brown would certainly have wished to have made some alterations to the text to take account of developments since the last edition. However, these would have been in the nature of minor revisions, a slight shift of emphasis here, a new example there, for the robustness of his original work means that it has stood the test of time and remains highly relevant. Those of us who had the pleasure of knowing Allen, and working alongside him on excavations, knew a man who was passionately interested in the whole subject of medieval castles and their place in society. Equally at home in a record office, wielding a shovel on site, or discussing the day's discoveries over a convivial pint or two in some local hostelry, he brought tremendous enthusiasm to everything he did. In his inaugural lecture as Professor of History at King's College, London, he remarked that teaching was a form of loving – his enthusiasm to share his knowledge with others, and to partake in turn of their discoveries, was palpable and endearing. It is this enthusiasm, so evident in the text, coupled with his rigorous academic and literary standards, that makes *English Castles* the book it is.

Jonathan Coad
Salehurst

Preface

Technically this is the third edition of a book first published in 1954 and revised for a paperback edition (which cost five shillings) in 1962. When it was originally written over thirty years ago, I and all the world were young, and there were few in the field of castle studies. Since then there has been a considerable and continuing revival of academic interest in the subject, not least in this country, in France and in Germany. As instances, which could be multiplied, the *History of the King's Works* has been written for the medieval centuries (1963); a series of bi-annual European conferences on *Castellologie*, of which the eighth will be held this summer, has been established (under the name of 'Château-Gaillard' because the first and most memorable of the conferences was held there, at Les Andelys, in 1962); and a research project into the origin of the castle has been launched and largely completed by the Royal Archaeological Institute. In view of all this activity it seemed necessary substantially to rewrite a large part of my book, especially the earlier chapters, to incorporate recent work: at least the first half of it is therefore new, as also are all the notes, which have now become very necessary, and many of the illustrations. Nevertheless, it is satisfying to report that the message even of the earlier chapters is what it was before, albeit presented with much more scholarly detail and with much more reference to France, whence came our castles and our feudalism. These, indeed, are the basic facts which stand, namely that castles are feudal, and in this country are, with feudalism itself, a Norman and French innovation, part and parcel of the Norman Conquest. As for the type of these early castles on both sides of the Channel, while it is nowadays emphasized that not all of them had mottes, and while it ought to be emphasized that not all of them were of earthwork and timber, it remains a certainty that the 'motte-and-bailey' castle was already well established in France and Normandy before 1066 and came to England thence.

The fact that the later chapters of this book have been much less substantially re-written does not, of course, imply that they could not be improved, but, rather, reflects the nature of the new work which is concentrated upon the early period, upon the origin of the castle in particular, and upon the origin of the motte most particularly of all. It is also in this country largely confined to archaeologists, which is a point to note when, in an age of academic overspecialization, archaeologists are not usually historians (and vice versa), and neither of them are usually architectural historians who, in any case, in the medieval period generally confine themselves to churches. What is especially needed now, it may be urged, is sustained attention to the later castle and, no less, to all those many aspects of the castle's history other than the archaeological and architectural. It should be obvious that artifacts including architecture are dry bones indeed without the living flesh of the society which created them. Meanwhile, since we do not yet live in a perfect world, this book, as before and with all its remaining faults, at least tries to be in outline a comprehensive history of the castles of England and Wales – though, again as before, not of Scotland, which remains a separate story.

In the prefaces of the first two editions of this book I thanked those who then helped me. They, I trust, will not forget, as I will not forget them. Those who have generously helped me this time are very many, and include a growing group of friends from the Ancient Monuments branch of what is now the Department of the Environment, past and present, namely Dr A.J. Taylor and Dr M.W. Thompson, together with Messrs. Gilyard Beer, Jonathan Coad, Peter Curnow (especially), Brian Davison, Patrick Faulkner, Beric Morley, and the present Chief Inspector, Andrew Saunders. It gives me especial pleasure also to express my thanks to Professor Michel de Bouard of the University of Caen for much help and kindness touching Doué-la-Fontaine and many other matters. I am likewise much obliged to Messrs Philip Barker (Hen Domen), Philip Mayes (Sandal) and Derek Renn (Skipton *et al.*), to my former research pupil Dr Charles Coulson, and to my present research pupil Mr Peter Lewis who thought nothing of leaping on a train to check a far-flung keep. I owe a particular debt of gratitude to another pupil, Miss Catriona Gordon, who drew the map.★ Many of the castles mentioned in the text, including many in France, for me at any rate are steeped in the memory of enthusiastic inspection and photography with my son and daughter, Giles and Philippa, and it seems appropriate gratefully to mention in this connection two friends, Professor Christopher Crowder and Mr David Thompson, whose respective houses in France made these delectable excursions possible, as well as other friends in Caen. Lastly, as something more than a literary convention, I am deeply indebted to my poor wife Vivien, who undertook much of the labour of the index, all of the labour of the typing, and a great deal else besides. As a postscript, my dog, who is very fond of castles especially when ruined, would like a mention. It only remains to add that I am very grateful to the publishers for the opportunity to issue and re-issue a book on a life-long interest, and to Celia Hollis for much help in seeing it through the press this time.

Thelnetham, Suffolk.   R.A.B.
    June 1976.

★ For the 2004 edition, the map has been redrawn by Philip Judge from Catriona Gordon's original.

Chapter 1

Continental Origins

Any book about castles should begin by saying what they are, for certainly the name 'castle' has been much abused by loose usage in the past and, indeed, still is. In France (significantly, as we shall see) the word *château* has now long been applied to any large country house of social distinction with or without fortification, and in this country, while all kinds of ancient fortifications are sometimes and wrongly called 'castles' (e.g. the 'British' Maiden's Castle in Dorset or the Roman Burgh Castle in Suffolk), the true nature of the castle proper, and its origins as a French and, more specifically, Norman importation, were scarcely established before the beginning of the present century, chiefly by Mrs E.S. Armitage in that most fundamental and seminal of books, *Early Norman Castles of the British Isles* (1912). All societies, it would seem, in all periods including our own, have fortifications and defences of some kind; but also all military organization, and all architecture, reflects the type of society which needs it and produces it. What is it, then, about the castle which is different, which sets it apart from other forms of fortification, and which ties it down to that period of Western society which we (rather absurdly) call the Middle Ages?

Much of the answer lies in correct definition, and the castle is basically a fortified residence, a residential fortress. It is this duality – residence and fortress, domestic and military – which goes far to distinguish the castle from other known types of fortification in the West. Thus, for example, when the great house ceases to be fortified, and the magnates of the land no longer build fortified residences, as happens in England and in France, let us say, from the sixteenth century onwards, then there the history of the castle as a viable institution is at an end, and though many will continue to be occupied and many more will survive at least as ruins until our own day, the great country house, unfortified, takes the place of the castle in succeeding centuries as the characteristic residence of the landed aristocracy and the ruling class. While it is significant that on the other side of the Channel such houses are still called *châteaux* as emphasizing the residential rôle of the medieval castle, on this side of the Channel the coastal forts built by Tudor monarchs in the sixteenth century – Deal, Walmer, Camber and the rest – are not castles (though they are often called so) because they are exclusively military and not residential. That duality, at one and the same time both residence and fortress, which is basic to the castle, has been lost.

It is to be noted next that we are dealing exclusively with the residences of the great, and we may take the next step and say that the castle is the fortified residence of a lord, which is to say any lord, not necessarily the king or prince. The point is an important one, for by means of it we may begin to see how the castle is in the history of the West, not so much 'medieval' (a rather meaningless word) as feudal (which is more meaningful), a characteristic institution of that society which we call feudal, and which was dominated by a military and militant aristocracy, at the apex of which the king sat in majesty but not unique in his lordship. But meanwhile the castle as the fortified residence of a lord who may, or may not, be the king, brings us to its private as opposed to its public or communal nature. Modern fortresses, in terms of English history from Tudor coastal forts onwards to Pitt's Martello towers and beyond to today, are different from castles in being exclusively military, as we have seen: they are also different in pertaining exclusively to the king or prince, or, in modern parlance, they belong to the state, they are a manifestation of public authority. Older forms of fortification than the castle, that is to say the fortresses of earlier and different types of society, evidently share the same difference. In the Roman Empire fortification was an affair of the state, the attribute and the monopoly of sovereignty and public authority. While the eastern half of the Roman Empire, based upon Constantinople, survived in the form of the medieval Byzantine Empire (though the conquest of Constantinople by western crusaders in 1204 would change things for a time, as western crusaders also took the castle to their crusading states in Outremer), the same attitude and practice, at once both classical and modern, were evidently inherited by the Frankish Carolingian emperors, Charlemagne and his successors, in the West, as they were also by Henry the Fowler (919–30) and his successors in the emergent Germany, and by Alfred and his successors in England.

Further, the fortifications raised and maintained by these emperors and kings, these sovereigns in the exercise of public authority, were generally communal, the defences of communities, whether we think of Roman camps (*castra*) or cities (though Roman fortifications show much variety in size), or of the *burghs* of Alfred and Henry the Fowler alike. Ethelfleda, the daughter of King Alfred, we are told, built the burgh of Worcester 'to shelter all the folk',[1] and Charles the Bald in Frankia fortified Le Mans and Tours 'as a defence for the people against the Norsemen',[2] while, on the other hand, the residences, the palaces, in which the Carolingian kings and emperors themselves lived are not known to have been fortified any more than are the residences of Old English kings in this country. The same communal purpose is again evident in the fortifications of other early societies of which we know less, not least Viking camps (including the striking geometrical fortresses like Trelleborg) or, from a remoter period, Iron Age fortresses like the original Dover or Old Sarum. Such places were or could become fortified towns or cities, and to say that is at once to point the contrast with the usually much smaller castle – the private fortified residence of a lord as opposed to a fortified community – and the contrast and the difference can still often enough be seen without need of further argument or analysis where the two things survive together, as witness Portchester, Old Sarum, or Carcassonne.

The castle, then, is the fortified residence of a lord, and as such differs from other known forms of fortification in the history of the West both earlier and later, by its duality as both residence and fortress and by its private as opposed to public or communal nature. Here we reach the centre of any definition and analysis. Of course there will be untidiness round the edges of this special category of fortification, and scholarly qualifications to be made, but we must focus on the essence of the thing if we would understand it and the society which produced it. Thus the castle will generally be smaller than the communal fortified town or city, but there can be a kind of physical overlap between the two categories of fortification in that, while some towns and cities in the earlier Middle Ages especially (e.g. in England Old Sarum or Portchester) were certainly very small by modern standards, some castles are very large. It may be suggested that exceptionally large castles have so developed from smaller beginnings, and having been first planted within some larger, old and communal fortification (e.g. Dover in England (**1**) or Chinon in France), or upon some strong natural feature (e.g. Chepstow – **28**), have subsequently been compelled by military logic to take over the whole position. Again, because the castle is a fortified residence and yet at no time during the Middle Ages were there not lordly residences which were unfortified or, it may be, not seriously fortified but lightly defended, the distinction between the castle and the great house could be blurred in particular instances. There was probably always the hybrid or half-way category which we call 'fortified manors' and to which Domesday Book refers as *domus defensabiles*.[3] It was the degree of fortification which made one's house a castle, and therefore we had better add some such word as 'strongly' to our definition of the castle as a 'fortified residence'. It is clear that on the borderline it could be as difficult for contemporary bureaucrats (to whom it was important because of the issue of the control of fortification) as it is for modern historians to decide what was a castle and what was not. There is evidence to show that in the eleventh century the criteria included the depth of ditches and the height of banks and ramparts together with the design of the walls or stockades which further strengthened them.[4] Later, in England, the king's officials evidently settled for the arbitrary criterion of crenellation, *i.e.* battlements.

It seems likely, too, that at all periods particular significance was attached to the *donjon*, where one existed, as the particular sign and symbol of lordship. This word, which in the English language, as *dungeon*, has been debased to mean a deep, dark and dismal cell or prison,[5] still retains much of its original meaning in French, and is used by both French and English-speaking scholars as more or less a synonym for the 'great tower' or 'tower keep'[6] which is the dominant feature of so many castles. While the word was certainly applied by contemporaries to the tower keep, it might also be applied to the motte of a certain type of early castle,[7] or to the central core of a later one,[8] or, we may suppose, to the so-called 'shell keep',[9] and thus evidently denotes something of which the tower keep is only one form. Architecturally, this will be the *pièce maîtresse* of the whole building, but in conception, one may suggest, it is at one and the same time both the castle's ultimate military strong-point and principal residence, *i.e.* of the lord himself. It is very significant that the word 'donjon', like 'dominion', is derived from the Latin *dominus*, lord[10] – which etymological fact also stresses again the essentially feudal nature of the castle, as does the fact that in Spanish the great tower or tower keep is the *turre del homenaje*, the tower of homage.[11]

Finally, one must also qualify the private, as opposed to public or communal, nature of the castle as a fortress until the distinction comes into focus in contemporary terms. First, it is probably correct to see an overall pattern in the West of the right of fortification, beginning in the Roman period as a state monopoly, then descending through the successor kings and princes lower and lower down the hierarchy of subsequently developing feudal lordship, lastly the process reversed, and the wheel coming almost full circle, with the kings and princes of the emergent national states of modern times, notably in France and England, slowly and probably unconsciously gathering up again into their hands the ancient monopoly. More work, as they say, needs to be done upon these things which are certainly no less important than archaeological and architectural studies. Meanwhile, if this pattern is valid, it is also to be realized that in the right of fortification exercised by feudal lords at any level there is a strong element of the delegation – some would say usurpation – of ancient public authority, and also that, though the castle was the fortified residence of its lord, it could be and was regarded as standing for the defence as well as the control of its neighbourhood. Also it is to be emphasized that feudal lords from kings and princes downwards commonly exercised a striking control over the castles of their only less lordly vassals, not least through what has been called 'rendability' or the right of repossession at will, such control obviously limiting the 'private' nature of the stronghold.[12] A castle was held by a vassal of his lord in a way far more circumscribed than land and even less like free-hold: there never was that kind of castellated free-for-all still implied in some text-books, any more than there was a normal state of something called 'feudal anarchy', and the bold, bad baron was as rare in reality as he is still all too common in the media and even in places where they teach. Secondly, there is something of a numerical qualification to be made of the proper distinction between the castle as the private fortified residence of a lord and the communal fortifications of earlier and contemporary periods, in that while there is always likely to be an obvious disparity between the numbers of the community occupying a fortified town or city, or a Roman or Viking camp or an Iron Age fortress, and the numbers of a lord's household within his castle, the latter could nevertheless be upon occasion very large indeed. It requires a considerable effort of the imagination to break out of the confines of our modern domestic standards, even those now of the greatest among us, to envisage the *dolce vita* of the past, and the retinue of a great lord as he moved, it may be, from one castle to the next, with a household not just large but probably multiple, comprising perhaps his own household and that of his lady and that of his guest(s), to be met upon arrival, as like as not, by the household of his resident constable.

The existence of fortified residences and therefore castles in other and earlier societies in the West than feudal society is sometimes argued, not least today when the problem of the origin of the castle is very much a centre of attention, and notably in the case of the *raths* of Ireland and the *brochs* of Scotland. The different and special case of pre-Conquest England will be dealt with in some detail in the next chapter of this book, but meanwhile it can only be said of Irish raths, which evidently date anywhere from Roman times onwards, and of Scottish brochs, which may belong more precisely to the first century A.D., that the evidence, almost exclusively archaeological, will not sustain the thesis, and that the thesis is unlikely. The brochs,[13] which are stone-built towers, may well be the refuge of communities from Roman slave traders. The raths,[14] which are earthwork enclosures, are either likely to represent, in the larger instances, communal settlements enclosed or even defended, or in the more numerous smaller instances, the enclosed residences of kings and chieftains, and as such to fall into that large but indeterminate category of the enclosed homesteads of greater and also lesser men − *cf* the Carolingian manse, the burgh of an Old English thegn,[15] some of the small circular enclosures of eleventh-century Normandy recently investigated,[16] or the innumerable 'homestead moats' of England (especially in East Anglia and Yorkshire) probably dating from the twelfth and thirteenth centuries.[17] The element of enclosure here is as much as anything a matter of demarcation and agricultural necessity, and for the rest motivated more by normal domestic security in uncertain times than by military aggression or lordly pretension. For Ireland as for Scotland, castles as the seriously fortified residences of military lordship appear with feudalism itself only as part and parcel of the Norman penetration from England in the eleventh and twelfth centuries, and for Ireland we have the word of Geraldus Cambrensis, writing, as a contemporary of the Norman conquest and settlement in the later twelfth century, that the native Irish did not have castles, but for their strongholds made use instead of woods and bogs − *'Hibernicus enim populus castella non curat: silvis namque pro castris, paludibus utitur pro fossatis'.*[18] And certainly the tribal or clannish society of early medieval Ireland, or Scotland or Wales (which last is also said to have had raths) was radically different from that feudal society of France and the Rhineland which produced the castle as its most characteristic architectural manifestation.

While there is no divine law which states that the fortified residence can exist in no other period or type of society, there is no doubt, as a matter of sheer historical fact, that the castle as we know it is the product of feudalism, the symbol and much of the substance of feudal lordship, finding its origins, however obscure, in the ninth, and more certainly in the tenth century with the origins and establishment of feudal society itself, thereafter spreading across feudal Europe (and beyond with the crusaders) with the migration of feudalism and as a sign thereof, and declining as a viable institution in any given country when that country's society ceases in any meaningful sense to be feudal. What then is this feudalism, and what do we mean by feudal? Or rather, what should we mean, since 'feudal' is a word even more abused by loose usage and ignorance than 'castle' itself?

Feudal society, it has been said, is society organized for war: which indeed it was, but yet is not unique in so being (England in 1941?). It was certainly also a society dominated by a secular military aristocracy, and that of a special, i.e. 'feudal', kind.[19] It is difficult not to accept the military theory of the origins of feudalism wherein the crucial and determining factor in what follows was the increasing dependence from the mid-eighth century of the Franks in Gaul, who had hitherto, like the other Germanic races in the West, fought principally on foot, upon mounted warriors in war. To fight upon horseback is specialized in a way that to fight on foot is not, requiring full-time training from an early age ('You can make a horseman of a lad at puberty, after that never' – thus an early Carolingian proverb), and after that continual practice and devotion to arms. It is, in short, professional. Also it is expensive, requiring specially bred and trained horses, and increasingly elaborate gear – not least the hauberk or long coat of mail which comes to mark off the knight from his inferiors. We are watching, in fact, the evolution of the knight as a specialist mounted warrior, and the evolution of knighthood as an increasingly exclusive class. For the new military élite became inevitably a social élite also, and their social status was confirmed and strengthened when they received grants of land for their costly maintenance, as was again inevitable in an age when land was the principal form of wealth. Hence we begin to see the emergence of a new landed aristocracy, as we also see the appearance of the 'benefice' or 'fief' (the latter word in Latin is *feudum*, and from it our word 'feudal' was derived in the seventeenth century), that parcel of land which the knight-vassal holds of his lord in return for the expensive, mounted, military knight-service which he owes. To complete the emergent pattern and the sociological revolution, for it was scarcely less, we have to add the huge event of the collapse of the Carolingian state and of Carolingian society which took place in the kingdom of the West Franks (the future France and the Rhineland) in the ninth and tenth centuries, for reasons which include most prominently the incursions of the Vikings especially, but also of the Magyars and the Muslims, upon Western Europe ('From the fury of the Norsemen, good Lord deliver us!'). With the disintegration of the state and the withering away of an increasingly ineffective central authority, society reformed itself painfully at the grass-roots, on the basis of local lordship. New men came to prominence, the war-lords, we may say, took over, carving out new lordships from the fragments – often enough former administrative divisions – of the ancient Frankish kingdom. 'War made them conspicuous, grants of land established their position, marriage consolidated it, and the acquisition of ancient titles of honour cloaked their usurpations'.[20]

Here, then, are the origins of the feudal principalities into which the medieval kingdom of France was to be divided, and here are the origins of the new ruling families, the feudal princes, their power derived in part from ancient public authority and royal office delegated or usurped – it is well known that the count, the former Carolingian local official, becomes now a local potentate – and still more in practice from the rights of new feudal lordship, not least the right to call upon the military service of their knights to enforce their will. Their power depended also, as we shall see, in much upon their castles. Meanwhile in a world in which the apparatus of the state, not least the paid official and the professional administrator, has very nearly vanished, the bonds of society, the sinews of the emergent principality, become increasingly the feudal bonds which bind lord and vassal together, formalized in the solemn ceremony of feudal commendation whereby one man becomes the vassal of another (and vassalage is an honourable estate). This ceremony comprised an oath of fealty, an act of homage and (if one was lucky and favoured) investiture with the fief which the vassal held of his lord as his tenant, and the relationship thus established involved above all maintenance and protection of the vassal by the lord, and service, especially military service, knight-service, by the vassal to the lord. Nor were these bonds, as is well known, confined only to the level of the prince and his vassals (in text-book terminology, tenants-in-chief) but spread upwards and downwards in the nexus of the feudal hierarchy. The prince, count or duke, was himself the vassal of the king – for kingship, which is older than feudalism, waned at first but never vanished, and came to profit mightily from its own feudal potential, since the king was now the suzerain, the lord of lords – while the great vassals of the prince had vassals of their own, and those yet others. We must not however, push the feudal hierarchy too far down the social scale. Knights are the essence of feudalism, vassals with very few exceptions must be knights, and knights are exclusive. Feudalism is thus, strictly interpreted, an upper-class affair. We have been dealing with the emergence and establishment of a new upper class, a new ruling class, for the most part a landed aristocracy, whose lowest echelons, the landless knights serving in the household of their lord, were yet members of a class apart. The bonds, increasingly servile, which bound the peasant to his lord upon the fief came to be of a different and a lower kind with nothing that was honourable about them, reflecting amongst other things the basic fact that with the coming of the mounted warrior to predominance the peasant on his flat feet without specialist skills was worth far less in war than was the case before.

Of course any such summary analysis as this will leave much to be desired, yet if we attempt further generalization we may say that feudalism institutionalized personal relations, and formalized reciprocal loyalty as the principal bond of society and the main means of achieving political order. It also involved the devolution of authority and responsibility, in the form of lordship, to a degree that may seem intolerable to the modern mind – though in the twentieth century one may surely ask what it is so marvellous and divinely ordained about the all-powerful, monopolistic state. In any case the state will triumph in the end, though it will owe much to the centralizing discipline of feudalism in so doing. Meanwhile we must add that the social and political arrangements and institutions devised in the ninth and tenth centuries to meet immediate needs, having evolved into an established order and a sociological pattern of attitudes and of law, will last half a millenium, though not of course without further development and slow change.

The events and developments of the ninth and tenth centuries, then, are the context of the origin of the castle, or rather, to speak more accurately, it is these events and developments which produced the castle as an integral part of the new feudal society, to last as long as that society itself. Indeed, we can no more separate the castle from feudal society than we can separate the Romanesque and Gothic churches from contemporary Latin Christendom – and the Church itself inevitably became feudalized in this society, and bishops, like other lords, might have castles. It was in 864 in the Capitulary of Pistes that Charles the Bald, king of the West Franks, prohibited the construction of fortifications without his permission and ordered their destruction – 'We will and expressly command that whoever at this time has made castles (*castella*) and fortifications (*firmitates*) and enclosures (*haias*) without our permission shall have them demolished by the 1st of August'.[21] This might seem the recorded beginning of fortifications raised by other than royal and public authority, and may well be, though in fact it is difficult to find any certain instances of castles as the fortified residences of lords until the next century. The difficulty arises partly from lack of evidence as the lights go out over Western Europe, and partly from the problem of terminology which bedevils the task of the historian of the origins of feudalism, since only slowly and ambiguously are new Latin words coined, or old ones altered in their meaning, to describe the changing situation. Thus we may not know the vital point at which in any given area the classical word *miles*, simply meaning 'soldier', comes more narrowly and exclusively to mean 'knight', the knight who is the special feudal type of warrior; and similarly at any time from the ninth to the eleventh century or later such words as *castrum, castellum, firmitas, municipium, munitio* and *oppidum* are used indifferently for town or castle or any kind of fortification. By the mid-tenth century, however, we may cease to have any doubts in general (notwithstanding individual problems) from the evidence of the literary sources that the castle has become a feature of the landscape, a central institution of events, and at this point also archaeological evidence and even architectural remains enable us in some cases almost to see it as it was.

Until very recently the earliest surviving and upstanding castle in France and in Europe was taken to be Langeais (**2**) built by Fulk Nerra, count of Anjou, in 994. Now, while the date of its one stone building, the keep, has been pushed by some scholars a little later (*c.*1017?), pride of place must in any case go to Doué-la-Fontaine (**3**), not far away, after the spectacular excavations of 1967–70. Here we seem to be in the very presence of the events we seek as, about the year 950, and probably by Theobald, count of Blois, a princely, stone-built but unfortified ground-floor hall of *c.*900, having been burnt out in war, was converted into a defensive but residential strong tower or donjon by the addition of an upper storey, its entrance now at first-floor level (and covered by a timber forebuilding), its ground floor now a basement and its former ground-floor entrances rigorously blocked.[22] We can also see at this time how castles were part and parcel of the process of the formation of the new feudal lordships then being established in France. They riveted one's rule upon the land which they controlled, and they controlled an area which was the range of the mounted garrison within them.[23] 'They were the guarantee of the stability of the régime' and, the other side of the coin since feudalism is reciprocal, 'they made loyalty easy'.[24] Thus in the history of the foundation of the county of Anjou (whose counts were to become kings of England and kings of Jerusalem in the twelfth century), count Fulk Nerra, Fulk the Black (987 1040) stands out as 'a pioneer in the art of feudal government' and, withal, a mighty castle-builder. His grandson later recorded of him that he built thirteen castles which he lists, and others too numerous to name. The listed ones are Langeais (above), Baugé, Château-Gontier, Chaumont, Durtal, Faye, Maulévrier, Mirebeau, Moncontour, Montrésor, Montreuil-Bellay, Passavant and Sainte-Maure: the many others are thought to have included La-Motte-Montboyau, Montbazon and Montrichard, Mateflon, Saint-Florent-le-Vieux and Trèves. Fulk's neighbours also, of course, were similarly fortifying themselves, as his enemy, the count of Blois, is the probable builder of the donjon (both a strong tower and residence combined) at Doué-la-Fontaine – to have it captured, as it seems, by Fulk about 1025.

So too in Normandy, which especially concerns us in pursuit of the origins of the castle in England, the growing power of the duke (*alias* count of Rouen) from the beginning in 911 is marked among other things by the castles which he raised.[25] It is known that the principal ducal palace at Rouen was fortified with a great stone tower or donjon and doubtless other defences about the mid-tenth century by Richard I (942–996) and there is reference (at a time when references are rare) to another fortified palace, i.e. castle, built by the same prince at Bayeux (*palatium sibi et arcem fabricans*). It was in Richard I's time also that the famous castle of Ivry was raised and conferred upon his uterine brother, Raoul d'Ivry. Under dukes Richard II (996–1026) and Richard III (1026–7) the castles of Tillières, Falaise, Le Homme (now l'Isle Marie), Cherbourg and Brix were founded. Robert I, the Magnificent (1027–35) added Cherrueix at least and, as all the world knows, it was at the castle of Falaise that he formed his liaison with Herleva or 'Arlette', and there that in consequence, and most appropriately, the future Conqueror was born. Under duke William I himself we may take as one more instance of the association of castles with lordship, his fortification soon after 1047 of the town of Caen, and his planting of a great castle within it, as a principal means whereby ducal authority was finally asserted over Lower Normandy.

By this time also there were other castles in Normandy and elsewhere than those of the duke or count. It is nowadays sometimes maintained, especially by

French historians, that castles, like other good things in life, spread socially *de haut en bas*, and that during the first period of emergent feudalism and castellation in the late ninth and tenth centuries they were confined to the greatest lords, the new rulers of the emergent feudal principalities (Anjou, Blois, Normandy, Flanders and the rest), only thereafter appearing in the hands of their vassals and lesser magnates. It may be so, though the thesis may also seem rather too schematic for a period of social disintegration and inchoate lordship, when anything could happen and very often did, and when in any case the evidence at our disposal is so slight as to make any statistical study hazardous in the extreme. One should also focus not only upon such success stories (which, with hindsight, seem neat and tidy) as the evolution of potent feudal principalities like Anjou, Normandy and Flanders, but also upon the no less significant non-events like the failure of the great house of Bellême, in the marches between Normandy, Maine and the Île de France, to wield their lordship into a principality or to become counts of Perche, though castle was added to castle. This, after all and above all, was an age of personal lordship, often enough the survival of the fittest, an affair of a generation since neither vassalage nor the fief was yet hereditary in law; of competing and overlapping spheres of influence (there is no English equivalent for the excellent French word *mouvance* applied to the web of vassalage) rather than territorial frontiers. Further, when the great feudal princes enfeoffed a vassal with one of their castles – as they did from an early date since this is how things were done, as Fulk Nerra enfeoffed his vassals and as duke Richard I conferred Ivry upon his brother Raoul – we have at once, albeit in the tenth century, the situation, so to speak, of the eleventh, since no baronial castle, as we have seen, was ever so private as to be held of no-one. *Nulle terre sans seigneur* the feudal lawyers will say, and the dictum was even more true of castles which, moreover, never or seldom descended very far down the social scale and the feudal hierarchy.

Meanwhile an excellent recent survey,[26] making use (as use should be made) of all historical methods – not archaeological alone but documentary and the study of place names and of church dedications – and advancing by all historical approaches – political, social and economic – has shown in depth for one small area the process of castellation at a lower level than the formation of the great feudal principalities. In the district of Le Cinglais, in Lower Normandy between Caen and Falaise, some twenty-six castles were founded in the course of the eleventh century, mostly, it would seem in the first half of it. They represent 'the rise of the knightly class', they represent the foundation of new lordships, and they represent also the taking-in of new land. They were the centres of these movements as they were the centres and headquarters of the new lordships, and the principal means whereby the whole nature of the district was changed. At the beginning of the eleventh century the central plain, which was the area of ancient settlement, was ducal demesne, land directly administered and exploited by the duke, and the outlying higher ground was largely uncultivated: by the century's end the castles have been planted in the uplands which have been settled and cultivated under their protection, and the central plain has been divided among the lords of the principal castles who are the vassals of the duke. While Le Cinglais is a general instance, we have a particular instance in the castle of Le Plessis-Grimoult (Calvados), also the object of recent study and excavation,[27] and also in Normandy. Here the castle had been founded and developed in the early eleventh century and before 1047 when its lord, Grimoult du Plessis, lost all his possessions as one of the defeated rebels against the young duke William, and the site was abandoned. Again, the castle was the centre, or in the language of feudalism the *caput* (head), of a new lordship or 'honour', the honour held in this case not direct of the duke but of the bishop of Bayeux, and again the lordship chiefly comprised newly colonized land on the margins of ancient settlement. Lastly, we may return from the particular to the general once more by noticing the large number of castles raised in Normandy, as the Norman chronicles tell us, in the exceptional circumstances of the disputed succession to the duchy which followed the untimely death of Robert the Magnificent in 1035, and during the troubled years of the minority of his heir, William the Bastard, many of which, we are also informed, were demolished after his triumph at Val-ès-Dunes in 1047. 'In his early youth', says William of Jumièges of duke William, 'many of the Normans, renouncing their fealty to him, raised earthworks (*aggeres*) in many places and constructed the safest castles (*munitiones*)', and of the victory at Val-ès-Dunes the same chronicler adds (to be echoed by his contemporary, William of Poitiers), 'a happy battle indeed which in a single day brought about the collapse of so many castles (*castella*)'.[28]

Because of the emphasis that has in this chapter necessarily been placed upon the castle as a fortified residence in order to distinguish it from other forms of fortification, we must, indeed, not go so far as to forget that it was no less a fortress than a residence. The illicit because unlicensed castles that were raised in Normandy in the troubled times of 1035 to 1047, or more famously in England in the reign of Stephen (1135–54), were often the intended bases of military aggression and defences against the same. For centuries after 1066 one may use the evidence in English records of the strengthening, garrisoning and provisioning of castles as a kind of barometer to political tension, and when in 1173 a serious rebellion broke out against Henry II the anonymous author (probably Roger of Howden) of the contemporary *Deeds of King Henry* lists not only the names but also the castles of the king's opponents.[29] We shall deal in some detail in a later chapter with the role of the castle in war, but meanwhile we must note that, because the castle controlled the surrounding countryside, he who would control the land must first hold, or take, the castles, and because also the castle became from an early date the sign and the symbol of lordship in an age which attached great importance to symbolism, so also it became a prime objective in warfare as well as an active base for its waging. Warfare, indeed, came to turn upon castles no less than upon the heavy cavalry of knights, and the knight and the castle became the chief instruments of war in the feudal period, which is why, quite rightly, we so closely associate them in our minds with feudalism. Thus in Norman history by the mid-eleventh century sieges of castles take their place beside battles in the annals of war, and in the assertion of his supremacy by the young duke William against internal and external foes alike, the great sieges of Brionne (1047–9), Domfront (1051–2), and Arques (1052–3) are scarcely less important than the battles of Mortemer (1054) and Varaville (1057). The Normans, of course, excelled in the art of war, and before 1066 the future Conqueror had never failed to take a castle as he had never lost a battle.

Finally in this introductory chapter we must turn to some discussion of the architectural form and development of the early castle on the Continent down to 1066, as a necessary introduction and background to the more detailed treatment of the form and development of the English castle which will follow in later chapters. This subject has received a great deal of attention in recent years when the revival of interest in castle studies (in French *castellologie*) has been particularly concerned with their origins and early forms, and, on this side of the Channel especially, has been largely confined to archaeologists rather than historians (a distinction which unfortunately still persists). Since these studies are very much continuing, the subject is *sub judice*, and in consequence anyone who attempts to summarize and generalize does so at his peril. Nevertheless, one may suggest that there were two basic principles in castle design, i.e. in fortifying a large residence, or building a strong house, and that these in fact were evidently applied, often in conjunction, throughout the castle's history from the beginning to the end.

One principle, which as a method of fortifying anything is both very obvious and very ancient, is to put a strong enclosure about it – ditch, bank and timber palisade, or, it may be, a stone wall, also probably with ditch and bank. This, the method of fortifying a township or other communal settlement, was no less applicable to the usually smaller area of the castle, not least when it is remembered that the castle is a great house, and the great house during much of the Middle Ages tended to be a thing of bits and pieces, its several components – hall(s), chamber(s), chapel(s) and the like – standing separately and not articulated into one building. (To what extent the castle, because of the discipline imposed by fortification, contributed to the development of the articulated house is itself an interesting point. The monastery, with its several components arranged in a planned relationship from an early date, must also have exerted influence.) The second method, a little less obvious and evidently more straitly confined to the Middle Ages and the particular function of the castle as a fortified residence, is to build a strong tower; that is to say, if the need is for a strong and fortified house, one method is to bring all or most of the necessary components together into one defensible unit, and the result will be a tower, especially since a lord's household requires many components and the defensive advantages of height are manifest. This tower also might be constructed of timber rather than stone in the early period, especially if, as we shall see, it was associated with a motte. Here then is the 'great tower', the 'donjon' or keep, at once both the principal strength and principal residence of many castles.

If the fortified enclosure and the great tower are the two basic principles of castle design from the beginning to the end, it is worth spending a little longer discussing them. In the first place, as has already been said, the two may (or may not) be used in conjunction, in the sense that while the castle may, and frequently does, in any period consist of an enclosure without a great tower, it is difficult to suppose that the great tower ever stood alone without an enclosure, if only because, however ingenious your architect in designing it, there will always be something desirable left out, not least the horses, and one will both need greater space for all the appurtenances of lordship, and also wish to keep an enemy at his distance. Next, the materials used, over and above earthworks, in the construction of the castle are a secondary consideration, and our two principles will apply whether the castle is built of timber or of masonry, or a combination of both. While it is true that many early castles are of timber, especially (and perhaps misleadingly so) in England because of the special and immediate circumstances of conquest and military occupation, it is also true that stone fortification is present from the beginning or at any rate from our earliest known examples, and, again, that timber fortification can be used very late (e.g. Edward I in Scotland). It is wrong to postulate a general and uniform development from timber fortification to stone fortification, and almost certainly wrong to press too hard the concept of the timber castle, by which earthwork and timber is meant, as though it were entirely a special category.

It is, of course, difficult and rare to identify with certainty surviving, still less unaltered, castle-works of the tenth or even the eleventh century, or to find any detailed evidence of the form which early castles took from written or pictorial sources. Our concern is especially with Normandy, and we may begin with the simple fortified enclosure since it was long ago suggested by Mrs Armitage[30] that this may have been the earliest type of castle, and the suggestion is nowadays being repeated, though the fashionable archaeological term 'ring-work' is used and the context is the present pre-occupation with the origin of the 'motte' or castle mound (to which we must shortly turn). The invention, to which archaeologists are especially prone, of terms of art which would be incomprehensible to contemporaries is nearly always a dubious procedure, and certainly the term 'ring-work' is best avoided as having become virtually meaningless in current usage. No longer confined to the fortified enclosure of ditch, bank and timber palisade (which in any case is not a separate category of castle distinct from the walled enclosure), it is applied equally to large, communal fortifications like Old Sarum or Trelleborg, to Irish raths and to many other things besides, many of which are not castles at all, and thus serves chiefly to confuse. That said, the particular importance of the recently excavated site at Le Plessis-Grimoult[31] is that it is one of the earliest castles in Normandy to survive and be securely dated, and its form is the fortified enclosure. It was evidently developed from a previously unfortified residence in the early eleventh century and, having been abandoned in 1047, has never been altered. Its principal fortifications comprised a strong earthen rampart four metres high, crowned by (it is to be noted) a stone curtain-wall with at least one mural tower and a stone gatehouse, the latter consisting of a tower pierced by the entrance passage. Arques, also in Normandy and certainly in existence by 1052 when it was besieged by duke William, though much larger was also in the beginning an enclosure of rampart and ditch, perhaps with a timber palisade and gatehouse, perhaps with a curtain and gatehouse of stone, until the present keep was added by Henry I.[32] Other early castles in Normandy[33] as elsewhere in France are obviously of this pattern whether their ramparts were crowned with palisade or stone wall, and the type of castle which basically consists of an enclosure (or more than one enclosure), though obviously increasingly sophisticated in its fortification and construction, will persist throughout the Middle Ages, as witness Caernarvon or Beaumaris (**21**, **24**).

Yet there is also much evidence – indeed, perhaps more evidence – to show that in Normandy as elsewhere the great tower could be the dominant feature of the castle from the beginning, or at least that it was so present in some of the earliest castles of which we have record or knowledge. Outside Normandy the donjon at Doué-la-Fontaine has already been mentioned, dating from *c*.950 and of particular interest because it was converted from a previously unfortified hall. Langeais is traditionally ascribed to Fulk Nerra, count of Anjou, in 994. Its original status as a donjon has recently been questioned, the suggestion being that it was only later strengthened and thus converted into one.[34] Nevertheless it seems to point to the origin of a type of donjon which will persist, less a proper tower whose principal dimension is the vertical and more a strong and defensible first-floor hall. As a Norman analogy, the chronicler William of Poitiers[35] refers to the main strength of Brionne when William the Conqueror besieged it in 1047 as its 'stone hall' – 'This castle (*oppidum*) both by the manner of its construction and the nature of the site, seemed impregnable. For in addition to the other fortifications which the needs of war require, it has a stone-built hall (*aula lapidea*) serving the defenders as a keep (*arx*)' – while the many later examples include Falaise, Norwich and Castle Rising (**15**), all of the twelfth century. Probably earlier than Langeais, the great tower of the Norman duke's castle at Rouen is known from written evidence to have existed from the second half of the tenth century. Others as early evidently existed in Normandy at Bayeux and at Ivry, where Aubrey, wife of count Raoul d'Ivry is said to have beheaded the architect to prevent his building a similar castle for anyone else.[36] Elsewhere in France the surviving stone keeps of Montbazon, Nogent-le-Rotrou and Mondoubleau are all attributed by French historians to the first half of the eleventh century, and the list could be extended.

Assuredly also the great tower, like the fortified enclosure, persists throughout the history of the castle, and it is not true (as we shall later see in detail) that in England especially it becomes obsolete after *c*.1200, any more than it is true that it belongs exclusively to the 'Romanesque' period of the eleventh and twelfth centuries, though certainly it was then very popular. Wherever it existed the great tower was the dominant feature, at any rate when it was built, of the castle which possessed it, and as such, and as also the military strong-point and the residence of the lord, it was in particular the sign and the symbol of lordship ('You shall have the lordship in castle and in tower'[37]). To this day 'the Tower' of London (**27**), first raised by the Conqueror, is the appellation given to the whole royal castle in London. The great tower was also, by virtue of its strength, majesty and lordly accommodation, the donjon *par excellence*, and one may suggest that those seeming great towers or keeps which survive with no evident signs of residence within them (e.g. the Peak in England or Loudun in France) were never, strictly speaking, 'donjons'.

We turn next to the motte, the present object of so much attention amongst archaeologists. The motte is an artificial or part-natural mound, usually with a ditch about its base, and was undoubtedly a prominent feature of many early castles. Whatever structures it bore upon its summit, the space is usually confined, and the motte, therefore, like the great tower, needed an enclosure to go with it. We are thus dealing with the so-called 'motte-and-bailey' type of castle which, though its origins are obscure and even controversial, was certainly very common, all would agree, in the later eleventh and twelfth centuries. The motte itself, however, does not thereafter persist (at any rate in what we should call the more advanced parts of Western Europe, and always excepting, of course, those very many castles which by then already possessed mottes), nor does it at first sight fit the pattern of evolving castle design based upon our two suggested principles of the great tower and the fortified enclosure. It does so fit, however, if we associate the enigmatic motte with the great tower and the donjon, and this seems to be the clue to its understanding. It has always been assumed, on the basis of much evidence, literary, archaeological and even pictorial, that the motte bore upon its summit not only an encircling palisade or stone wall round the perimeter (the so-called shell keep, another confusing and unnecessary archaeological term) but also very often a tower, most frequently in the beginning a timber tower. The mottes shown by the Bayeux Tapestry at Dol, Rennes, Dinan and Bayeux (**4–6**) itself are thus represented. We are told how, in 1026, Eudes II, count of Blois, raised 'a timber tower of marvellous height upon the motte' of the castle of La-Motte-Montboyau near Tours[38] – *turrim ligneam mire altitudinis super dongionem ipsius castri erexit*, in which text 'dongio' evidently means 'motte', as witness another text relating how in 1060 Arnold, seneschal of Eustace count of Boulogne, raised at Ardres 'a very high motte or lofty donjon' (*motam altissimam sive dunjonem eminentem*).[39] Again, the excavations at Abinger in Surrey in 1949 revealed clear traces of a timber tower upon the motte as well as of the palisade which encircled it about the summit.[40]

At Abinger the archaeological evidence suggested that the tower stood, as it were, upon stilts, that is to say the ground floor of the timber-framed structure was left open between the corner-posts to allow of more space upon what is the rather confined fighting-platform of the motte top, which is evidently also the type of construction of the tower on the motte at Dinan as it is shown on the Bayeux Tapestry (**5**). It also seems to be represented by the besieged castle tower carved on a late eleventh-century capital from Westminster Hall (now displayed in the Jewel Tower), where one of the posts is being attacked by a warrior with an axe, and at this point one is also reminded of the twelfth-century description of the tower or 'house' (*domus*) on the motte at Durham – 'four posts are plain, on which it rests, one post at each strong corner'.[41] Equally the timber tower might rise solid from the summit of the mound as was shown to be the case at the recently excavated Hoverburg near Cologne in the Rhineland.[42] Most excitement, however, has been aroused of late by two recent excavations in England, at South Mimms in Hertfordshire and at Farnham in Surrey (**8**).[43] In the former case a timber tower, and in the latter case a stone tower, were shown to have their foundations upon the natural ground level at the base of the motte itself, and their basements thus within the motte which had been raised *pari passu* with them. Both cases are thought to date from about 1140, which is late in the history of motte construction. A further case has recently been noted with the much later (fourteenth century) timber tower and motte at Kaersgärd in Denmark (where everything is late), though an early instance seems to be recorded at Penwortham in Lancashire, where nineteenth-century excavations are said to have revealed what was evidently the circular base of a timber tower within the eleventh-century motte, and the dry stone foundations for what was probably a timber tower were recently found buried within the early motte at Totnes in Devon.[44] The significance of these instances of conjoint construction would seem to be that in the minds of the builders of these castles the tower was the primary element and the motte an adjunct to strengthen it. The actual details of the construction of the stone tower itself at Farnham, with its masonry flange binding tower and motte together, were peculiar, and their chief interest to suggest an existing tradition of raising timber towers conjointly with their mounds when Farnham was built, but there are other known instances of stone keeps standing within mounds which thus cover their lower levels, for example at Ascot Doilly,[45] Oxfordshire, and Wareham[46] in Dorset. There are also several known instances of a motte being added later, i.e. piled up round, an existing tower, as was done at Lydford in Devon[47] evidently in the late thirteenth century, at Aldingbourne in Sussex in the twelfth,[48] and also at Doué-la-Fontaine where a motte was somewhat surprisingly added to the tower as early as *c*.1000.[49]

All the evidence reviewed therefore suggests that the motte with its palisade is generally to be associated with a tower and, presumably, originally a timber tower. Since later surviving examples of stone 'shell-keeps' upon mottes (below p. 59) can contain other accommodation than a tower within them, we must allow the probability of similar and earlier arrangements in timber, but where the motte bears a tower, which seems to be most frequently, that tower will also be the principal tower of the castle, the great tower. One may also therefore suggest that the motte did not persist as a contemporary feature over most of Latin Christendom because the stone-built great towers increasingly raised from the twelfth century onwards, with their immensely thick walls, often splayed out at the base in a battered plinth, did not really need its additional protection in spite of the occasional examples we have cited. Where a motte is found in conjunction with a great tower of stone, its practical function can scarcely be other than to protect the base of the tower and, of course, to add height if the tower is built upon it, but it may also point to the traditional importance and significance of the motte at the time, as must surely be the case when a later stone keep is awkwardly and, so to speak, unnecessarily added to an existing motte, as happens for example in England at Clun and at Guildford in the twelfth century.

Certainly during much at least of the eleventh and twelfth centuries, the very centuries of the most frequent and wide-spread castle building when feudal customs and traditions were established, the motte was the dominant feature of those very many castles which possessed it. When, in his twelfth-century *Roman de Rou*, in one of those authentic snap-shots of the past, Wace has the young duke William, on his great ride to Falaise in 1047, meet Hubert de Ryes, the latter is standing between the church and his castle, but the poet simply expresses it, 'entre le mostier et sa *mote*'.[50] Like the free-standing great tower, the motte acquired a symbolism of its own as the particular mark of lordship, and it seems very significant that the same word, 'donjon', could be applied to both (above, p. 15). As late as 1789 in the France of the *ancien régime*, homage and feudal dues could still be owed 'à cause de la motte', i.e. in right of the motte.[51] The late eleventh-century Bayeux Tapestry represents five of its possible six castles simply by their mottes (Dol, Rennes, Dinan, Bayeux and Hastings – **4–7**), and if it is a fact that its Scene 14 shows Rouen,[52] then that castle is represented simply by its great tower: in other words, the designer of the Tapestry, forced here and elsewhere to use an artistic short-hand, represents castles by their donjons, whether mottes or free-standing towers. The motte, one may suggest, like the freestanding great tower, could be referred to as 'donjon' because it was fulfilling the same function and with the same symbolic importance, at once both the military strong-point of the castle and, at least in very many cases, the elevated residence of the lord. At the fortified palace which Windsor castle has become in England, the Conqueror's motte still crowns the whole position (**36**), and the buildings within the shell keep upon its summit could still house the king's majesty in the fourteenth century, just as Henry II's great keep at Dover (**1**) housed Charles I and his bride, Henrietta Maria, in the seventeenth. The excavations at South Mimms suggested the former sophistication of the internal appointments of the timber tower which there rose from within the motte, and that even such timber towers could be lordly within as well as in their external appearance is adequately shown by the rare but precious literary descriptions we have of them. Laurence the prior of Durham says of his timber tower upon the motte, which we have already cited as standing on four posts 'one post at each strong corner', that 'each face is girded by a beautiful gallery which is fixed in the warlike wall'.[53] The timber tower-house (*domus lignea turris*) of the castle of La Cour-Marigny, near Montargis (Loiret), in the mid-eleventh century was of two

storeys, the ground floor containing a storeroom (*cellarium*) and the upper floor
the solar (*solarium*) where the noble (*sic*) lord of the castle lived, conversing,
eating and sleeping with his household.[54] The contemporary description by
Lambert of Ardres of the 'great and lofty house (*domus*)' which Arnold, lord of
Ardres, built in his castle there about 1117 is well known, but must nevertheless
be printed at this point:[55]

'Later, when peace had been established between Manasses count of Guisnes
and Arnold lord of Ardres, Arnold built upon the motte (*super dunjonem*) at
Ardres a timber house which was a marvellous example of the carpenter's craft
and excelled materials used in all contemporary houses in Flanders. It was
designed and built by a carpenter from Bourbourg called Louis, who fell little
short of Daedalus in his skill; for he created an almost impenetrable labyrinth,
piling storeroom upon storeroom, chamber upon chamber, room upon room,
extending the larders and granaries into the cellars, and building the chapel in
a convenient place overlooking all else from high up on the eastern side. He
made it of three floors, the topmost storey supported by the second as though
suspended in the air. The first storey was at ground level, and here were the
cellars and granaries, the great chests, casks, butts and other domestic utensils.
On the second floor were the residential apartments and common living
quarters, and there were the larders, the rooms of the bakers and the butlers,
and the great chamber of the lord and his lady, where they slept, on to which
adjoined a small room which provided the sleeping quarters of the
maidservants and children. Here in the inner part of the great chamber
there was a small private room where at early dawn or in the evening, or in
sickness, or for warming the maids and weaned children, they used to light a
fire. On this floor also was the kitchen, which was on two levels. On the
lower level pigs were fattened, geese tended, chickens and other fowls killed
and prepared. On the upper level the cooks and stewards worked and
prepared the delicate dishes for the lords, which entailed much hard work on
the part of the cooks, and here also the meals for the household and servants
were prepared each day. On the top floor of the house there were small rooms
in which, on one side, the sons of the lord slept when they wished to do so,
and, on the other side, his daughters as they were obliged. There too the
watchmen, the servants appointed to keep the household, and the ever-ready
guards, took their sleep when they could. There were stairs and corridors
from floor to floor, from the residential quarters to the kitchen, from chamber
to chamber, and from the main building to the *loggia*, where they used to sit
for conversation and recreation (and which is well named, for the word is
derived from *logos* meaning speech), as also from the *loggia* to the oratory or
chapel, which was like the temple of Solomon in its ceiling and its
decoration.'

There remains the question of the origin of the motte and therefore of the motte-and-bailey type of castle. The suggestion that the earliest type of castle may have been simply a fortified enclosure about a lordly residence has already been noted, and the tendency at the present time among archaeologists in this country especially is, so to speak, to delay the advent of the motte. We do not know, in fact, where and when it first appeared, any more than we know precisely when and where the castle first appeared, and there is still no compelling reason to separate their origins since the mound, after all, is a fairly obvious form of small fortification at least if earthwork and timber is to be used. The evolution of the low dwelling-mound (*hauptburg*) above an inferior courtyard (*vorburg*), on riverine sites in the Rhineland in the tenth century as the result of flooding, does not seem to provide a satisfactory origin for mottes in general, and at the Husterknupp (near Frimmersdorf), where the full evolution to a motte-and-bailey castle took place, it was evidently not completed before the twelfth century.[56] There is no doubt of the prevalence of the motte-and-bailey type amongst early castles in England after 1066, and the accepted view since Mrs Armitage's day has been that it was introduced with the castle itself by the Normans. Since, however, it is not easy to point to a motte in Normandy known without the slightest doubt to have existed before the conquest of England, and because it has recently been shown that a motte can be added later to a castle which began without one (Castle Neroche, Somerset. See below, p. 36), the latest and most dramatic hypothesis has been that the origin of the motte is to be sought in the peculiar circumstances of the Norman Conquest of England itself,[57] which certainly included, as the imposition of the supremacy of a comparatively small and feudal military aristocracy, one of the most extensive and rapid castle-building programmes in history.[58]

That the Normans or the rest of the French do not seem to have taken the motte-and-bailey with them to the Middle East on the First Crusade (1099) might be argued in support of this suggestion, though the fact that the type seems duly to appear in southern Italy and Sicily,[59] conquered by the Normans of the same generation as the conquest of England, does so rather less. In the main, however, neither French historians nor the evidence will allow the ingenious hypothesis. The motte at Doué-la-Fontaine was added to the great tower, it will be remembered, about 1000.[60] There is literary reference to Eudes II building his 'timber tower of wondrous height' in 1026 at La-Motte-Montboyau upon the motte (*dongio*), which, therefore, already existed (presumably raised by Fulk Nerra ten years before), as there is to Arnold lord of Ardres constructing his motte at Ardres in 1060.[61] A recent study of the castles of Fulk Nerra, count of Anjou (987–1040), based upon both archaeological and textural evidence, finds the motte as one of their characteristics.[62] As for Normandy, the case for attributing a pre-Conquest date to the surviving mottes of Manéhouville (the best attested), Gaillefontaine and La Ferté-en-Bray has recently been argued.[63] Meanwhile the close study of Le Cinglais by M. Fixot seems to put beyond doubt the raising of motte-and-bailey castles in that area during the whole course of the eleventh century, and of the same date as other castles of the simple fortified enclosure type to which they were therefore merely an alternative contemporary form.[64] It is also very much worth noting that in the passage from William of Jumièges already cited[65] relating how many Norman magnates during duke William's minority 'having raised earthworks ... constructed for themselves the safest castles', the word here translated 'earthworks' is in fact the Latin *aggeres* which could quite legitimately be rendered 'mounds', i.e. mottes. Perhaps, indeed, it should be, for there is no doubt that the same word *agger* means motte in the well-known early twelfth-century description of the castle at Merchem quoted later in this book,[66] and this also seems to be its meaning in the reference to the castle raised by Fulk Nerra and Geoffrey his son in 1030 at St-Florent-le-Vieil – 'they raised an *agger* with a timber court'.[67] Our conclusion therefore must be the traditional one, even if it can be no more precise, namely that the motte-and-bailey as an early type of castle has its origins in France and the Rhineland at a date certainly before the mid-eleventh century, and that, being already known in Normandy by that time, it was brought by the Normans and their allies to England in and after 1066.

Chapter 2

The Norman Conquest of England[1]

'For the fortresses (*munitiones*) which the Gauls call castles (*castella*) had been very few in the English provinces, and for this reason the English, although warlike and courageous, had nevertheless shown themselves too weak to withstand their enemies.'[2] Thus Ordericus Vitalis writing, it is true, in *c*.1125, yet the chronicler to be valued above all others for the depth and detail of his information about Anglo-Norman feudal society in the late eleventh century as well as the early twelfth, and, though not contemporary, an authority also for the history of the Norman Conquest of England, because of his careful use of a wide range of sources and his well-placed position in the monastery of St Evroul. It is good thus to begin with a reliable early twelfth-century statement that the origin of the castle in England is to all intents and purposes to be found in the Norman Conquest because, although this has been the accepted view amongst historians at least since Mrs Armitage's day, the absence of native castles in pre-Conquest England is again being questioned at the present time, together with the absence of feudalism. In fact, as has been sufficiently argued in the last chapter, the two things go together, though those who argue for pre-Conquest English feudalism on the one hand, and those who argue for pre-Conquest English castles on the other, too seldom realize their alliance, so far is the social significance of the castle short of general acceptance in this country (though not in France – *le vieux château féodal*). Indeed one may suggest at this stage, by way of introduction, two curious and recurrent traits amongst many English historians of all generations past and present. The first is an anachronistic nationalism which, coming to the boil in 1066, leads to a disinclination to admit the importance of the Conquest and to a conviction that anything important the Normans can claim to have introduced was already here before they came, whether castles or Romanesque churches, feudalism or the reformation of the Church. The second, which logically is incompatible with the first though the two are sometimes found together, is the belief that feudalism is a foreign and a bad thing to which the English (whoever they may have been) never really took, but got rid of with native genius as soon as ever they could.[3]

Unfortunately this is not the place to argue in detail the case for the conventional view that feudalism in England is a Norman importation, nor, indeed, for the less conventional view that feudalism is a good thing, greatly contributing to the cohesion of society and the authority of kings and princes. We can at least, however, assert the truth of both contentions. At least, also, the true nature of Old English government and society is very relevant to its system of defence and fortifications. These were the Old English *burhs* or burghs or boroughs,[4] large, communal fortifications which by the mid-eleventh century were fortified towns and cities, and communal also in that all of them were raised by public authority, royal authority, under Alfred and his successors, originally as defences and bases against the Danes. Many (Wareham, Shaftesbury, Cricklade, Tamworth, Wallingford) were rectangular, others irregular in shape through the dictates of topography (Lydford, Lyng) or because they occupied the predetermined site of, e.g., an Iron Age hill-fort (South Cadbury, the legendary Camelot, or Dover). In the beginning their defences were evidently of ditch, bank and timber palisade (with perhaps timber revetment of the bank), stone walls replacing the palisades only later (at Tamworth in 917, more usually in the eleventh century), unless the new borough was from the beginning established in a Roman fort or town and made use of surviving masonry defences (Winchester, Exeter). An average size for an Alfredian borough is thought to have been about 100 acres, whereas Mrs Armitage put the average size of her early Norman castles in England at three acres, and it is particularly significant for the nature of these places as the defences of whole communities that some of them occupy former Roman cities (Winchester, Exeter, or *cf.* Portchester in the former Roman Saxon Shore fort), just as probably all of them included a minster church, the *matrix ecclesia*, serving the community and doubtless the adjacent countryside. It is even more significant for our purposes, as pointing the difference between the borough and the castle, that in many surviving cases the castle stands within the borough occupying only a small part of it (Tamworth, Wallingford, Lydford, Portchester, Old Sarum), and we may note also that Stenton's description of the typical Old English borough on the eve of the Norman Conquest includes the feature of the men of different lords living within it,[5] a feature inconceivable in the feudal castle which is the fortified residence of one lord.

In short, the Old English system of fortifications was a national system, like the Old English military system which was based upon the royal right to call upon the military service of all free men, and as witnessed also by the elaborate organization of the Burghal Hidage[6] whereby the king applies this right to the manning of his fortresses, one man from every hide. Such a system, which is both ancient and modern in imposing common obligations upon all free men as subjects of the king, is manifest also in the Old English geld which was a national tax, and is entirely characteristic of a Germanic and Carolingian-type kingdom such as England remained down to 1066. It is to be remembered that everywhere in Western Europe kingship is older than feudalism, just as Germanic society in the beginning was not feudal. In the kingdom of the West Franks which will be France, the old order, as we have seen, was changed in the course of the ninth and tenth centuries especially, when the central authority of

Carolingian monarchy collapsed and a new and feudal society established itself based upon local lordship. In England, by contrast, though the Danes overran the rest of the land and its former particularist kingdoms, Alfred held out in Wessex, allied with the surviving part of Mercia, and began that reconquest of the 'Danelaw', the area of Viking hegemony, which was completed by his successors. In this way the kingdom of Wessex expanded to become, by 954, the kingdom of all England; time-honoured monarchy in consequence, far from waning, waxed; and the society over which it reigned suffered no break in the continuity of its development, even the Danes and Norsemen in the Danelaw, however predominant, being themselves of Germanic stock and probably more influenced by than influencing the society they had overcome. Nor was the situation fundamentally changed by the second Danish onslaught of the early eleventh century which resulted in the outright conquest of the whole English kingdom by Swein Forkbeard and Cnut his son in 1014–16, just fifty years before the Norman Conquest. Defeat when it came was nation-wide and brought about neither political fragmentation nor any weakening of the monarchy. The alien Cnut and his two sons ruled over England as the beneficiaries of a superior culture rather than its destroyers, until in 1042 the ancient Wessex royal house was restored in the person of Edward the Confessor, and though by the mid-eleventh century Anglo-Scandinavian rather than Anglo-Saxon may be a better description of Old English society, especially at the top, there was no fundamental change either in that society or its institutions. The old order, the Old World, survived until at Hastings it went down before the Brave New World of feudal northern France as represented by the Normans.

Although the fact that Old English society down to 1066 was in no sense feudal, combined with the known nature of the Old English fortifications and defensive system, forms the major part of the argument for the absence of castles in England until their introduction, together with feudalism itself, by the Normans, it is also nowadays necessary to conduct the argument in terms of castles *per se*, as Mrs Armitage was constrained to do over fifty years ago. To prove the absence of native castles in pre-Conquest England in these terms, of course, we are bound first to use negative evidence, though, as Mrs Armitage pointed out, even that may seem very conclusive.[7] Thus, save in the few exceptional instances to be discussed below, we simply do not hear of castles, nor meet the word, in England before 1066 in any of the sources of whatever type, nor has any Old English castle ever yet been found or identified. To cite one particular occasion which must seem particularly significant, it is surely inconceivable that, had king Edward, earl Godwin and the other English magnates possessed castles or been accustomed to use them, we should not hear of it in the chronicles at the time of the political crisis of 1051–2, when Godwin and his sons defied the king and brought the kingdom to the brink of civil war – as the Norman chroniclers refer at once to the raising and fortification of castles in the crises in Normandy of 1035 and 1047, and to the demolition of castles by the victorious duke William thereafter.[8] By contrast the English sources for

1051–2 refer only to the very few castles of the 'Frenchmen', i.e. Edward's so-called Norman favourites who, with all they stood for, were themselves a cause of the trouble.[9] Nor for that matter do we hear of any English castles when they were most necessary in 1066 and the troubled years that immediately followed. We may add, too – and here the evidence is more positive – that none even of the royal residences in pre-Conquest England are known to have been fortified, any more than are the Carolingian palaces of pre-ninth-century Gaul, and in this king Edward's Westminster stands in sharp contrast to duke William's Rouen. Most significant of all, however, is the very positive and overwhelming evidence for the huge programme of castle-building carried out by the Normans as part and parcel of the Conquest, and a principal means whereby it was effected and made permanent.

Before we turn to that, however, we must deal first with the exceptional cases of those few castles already present in king Edward's day. They are in fact exceptions of that best sort which prove the rule, namely that the castle in this country is a Norman and French importation, for the only known castles to which we have reference before Hastings are in every case the foundations of French lords already here, the 'Norman favourites' of Edward the Confessor and, as it turned out, the forerunners of the Conquest. Ordericus Vitalis, it will be noted, does not say there were no castles in England but that they were very few, and it is also to be noted that the Old English chronicles themselves in mentioning them seem to do so with disapproval as both alien and oppressive – 'the foreigners then had built a castle (*castel*) in Herefordshire in earl Swein's province, and had inflicted every possible injury and insult upon the king's men in those parts', thus the 'E' version of the Anglo-Saxon Chronicle for 1051.[10] In the next year there is specific reference to two named and alien castles when the same version of the Anglo-Saxon Chronicle, speaking of the flight of 'the Frenchmen' from London in 1052 when earl Godwin returned from his brief banishment, says that 'they took horses and departed, some west to Pentecost's castle (*castele*) and some north to Robert's castle (*castele*)'.[11] These two have been identified with some probability as the existing castle sites at Ewyas Harold in Herefordshire and Clavering in Essex respectively.[12] We hear again of Pentecost's castle *alias* Ewyas Harold, together with at least one other castle in Herefordshire belonging to a certain Hugh, in Florence of Worcester, a chronicler of the early twelfth century but thought to have been using a lost version of the Anglo-Saxon Chronicle for this period, who, writing of the events of 1052 and the banishment of many of those whom he specifically calls Normans on earl Godwin's return, says that Osbern surnamed Pentecost and his associate (*socius*) Hugh surrendered their castles (*castella*, in the plural).[13] In addition, the existing castle site at Richard's Castle (still the place-name – **II**), again in Herefordshire, has a strong claim to pre-Conquest origin, as its known lord, Richard son of Scrob, was already established in the district in 1052 and was allowed to remain there by the Godwin faction on their return.[14] We are dealing here, in fact, with the veritable French and Norman colony planted in

Herefordshire by king Edward under his nephew Ralph 'the Timid' (the son of the king's sister, Godgifu, and Drogo, count of the Vexin), who was made earl of Hereford in 1053 or earlier, and it is extremely probable that earl Ralph himself had a castle at Hereford, probably as early as 1051 though the actual date of its foundation is unknown.[15]

Clavering, then, in Essex, with Ewyas Harold, Richard's Castle, Hereford and at least one other all in Herefordshire, are the only known or probable castles in England before the Norman Conquest, and all pertain to French lords already here as king Edward's 'Norman favourites'. It is not, however, quite true to say that the only references to castles by that name before 1066 are in this alien context, for there is also the double exception of Dover (1). It is well known that in the fullest and best account we have of Harold's famous oath to duke William in 1064, in William of Poitiers' contemporary life of the Norman duke, Harold is made to swear amongst other things that he will hand over to William, to be garrisoned by Norman knights, 'the castle (*castrum*) of Dover fortified at his (Harold's) own cost and effort' (as well as other 'castles' similarly in other unnamed places), as a pledge or surety for the duke's ultimate succession to the English throne.[16] If this were all, by taking the passage at face value we might say that here is another exceptional case of a castle raised in England before 1066, in this instance under Norman influence rather than by, as it were, resident lordship. But Dover is also referred to as *castelle* and *castrum* earlier than this, in the English sources recounting the dramatic events of earl Godwin's rebellion in 1051. Although there is good reason to believe that the deeper issue of the succession to the English crown underlay this enigmatic affair, the Anglo-Saxon Chronicle merely has it caused by a *fracas* between the men of Dover and those of count Eustace of Boulogne who was on a visit to king Edward. The king ordered the harrying of Dover in punishment and Godwin, in whose earldom it lay, refused. It may seem very probable that count Eustace's visit was in connection with Edward the Confessor's promise of the succession to duke William which, from other evidence, can only have taken place at this time, and that the duke was already seeking Dover in pledge as he was to do again in 1064, but however that may be the 'D' version of the Chronicle states that earl Godwin and his sons threatened the king with war 'unless Eustace were surrendered and his men handed over to them, as well as the Frenchmen who were in the castle (*castelle*)'.[17] The whole context of this passage indicates Dover as the unnamed 'castle',[18] and Florence of Worcester in his account, which closely follows the 'D' version of the Chronicle but has extra information, specifically names it as Dover, as well as identifying the 'Frenchmen' in it as Normans and men of Boulogne – 'They sent messengers to the king at Gloucester demanding on threat of war count Eustace and his companions, together with the Normans and men of Boulogne, who held the castle (*castrum*) on the cliff at Dover'.[19] We hear of this pre-Conquest 'castle' at Dover once more when in 1066, immediately after his victory at Hastings (and significantly in view of the political importance of Dover suggested above), we are told by

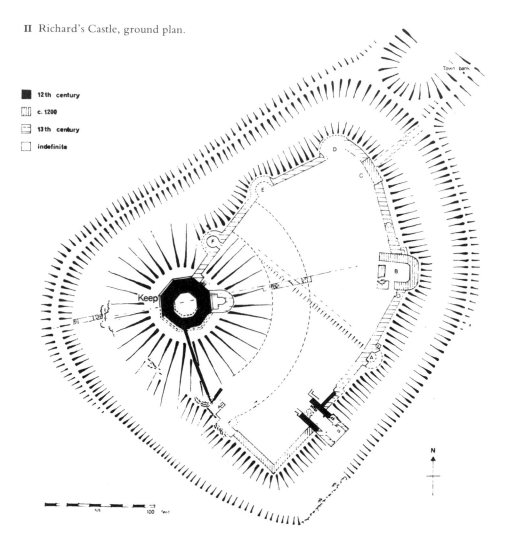

II Richard's Castle, ground plan.

■ 12th century
▥ c. 1200
▦ 13th century
▢ indefinite

Keep

Town bank

N

the contemporary Norman and French accounts that the Conqueror marched upon Dover and took it, on which occasion William of Poitiers says that the duke 'spent eight days adding to it those fortifications which it lacked'.[20] The explanation offered here[21] of this 'castle' on the cliff at Dover in the last decades of the Old English state is that it was not a castle at all but the Old English borough occupying the whole area enclosed by the former Iron Age earthworks,[22] and that the fortifications which it lacked and William added comprised or included a castle which he raised within it, on the analogy of many other places including, in all probability, Pevensey and Hastings a few weeks before.[23]

For this hypothesis there is a fair amount of direct evidence as well as all probability in favour of it. In the future, and by the thirteenth century at least if not the later twelfth, the Conqueror's castle at Dover was to expand by military compulsion to occupy the whole position as it does now (**I**), but a large and late Anglo-Saxon church (St Mary-in-Castro), dated to the late tenth or early eleventh century albeit disagreeably restored in the nineteenth, still stands in the midst of it, indicative of a former late Old English borough.[24] Further, although Dover is called *castelle* in the 'D' version of the Anglo-Saxon Chronicle for 1051, in the 'E' version for the same year it is called *burge* and *burh*.[25] We are also told in that latter version that in 1051 count Eustace and his followers 'went *up* towards the burge' (and slew more than twenty men in return for their own losses of nineteen plus wounded inflicted by the 'burh men'),[26] i.e. this borough is clearly the present fortress up on the cliff. Again, in Guy of Amiens' account of the events of 1066, the victorious duke after Hastings took and entered Dover *castrum* and commanded the English within 'to evacuate their houses',[27] which surely indicates this 'castle' was a town. Finally there has recently come to light[28] some measure of archaeological confirmation for the suggestion that the fortifications which the Conqueror added during the eight days of 1066 included a comparatively small enclosure, i.e. a castle, within the undoubtedly pre-existing Iron Age earthworks, in the vicinity of the church and now deep beneath the huge horse-shoe shaped rampart about the church, mistakenly called 'Harold's Earthwork' (the same excavations showed it to be thirteenth-century). Archaeologically speaking, the ditch and bank far below the present earthworks were mid-eleventh century and could belong either side of the crucial date of October 1066, but their close proximity to the south transept of the church and their interference, indeed, with an Anglo-Saxon burial ground adjoining it, strongly suggest the urgent irreverence of war rather than the work of a native earl in time of peace, and the weight of all the other evidence strongly suggests that this excavation did reveal in fact a glimpse of the Conqueror's castle. In short, Dover castle, properly so called, is not to be added to the few exceptional pre-Conquest English castles, but is a Norman foundation of 1066. The difficulty to be resolved in this case is simply one of terminology and of the ambiguous use of words in our sources. There are other instances in Anglo-Saxon sources of the application of the word 'castle' (*castellum* in Latin or *castelle* in the vernacular) to a town, and from an early date.[29] Even in France by the mid-eleventh century feudal vocabulary was still in a state of evolution and in non-feudal England, naturally enough, the process had scarcely begun.[30]

One piece of documentary evidence has lately been adduced in support of the suggestion that the Old English thegns, i.e. the upper and landed class, may have had fortified residences, i.e. castles.[31] This is the compilation known as 'Of People's Ranks and Laws', and is a kind of moral tract for the times, probably written by archbishop Wulfstan of York between 1002 and 1023. It is a strange piece of writing, anachronistic in sentiment and approach, belonging to that large category of literature which appeals to the lost if exaggerated virtues of the Good Old Days. It is thus an unlikely context in which to find reference to

III Castle Tower, Penmaen, ground plan.

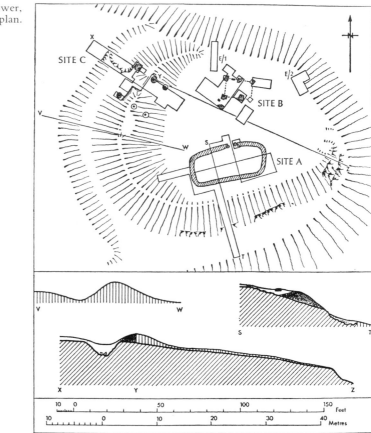

castles which in the early eleventh century would be, so to speak, the latest thing, and certainly the idealized society otherwise described by the writer is uncompromisingly Germanic and pre-feudal. The section, however, to which attention has been drawn is that which lists the qualifications of thegnhood, and reads as follows:[32] 'If a ceorl (i.e. free peasant) prospered, so that he possessed fully five hides of land of his own, church and kitchen,[33] a bell and a *burh-geat*, a seat and special office in the king's hall, then was he thenceforth of thegn-right worthy'. The *burh-geat of* this passage must be rendered 'borough-gate', and therefore, the argument goes, this is the gate of a fortification, therefore the thegn's residence being described is fortified, i.e. it is a castle. The gate, too, must be particularly impressive to be thus singled out for mention, and one's thoughts are thus directed to the kind of (Norman and post-Conquest) 'ring-work' or enclosure castle recently excavated at Penmaen in Glamorgan (**III**).[34]

But this interpretation will not do. For the gate of the borough to be specified as thegnly is much more likely to imply that it had some lordly and thus symbolic function – probably, as Maitland thought, the dispensation of justice[35] – than that it was architecturally outstanding. More important is the point that the word *burh* or borough as used here does not imply fortification. One meaning of the word is certainly 'fortification, fortified place'[36] and hence its application to the communal fortresses built by Alfred and his successors which have been described in this chapter, but the noun is derived from the Old Teutonic verb *bergan*, to shelter or protect.[37] In consequence, while the noun *burh, burg*, borough, is used in the sources from an early date to signify a fortified place or military encampment, so also was it used from an early date to signify an enclosure about a dwelling without any element of fortification at all. This usage is abundantly illustrated in the Old English law codes, not least in connection with *burg-bryce*, the offence of breaking into such an enclosure or, as we should say, forcible entry, for which the punishment was (as usual in Germanic law) a compensatory payment or *bot* (hence *burgbot*) to the injured party, scaled according to his rank. Thus Ine's laws declare in the seventh century,[38] '*Bot* shall be paid for the king's *burgbryce* (*i.e.* for breaking into the enclosure of his residence) and for a bishop's where his jurisdiction is with 120 shillings; for an ealdorman's, with 80 shillings; for a king's thegn's with 60 shillings; for a gesith-cund man's (i.e. a nobleman's), having land, with 35 shillings' – and this, it is to be noted, at a date (688–94) when castles had not been invented on the Continent, let alone in England. Examples could be multiplied from the laws of other Old English kings, and even the peasant's or ceorl's dwelling was similarly enclosed (no question of a castle here), Ine's laws decreeing that his homestead (*worthig*) must be fenced both summer and winter to prevent the straying of beasts,[39] and Alfred's rating the ceorl's *edorbryce* or compensation for breaking into his enclosure (*edor* is fence) together with the *burgbryce* of his social superiors, though of course at a lower rate (5 shillings).[40]

We are dealing here in fact with a fundamental unit of Germanic society and agricultural organization, and that which is *burh* and *worthig* in the laws of Wessex is the manse or *mansus* of Carolingian capitularies and other documents upon the Continent. Here thus is the peasant manse of the ninth and tenth centuries as described by one of its latest historians, Georges Duby:[41] 'We understand by this an enclosure, solidly rooted to its site by a permanent barrier such as a palisade or a living hedge, carefully maintained, a protected asylum to which the entry was forbidden and the violation of which was punished by severe penalties: an island of refuge where the occupant was assumed to be the master ... a haven for possessions, cattle, stocks of food ... the kernel of the village'. The lord's residence, his borough, his manse, his demesne, was no different in kind, albeit bigger and grander. 'A demesne bore the same appearance as a manse, for it was after all the manse of the master, the *mansus indominicatus*. But it was an outsize manse, because it corresponded to a specially numerous, productive and demanding household.... Even so, its structure was no different from that of other manses. At the centre was an enclosure, the courtyard, the space surrounded by a solid palisade, enclosing as well as the orchard and kitchen garden a collection of buildings which amounted to a hamlet.'[42] M. Duby then goes on to cite a documentary description of the royal 'hall' at Annapes (on the borders of Flanders and Artois) which comprised a stone-built 'palace' and had about it a great enclosure 'provided with a strong palisade and a gate of stone surmounted with a gallery'.[43] Here, then, we evidently meet our *burh-geat* again, but the point is that none of these residences and homesteads, lordly or humble, manse, *burh* or *worthig*, are fortified. An enclosure does not have to be a fortification nor have any military intent. There is a difference between one's garden fence or wall and the walls of Caernarvon castle. The *burh* of the Old English laws and archbishop Wulfstan's tract is a domestic, a social, an agricultural enclosure, an affair of demarcation. It is what Duby calls it, an asylum, wherein the privacy and property of its occupant is to be respected and protected at law. From all this, no doubt, the dictum that an Englishman's home is his castle arises, but in no other sense, be he never so grand, was his home a castle before 1066.

There is no evidence to show the existence of the fortified residence, i.e. the castle, in England before the Conquest beyond those alien exceptions raised in Edward the Confessor's day which we have discussed. Recent excavations at Sulgrave in Northamptonshire,[44] largely conceived in the hope of finding such a thing, were undertaken there because of the near-unique opportunity of what seems to be a Norman castle occupying the site of a former pre-Conquest thegnly residence. Because of a complete absence of documentary or literary evidence it is not in fact known if Sulgrave ranked as a castle after 1066, but the excavations, so far, have shown that the reasonably impressive enclosure (*alias* ringwork) of ditch and bank there now is of post-Conquest date, and differs radically from whatever Old English enclosure preceded it (as yet unknown). If, therefore, the residence at Sulgrave became a castle in Norman England, it looks as if it did so by the addition of fortifications about it, and in the Norman world of the late eleventh century the criteria of fortification could be the depth of ditches and the height of banks together with the construction of their palisades – 'No one in Normandy might dig a fosse in the open country of more than one shovel's throw in depth, nor set there more than one line of palisading, and that without battlements or alures.'[45]

We turn lastly to Norman castle-building in and after 1066 as, surely, entirely positive and equally convincing evidence for the absence of castles in pre-Conquest England. For why else should this have been necessary? If, for example, the Normans felt compelled to plant castles in London (three), York (two) and Winchester, as the principal cities of the conquered land, to say nothing of countless other places, it must be at least difficult to sustain any argument for native castles in the last years of the Old English kingdom. In fact the Norman Conquest, and the subsequent Norman settlement which sociologically is the imposition of an alien ruling-class upon the countryside, is marked at every stage by new castles as the new men literally dug and walled themselves in. By the end of the Conqueror's reign in 1087 entirely casual references to castles in Domesday Book alone (in no way a systematic record of fortification) amount to fifty, and by the end of the century casual references in all written sources amount to some eighty-four, both figures being, without any doubt, a fraction of the total. There were never to be more castles in England than there were in the first century after the Norman Conquest, when they stood thick in every county. Most have left at least some trace and together they have been called 'the most authentic memorials remaining of the age of militant feudalism'.[46] The great proportion of them raised in the first years and decades after 1066 represent, together with the new knights and chivalry, the principal means whereby Norman rule was riveted upon the land, and they represent also what must have been the most extensive and concentrated programme of castle-building in the whole history of feudal Europe.

Almost the first act of the Conqueror after his disembarkation at Pevensey on 28 September 1066, was to raise a castle there, and when, a day or two later, he moved his forces on to Hastings another was raised which the Bayeux Tapestry shows being constructed (7).[47] Immediately after his victory at Hastings on Saturday, 14 October, the duke, as we have seen, marched upon Dover and placed a castle in it (1). At the end of the long, circuitous and intimidating advance upon London in the autumn and early winter, after the English leaders had come in and made their submission at (Little?) Berkhampstead, William sent lieutenants ahead to construct a fortress (*munitionem*) in the city and otherwise prepare for his triumphal entry, while after his coronation on Christmas Day, 1066, the new king withdrew to Barking while fortifications (*firmamenta*) were completed within the city 'against the inconstancy of the huge and savage population'.[48] In these events we may well see the origins of all three London castles, Baynard's Castle in the south-west corner, Montfichet to the north of this, and, in the south-east corner, the castle where the Tower, i.e. the donjon, of London was to rise before the end of William's reign.[49] Early in 1067, with very little of his new kingdom as yet under his direct control or occupied, the Conqueror moved off on a military expedition, probably into East Anglia where, amongst others, the castle of Norwich was planted.[50] William of Poitiers relates how from Barking he pursued his march into divers parts of the kingdom, everywhere making such dispositions as he pleased without opposition, and that 'in castles he placed capable custodians, brought over from France, in whose loyalty no less than ability he trusted, together with large numbers of horse and foot. He distributed rich fiefs amongst them, in return for which they would willingly undertake hardships and dangers'.[51] In March the king returned to Normandy for a prolonged and joyful celebration of his victory and elevation to the throne of England, leaving his half-brother Odo, bishop of Bayeux, and his closest friend, William fitz Osbern, to govern in his absence, and, says the Anglo-Saxon Chronicle, they 'built castles far and wide throughout the country, and distressed the wretched folk, and always after that it grew much worse. May the end be good when God wills!'[52] In the king's absence[53] his new castle at Dover proved its worth by holding out against an attack by the men of Kent led by count Eustace of Boulogne, and on his return he was compelled, early in

1068, to march upon Exeter which had rebelled against him, and where he planted the castle in the northern corner of the city after its submission. Later in the same year 'the king was informed that the people in the north were gathered together and meant to make a stand against him if he came',[54] and there followed William's first northern expedition and the foundation, amongst others, of his first castle at York (a second was planted in 1069 on the Conqueror's second northern expedition). Ordericus Vitalis describes how the king on this occasion 'rode to all the remote parts of the kingdom and fortified suitable places against enemy attacks'[55] and goes on specifically to refer to the raising of castles at Warwick, Nottingham, Lincoln, Huntingdon and Cambridge as well as at York.[56]

It is scarcely necessary to continue this ball by ball and castle by castle commentary on the Norman Conquest of England. One cannot miss, in general, from any reading of the sources, the contrast between the plethora of references to castles in and after 1066 and the paucity and exceptional nature of such references before, nor fail to mark how the very progress of that conquest and settlement is marked by the castles which were raised. A glimpse of Norman England, held down by a network of castles as early as 1074, is afforded by the Anglo-Saxon Chronicle in its account of the journey undertaken in that year by Edgar 'aethling' (prince) and his household from Scotland to the Conqueror in Normandy – 'And the sheriff of York came to meet them at Durham and went all the way with them and had them provided with food and fodder at every castle they came to until they got overseas to the king'.[57] Nor is the overwhelming evidence of Norman castle-building confined to the narrative sources. Domesday Book frequently refers to the number of houses or tenements destroyed in towns and cities to make way for castles which thus self-evidently are new (166 at Lincoln, 113 at Norwich[58]), and castles also now appear, though they did not before, in charters, writs and letters, as when, in 1075 with rebellion brewing, archbishop Lanfranc writes to Roger earl of Hereford commanding that the greatest care be taken of the royal castles.[59] We have already quoted the lament of the Anglo-Saxon Chronicle at the raising of castles by bishop Odo and William fitz Osbern in 1067 and its association of castles with oppression. The same note is struck by the same source in its obituary of William the Conqueror –

> 'He had castles built
> And poor men hard oppressed'[60]

– and we can still hear across the ages the curse of archbishop Ealdred of York upon Urse d'Abbetot the sheriff for raising the castle at Worcester so close to the church that its ditches encroached upon the monks' cemetery: 'Hattest thou Urs, have thou God's kurs'.[61] The native English evidently saw the castle as the symbol and the substance of oppression as we, as historians, see it as the symbol and the substance of feudal lordship. 'You shall have the lordship in castle and in tower'.[62] If one wants a still visible, vivid impression of the impact of the Norman Conquest upon the English countryside and Old English society one cannot do better than look at because we're not using aerial view, for example, Pleshey in Essex (**9**), where everything is new – castle, fortified township, and even the name – in a place which did not exist before 1066 but was thereafter chosen by the new, Norman, Mandeville lords, as the *caput* or head of their Essex honour. This is the indelible imprint of the Norman Conquest upon the land, signifying a social as well as a political revolution. And like so much else established in the strenuous days and years of 1066 and after as the means to an immediate end, the castle was to remain for centuries as part of the fabric of society and the state, and in a certain sense is with us still.

Chapter 3

The Norman and Angevin Period
1066–1215

Wε shall deal in the next three chapters with the architectural history of the castle in England and Wales, its development and subsequent decline, from the period of the Norman Conquest, which is the beginning of the history of castles in this country, to the end, which we may place in the sixteenth century. Scotland, though greatly affected by Norman penetration and owing its castles in the beginning no less to their influence, retained its independence as a separate kingdom throughout the Middle Ages and beyond, and therefore must remain a separate story.[1] We shall deal first, in this chapter, with the years from c.1066 to c.1215, with Norman and Angevin England (and Wales whose conquest in effect begins in 1066 to be completed by Edward I), that is to say with the feudal kingdom of William I (the Conqueror, 1066–1087) and his two sons William II (Rufus, 1087–1100), and Henry I (1100–35); with Stephen (the Conqueror's nephew, son of his daughter Adela and Stephen Henry, count of Blois); and with the three Angevin monarchs (succeeding through Henry I's daughter Mathilda, married to Geoffrey count of Anjou), namely Henry II, Richard I and John (respectively 1154–89, 1189–99, 1199–1216). We must not unduly emphasize the kings, since their great vassals will have castles too, and some rear-vassals also. Nevertheless it is to be remarked that William I, of course, was duke of Normandy, as was Henry I after 1106. William Rufus sought to become duke of Normandy, and Stephen lost the duchy to Geoffrey of Anjou, the husband of his rival Mathilda, in what was perhaps his most important failure. As for the Angevins, they were counts of Anjou, also dukes of Normandy and also dukes of Aquitaine as well as kings of England. If we add the obvious fact that, as from 1066, the vassals and rear-vassals of these 'English' monarchs, the barons and the ruling-class of England who established great lordships also in Wales, were predominantly Normans or otherwise 'French' almost to a man, we may begin to understand something of what the Norman Conquest means in the history of England, and to realize in particular that 'English' castles are in the beginning the castles of these men in England and Wales, and scarcely to be understood without reference especially to Normandy and Anjou.

The Norman and Angevin period chosen as our first for this chapter may

seem a long one but, while all chronological divisions of the continuous process
of history are arbitrary and potentially misleading, this period has a certain unity
of its own in general history and, in the narrower context of castle studies, may
do less harm than anything shorter. Much that is misleading, for example, has
been written in the past about 'the castles of the Anarchy', i.e. the reign of
Stephen, as though they were somehow a separate category, and similar
disadvantages could arise from a separate treatment of 'the castles of the
Conquest', not least in the possible implication that castles of earthwork and
timber, which undoubtedly predominated at that time, were, again, a
fundamentally distinct category of castle. In reality, though there is a great
deal of progress in the design and construction of castles in England and Wales
between 1066 and 1215 as we shall see, and amongst it a transition from the
prevalence of timber fortification to a predominance of stone, the emergent
pattern of the late twelfth century is already implicit in the late eleventh.
Moreover, by the end of the twelfth century we are on the threshold of that
period of supreme achievement which comes about, for a variety of reasons, in
English castle-building in the thirteenth and early fourteenth centuries and
which deserves separate treatment in its own right – thus leaving us with the
underworked period of the castle's decline as an architectural form for the third
and final chapter of the three.

In an earlier chapter something was said of the form as well as the origin of
early castles on the Continent, not least in Normandy and the valley of the Loire,
as a necessary introduction to the history of the English castle. It was then
suggested that there were two basic principles of castle design from the
beginning to the end, the enclosure and the great tower, and that these were
sometimes combined and sometimes not, in that one could have an enclosure
without a great tower but not a great tower without an enclosure. It was also
suggested that the material of construction, in practice either timber or masonry,
since both are likely to be combined with earthwork, is a secondary matter:
both, of course, may at any time be used together, but in any case, while it is
generally assumed that timber construction prevailed in the early period even on
the Continent, and certain that masonry predominated at least from the later
twelfth century onwards, stone defences are present from the beginning of the
castle's history, and that history is not a straightforward question of progress and
conversion from one to the other. Finally, it was suggested that the seeming
enigma of the motte, already used in Normandy as elsewhere in France before
1066, best fits the overall pattern of enclosure and great tower if it is associated
with the latter, which by all the evidence seems to have been the case.

This, then, is the background to the castles of the Conquest which, as we have
also seen, began to rise as soon as the Norman invasion force disembarked at
Pevensey in 1066, and, indeed, before if we recall the castles of the 'Norman
favourites' of Edward the Confessor. It seems clear that the great majority of the
innumerable castles of the first generation of the Norman Conquest were of
earthwork and timber, and it may well be that we should attribute this less to

contemporary custom and fashion in Normandy and France and more to the circumstances of the Conquest itself and the over-riding necessity for speedy fortification and digging in, with for the most part an unskilled labour force. The combined resources of England and Normandy, we may surmise, could not have produced so many castles so quickly in any other way. It is also clear that while a considerable number of the earliest castles in England were simply of the enclosure type, and others had great towers of stone more or less from the beginning, a great many more had mottes and were of the motte-and-bailey pattern. The most recent figures available from field studies of early castles raised between *c*.1066 and *c*.1215 are 741 castles with mottes as opposed to 205 'ringworks' or enclosures without them,[2] and while no-one would wish to claim mathematical accuracy for the exact figures, the proportions are not likely to be far wrong. Further, though perhaps a large motte may take longer to raise, and longer to consolidate, than the banks of an enclosure, and though recent excavations have shown that a motte can be added later to an earlier enclosure as at Castle Neroche in Somerset,[3] or converted out of one as at Aldingham in Lancashire,[4] there is as yet no compelling reason not to suppose that the motte-and-bailey type of castle was constructed in England from the beginning. The Bayeux Tapestry, which seems surprisingly accurate in architectural and archaeological matters,[5] shows the Normans raising a motte at Hastings in the first days of their invasion in October 1066 (**7**). The existing motte at Hastings castle, albeit much mutilated, has not been archaeologically disproved to be an original feature, and nor, for that matter, have the formidable mottes at the pre-Conquest castle sites of Richard's Castle (**II**) and Ewyas Harold.[6] It is not easy to date precisely surviving features of the castles of the Norman Conquest and settlement, but amongst mottes which can be reasonably securely dated those at York (1068–9),[7] Carisbrooke ('at least' the 1070s[8]) and Hen Domen, Montgomeryshire 1070–74[9]) (**IV**), are evidently both early and original. The motte-and-bailey castle, as indeed one would expect of a successful architectural form, was as admirably suited to the needs of the Norman *conquistadores* in England and Wales as it was to their society and the warfare which they waged, but the attractive theory that it was in fact evolved in the strenuous years which followed 1066 cannot be sustained, as we have seen, not least because it was already known in Normandy and France before they came.[10] Unfashionable as it may therefore seem, by contrast with the current publicity given to 'ringworks' by English archaeologists, we shall begin with the motte-and-bailey as a very common, and thus characteristic, type of early castle, and one, too, which entirely fits the chronological confines of this chapter, since it is probable that at least in England none were raised, though many survived, after the close of the twelfth century.[11]

The classic motte-and-bailey castle, then, consists of two elements, the motte and the larger enclosure of the bailey. The former dominates the whole and it is significant that some early texts refer to it as the donjon.[12] It is a part natural or wholly artificial mound of earth, roughly circular or oval in plan, with a flat top

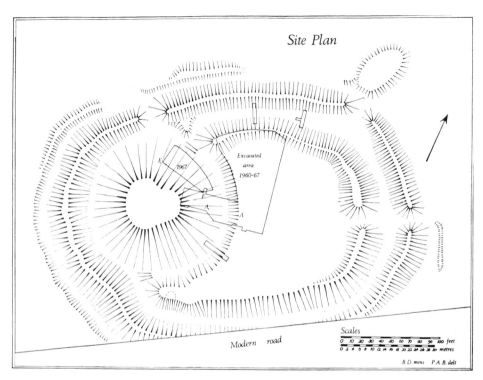

IV Hen Domen, Montgomery, ground plan.

and varying, as one might expect, considerably in size. A recent survey of English mottes shows their height ranging from less than 5 metres (*c*.15 ft) upwards to above 10 metres (*c*.30 ft), suggests that their diameter will always be at least twice their height, and finds also that the biggest mottes tend to be the earliest.[13] By contrast, some are so low as scarcely to be mounds at all but banked enclosures evidently serving as the strong-point and headquarters of the castle in the same way as a motte. For them the regrettable term 'ring-motte' has lately been invented. Castle Acre in Norfolk (**10**) is an instance of the type which is also common in Hampshire. The normal motte has a ditch about its base, either dry or water-filled, with probably a counter-scarp on the outer edge. At Hen Domen (**IV**) there was a palisade as well as a ditch about the foot of the motte.[14] The motte itself is at least partly constructed from the material thrown up from the ditch, and one method of construction to achieve the necessary solidity was by an ascending series of rammed-down layers of material, as is evidently indicated by the Bayeux Tapestry's representation of the raising of the motte at Hastings (**7**), is revealed by some aerial photographs of Pleshey in Essex and has been archaeologically detected at Norwich, Carisbrooke and the Baile Hill at York. Cut off by its ditch and raised aloft, the motte is thus distinct from the bailey which generally lies to one side of it. It is as difficult to envisage the motte as it is the great tower without a bailey since, save in the very largest instances (e.g. Norwich), the space upon the summit must be insufficient both for all the appurtenances of lordly residence and for sufficient military action. The larger enclosure of the bailey will be defended by its own ditch, dry or wet, and bank, the former joining up with the ditch of the motte, and will contain all those domestic and military requirements which the motte cannot provide. Its entrance will be the main entrance of the castle. Its shape will obviously vary, but a kidney or bean shape partly clasping the motte, again as at Pleshey (**9**, **V**), is not uncommon. Variations on this classic overall plan include the motte standing entirely within the bailey as at Bramber and Aldingbourne, both in Sussex, and two baileys as at Arundel and Windsor (**36**) (in both those cases with the motte between them). Much less common is to find two mottes as at Lewes in Sussex (**VI**) and, less certainly, at Lincoln. A double ditch about the whole castle, as at Berkhamstead (**18**) and Hen Domen (**IV**), is also rare, and there is reason to suppose that this kind of double strength was a regalian right closely controlled in the early period.[15] One may, of course, find motte-and-bailey castles (e.g. Pleshey, Tonbridge), as one may other types of early castle (e.g. Castle Acre) and later castles (Caernarvon, Conway, etc.), in association with contemporary fortified townships, and so marking, in text-book fashion which even he who runs may read, the difference between the castle and communal fortifications.

It is comparatively easy to generalize about the earthworks of the motte-and-bailey castles since in innumerable instances they survive, however eroded or otherwise disguised. It is much more difficult to speak plainly of the buildings and other defences of early castles when these very seldom survive, never survive if they were of timber construction, and may, indeed, have vanished without trace even for the archaeologist. It is still true to say, moreover, that few motte-and-bailey sites have as yet been thoroughly archaeologically investigated with all modern techniques. Nevertheless, archaeological evidence is slowly accumulating with the present revival of interest in castle studies, more especially in early castles and most especially in mottes, while we also have, as we have always had, some few but precious contemporary literary descriptions and even pictorial representations. Round the summit of the motte we should expect to find, in the first generation, a timber palisade, crenellated and with a fighting platform, as was evidently revealed by excavation at Abinger in Surrey,[16] and as seems to be shown in all five of the mottes on the Bayeux Tapestry – Dol, Rennes, Dinan, Bayeux and Hastings (**4–7**) – with the possible exception of the odd and elaborate structures shown on the first and fourth.[17] Within the palisade, or in any case rising from the summit of the motte, we should also expect to find a timber tower. The close association of motte and tower has already been emphasized,[18] and indeed in one twelfth-century literary text the two words are used synonymously – *in mota, scilicet turre lignea superiori*.[19] Towers seemingly of timber are shown on four of the five mottes on the Bayeux Tapestry where the fifth, the unfinished motte at Hastings, bears only a palisade, and the excavations at Abinger revealed a timber tower evidently standing upon stilts, i.e. open at

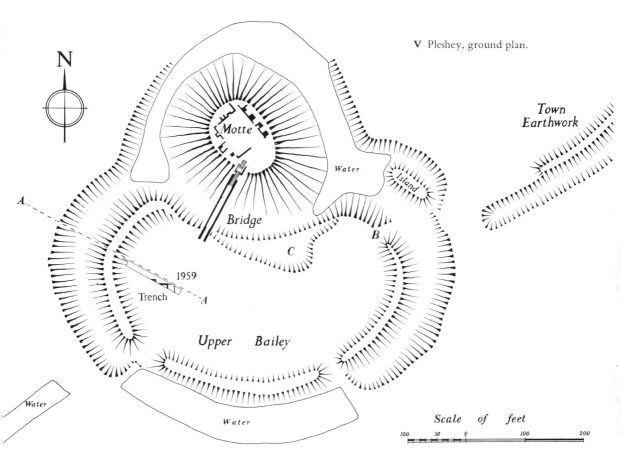

N

Town
Earthwork

Motte

Water

Island

A.

Bridge

B

C

1959

Trench   A

Upper   Bailey

Water

Water

Scale   of   feet

100   50   0   100   200

ground level, after the manner of the Tapestry's Dinan (**5**).[20] At the later (*c.*1140?) site at South Mimms, the timber tower went right down to the natural ground level within and beneath the motte, which was itself revetted with timber to make it vertical and sheer externally.[21] At Farnham a contemporary stone tower was again carried down within the motte (**8**), and a similar method of construction was evidently followed for timber towers at Totnes and Penwortham.[22] There is, however, as yet no reason to suppose that this latter method is anything other than a variant, possibly later, of the norm of setting one's tower securely upon the summit of the mound, and, indeed, it is difficult to envisage any other sequence of construction in the case of the biggest 'Class I' mottes like Thetford, Haughley or Norwich, Ongar or Clare, Ewyas Harold, Dunster, Arundel or Tickhill.

That the motte was the military strong-point of the motte-and-bailey castle is self-evident and borne out by contemporary accounts of sieges.[23] It also seems very likely that it normally bore the residence of the lord and thus had both that

VI Lewes, ground plan.

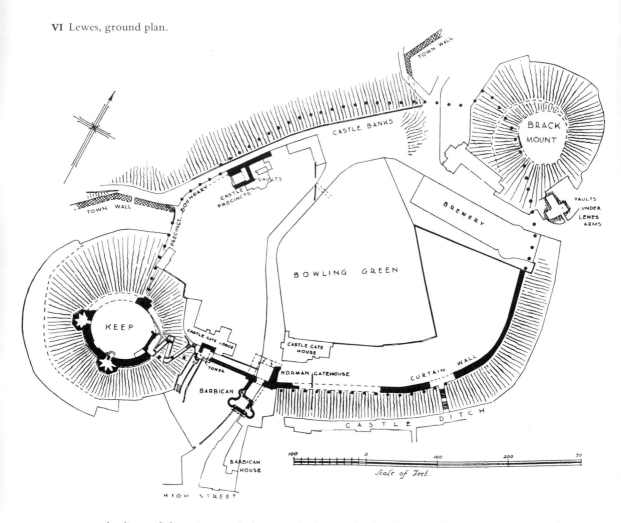

duality of function and that symbolism which allowed the word *donjon* to be applied to it.[24] That even the timber tower which customarily stood upon it in the first generation could comprise lordly accommodation is sufficiently shown by surviving literary descriptions, not least by that of the tower on the motte at Ardres in the early twelfth century already quoted,[25] as well as by the archaeological evidence from South Mimms, and is suggested also by the elaborate structure shown upon the motte at Bayeux on the Tapestry (**6**). It is appropriate at this point to quote a further well-known but precious description of a motte and its superstructure, this time in Belgium or northern France about 1130.[26] We are told by his contemporary biographer, Walter the archdeacon, how bishop John of Thérouanne (d. 1130) was accustomed to stay at 'Merchem' when travelling in his diocese, and here

'There was, near the *atrium* of the church, a fortress (*munitio*), which we may call a castle (*castrum*) or *municipium*, exceedingly high, built after the custom of that land by the lord of the town many years before. For it is the habit of the magnates and nobles of those parts, who spend most of their time fighting and slaughtering their enemies, in order thus to be safer from their opponents and with greater power either to vanquish their equals or suppress their inferiors, to raise a mound (*agger*) of earth as high as they can and surround it with a ditch as broad and deep as possible. The top of this mound they completely enclose with a palisade of hewn logs bound close together like a wall, with towers set in its circuit so far as the site permits. In the middle of the space within the palisade they build a residence (*domus*), or, dominating everything,[27] a keep (*arx*)'.

The archdeacon goes on to say that the gate into the enclosure on the summit of the motte was reached only by 'a bridge which rises gradually from the counterscarp of the ditch, supported by double or even triple columns at suitable intervals'. There follows the story of how one day this bridge at Merchem broke under the press of the good bishop's followers as he was descending after changing his vestments in the keep where he was lodging: all fell 35 ft and more into the water, though all by God's mercy were saved.

A flying bridge of timber such as is here described at Merchem, connecting the bailey with the motte top and stepped for the better passage of men and horses, is shown on the Bayeux Tapestry at Dol, Dinan and Bayeux, though perhaps less certainly at Rennes (**4–6**).[28] This, too, was the type of the successive bridges at Hen Domen. At Abinger, however, the bridge from the bailey was horizontal to the foot of the mound,[29] and at the Baile Hill at York possibly original steps,[30] such as may be shown at Rennes (**4**), were found cut into the mound, implying a similar arrangement. As for the bailey itself, we should expect its bank to be crowned by a stout timber palisade with crenellation and parapet, pierced by the entrance to the castle, doubtless in the form of a timber gate-tower,[31] and quite possibly set about with other timber towers such as have been found at Hen Domen.[32] It is generally assumed that the bailey palisade would sweep up two sides of the motte to join the palisade on its summit, on the analogy of the wing walls joining the curtain wall of the bailey to the 'shell keep' on the motte in certain motte-and-bailey castles which have acquired stone defences (e.g. Arundel, Carisbrooke), though this arrangement was not followed at Hen Domen.[33] Within the bailey we should find all the buildings and accommodation required in addition to what is provided on the motte, and in our classic motte-and-bailey these are assumed to be of timber in the first generation though this may not have always been the case. A sequence of four or five phases of timber framed buildings, including a chapel, has been traced in the bailey of Hen Domen dating between *c*.1070 and *c*.1300[34] Though timber-framed buildings can, of course, be structurally very sound, long-lasting and also impressive, none are known to survive from the castles of the late eleventh and twelfth centuries and we can only refer here by way of illustration to early examples in stone like the halls at Richmond and Oakham or the chapels at Durham and Ludlow.

Increasingly common as was the motte-and-bailey type of castle in early Norman England and during what has properly been called the first century of English feudalism, it is nevertheless certain that not all early castles conformed to that pattern, and that some from the beginning consisted simply of an enclosure without a motte or, indeed, a donjon of any kind. Thus the first castle raised in England by the Conqueror, at Pevensey immediately upon his landing in 1066, was the enclosure represented by the present castle (which received its keep in the early twelfth century and its curtain, gate and mural towers in the thirteenth) in the south-east quarter of the Roman fort of Anderida, then an Old English borough.[35] One of many analogies is provided by the original castle of the Conqueror in London in 1066 before the 'Tower of London' was built, which was a small enclosure between Roman wall and river in the south-east angle of the city.[36] The castle planted by the victorious duke within the borough at Dover after the victory at Hastings seems also to have been an enclosure in the vicinity of the church and about the Roman pharos (**I**), and has certainly left no trace of any motte.[37] Old Sarum,[38] where the Norman castle occupies the centre of the Iron Age earthwork and Old English borough forms an analogy with Dover, and Exeter (1068), where the castle was raised in the northern angle of the Roman walls of the city, with London. The cutting-off by bank and ditch of one corner of a pre-existing and larger fortification (Portchester is another instance, albeit of uncertain date) seems almost to be a type of early castle. Meanwhile enclosures without mottes, free standing, so to speak, in open country, are also found. The earliest so far to be archaeologically examined is at Sulgrave in Northamptonshire, dated to the period of the Conquest,[39] though until the excavations there are completed the twelfth-century Penmaen in Glamorganshire (**III**) stands archaeologically as the classic of its type. This had bank, ditch and an elaborate timber gateway, though no trace of any palisade.[40] Neither Sulgrave nor Penmaen in fact are particularly impressive for their strength, and indeed the absence of any contemporary written reference to either as a castle prevents us from being certain that they ranked as such, but there is no doubt, of course, that the enclosure with neither motte nor great tower persists from start to finish as a basic type of castle and includes some of the finest in the land – as witness, amongst many possible examples, Framlingham (**12**) in our present period of the eleventh and twelfth centuries, or Conway (**XIV**) and Caernarvon (**XIII**) for the thirteenth and the fourteenth.

Further, if the conventional assumption is valid that the motte-and-bailey castle in its first and 'pure' phase bore only timber buildings and defences (an assumption perhaps more valid for the motte than the bailey), the same is not true for the enclosure type of castle which can show some of the earliest stone fortification as a primary feature. Thus the gate-tower at Exeter evidently dates from the castle's foundation in 1068, while both Richmond (Yorks) and Ludlow

(**11**) were evidently stone-walled enclosures from the beginning, each with a contemporary gate-tower like Exeter (though in each case converted into a donjon in the twelfth century), and each, be it noted, with stone mural towers to strengthen their *enceinte*. The last point is important since the use of mural towers to provide flanking fire onto the exposed outer face of a wall was formerly considered a thirteenth-century technique (though used, of course, in classical times), while the fact that the same technique could be applied in the earliest period in timber, as at Hen Domen, is a further indication of the falsity of a too rigorous distinction between timber and masonry castles. The castle of the Peak in Derbyshire also seems to have had a stone curtain wall from the beginning, while very little later than Richmond and Ludlow is the second and present castle at Rochester (**39**), known from the *Textus Roffensis* to have been built for William Rufus by Gundulf bishop of Rochester, and begun some time between 1087 and 1089. Later much developed and the existing great tower (**14**) added in Henry I's reign about 1127 (see below), Gundulf's was an artificially levelled enclosure with a stone wall on the line of the present one, surviving in large part, though heightened, along the west or river front of the castle, where it made use of a section of the old Roman wall of the city for its base. It had at least one mural tower (on the site of the southerly of the two eastern towers of Edward III facing the cathedral) and probably others, a main gate-tower on the site of the modern entrance from Castle Hill, and a great ditch on the three landward sides.[41]

A fine castle of the same type dating from the end of the period covered by this chapter is Framlingham in Suffolk (**12**).[42] Rebuilt as it now stands, it is principally the work of Roger Bigod, earl of Norfolk, in *c.*1190, and is again the second castle, the first, on the same site, having been demolished by Henry II after the rebellion of the previous earl, Hugh Bigod, in 1173–4. The principal strength of the castle is and always was (the large outer bailey to the south and east never apparently having been defended by more than a palisade about its bank and ditch) the oval-shaped inner ward, enclosed by its stone curtain wall strengthened by a systematic series of thirteen mural or flanking towers which project from it and rise above it. Save for the multiangular tower at the south-east angle (a little reminiscent of the contemporary Avranches Tower at Dover, for which see below), these towers are rectangular and most of them open to the gorge. They strikingly resemble the towers of Henry II's Dover (below) which slightly antedate them, though their immediate analogy was probably the mural towers of the now vanished curtain of the same king's castle at Orford, again built a few years before (below). That there can be such close affinities between a baronial and a neighbouring royal castle, perhaps even suggesting the employment of the same master mason, is a useful reminder of the nature of feudal society, where the king's lordship is superior but in a sense not different in kind from that of other lords.

It is also a fact that the great tower built in stone was a feature of some castles in England from the beginning – though all due allowance must, of course, be made for the consideration that such things could not be raised at the drop of a hat, as William the Conqueror is said to have spent eight days in raising the castle at Dover.[43] Though we have no precise date 'the Tower', i.e. the White Tower (**27, XXI**) – which ever since has so dominated the royal castle in London as to give its name to the whole – was begun in the Conqueror's reign, probably in the 1070's, though it may not have been finished until after his death. This is truly formidable, impressive by any standards, a building, it has been pointed out, 'the like of which had not been seen in England since the grandiose days of the Roman occupation',[44] and a measure thus of the impact of the Norman Conquest. For our purposes, it is not only the earliest stone keep or great tower in England but also, with the one exception of Colchester (below), the largest, and amongst the largest in Latin Christendom. It measures 118 ft by 107 ft and rises 90 ft high from ground level to battlements, its four angle turrets rising above this again, and its walls 15 ft thick at the base (narrowing to 11 ft at the top). It was, of course, intended to be the principal strength of the castle to which the Conqueror added it, but it also contained, on two floors above the basement, suites of accommodation for the king and his immediate household (as witness the fireplaces and garderobes), the royal suite evidently being on the second floor with direct access to the splendid chapel of St John the Baptist on the same level. (Here one can get closer to the Conqueror and the Conquest than anywhere else in England.) The original entrance was at first-floor level, at the west end of the south or river front, and must have been reached by timber stairs, perhaps through a timber forebuilding after the manner of Doué-la-Fontaine.[45] In plan, the White Tower, like most early tower keeps, is rectangular, though its north-east angle turret is cylindrical (containing the main stairway) and it has, at the south-east corner, a bold apsidal projection running through the whole height of the building and housing in fact the east end of the chapel, its crypts and triforium. At the Tower, recently discovered structural evidence has shown that this apsidal projection represents a change from the original intention of a straightforward rectangular keep, but precisely the same feature, otherwise unique in Western Europe, is found in the great tower at Colchester which also dates from the Conqueror's time. No surviving precursors are known for this design, which certainly seems antique and 'Carolingian', and it has been suggested that it may derive from the great tower at Rouen, built by Richard I in the mid-tenth century and demolished with the whole ducal castle there by Philip Augustus of France after his conquest of Normandy in 1204.[46] Colchester (**13**), which otherwise closely follows the Tower of London in plan and design, is even bigger, a colossal $151\frac{1}{2}$ ft by 110. It too, had its original entrance at first-floor level, the present handsome entrance being an early twelfth-century insertion. While the Tower of London has been much restored, and altered in appearance, not least by Sir Christopher Wren's window openings of late seventeenth and early eighteenth-century date, the majestic tower at Colchester has lost its upper stages altogether as the result of attempted demolition in and after 1683. Both, it may be added, now suffer the same modern and unhappy fate of being used as museums, which prevents their being seen inside for what they were and are.

As in France, so in England and Wales, the great tower is one of the basic principles of castle building from the beginning to the end, and in this country steadily increases in number during the period covered by the present chapter, so that it has come to be regarded as especially characteristic of the twelfth century and the later twelfth century in particular – which is true enough in terms of contemporary fashion but erroneous if it implies the assumption that the great tower or tower keep was thereafter obsolete or obsolescent. Another example from the reign of the Conqueror is found at Chepstow in Monmouthshire (**28, XXIII**), attributed to William fitz Osbern, the king's closest friend and earl of Hereford (also lord of the Isle of Wight), already established here and pressing on into Gwent and south Wales before his death in 1071.[47] At Chepstow there is something for everybody interested in medieval military architecture, but the keep in the centre of the castle, at the narrowest part of the ridge on which it stands, together with surviving sections of the adjacent south curtain of the Upper and Middle Baileys, are evidently primary features. The former is notably oblong (100 ft × 40) and was heightened and otherwise 'modernized' in the thirteenth century. As built in the eleventh, it had two storeys only, a basement and a main residential floor comprising the great hall, with a fine entrance in the east wall leading into the basement but elevated and stepped up from the Middle Bailey. It was in short, that type of low and oblong donjon, as opposed to the towers proper, which we first met at Langeais[48] (**2**) and shall meet again at Castle Rising (in turn affiliated to Norwich and Falaise) and elsewhere.[49] At the present time, indeed, examples of stone tower keeps dating back to the eleventh century, though inevitably rare, show signs of being multiplied. As this book is being written a great donjon 71 ft square is emerging from current excavations within the 'shell keep' and inner enclosure of the Warenne castle at Castle Acre (**10**). There are many puzzles and enigmas, not least that its walls were doubled in thickness in the course of its construction, but for the moment there it is and with every indication of a very early date. At Canterbury the shattered keep (*c.*90 ft × 75), which in the nineteenth and twentieth centuries was used as a coal store for the gasworks, is attributed at least to Henry I (1100–1135) and has affinities with Domfront which is also thought to be his, but it also has features in common with Colchester and a claim to date back to the eleventh century.[50] The keep at Norwich, again, standing on the Conqueror's motte and, in spite of past mutilation and subsequent restoration, one of the largest and finest in the kingdom, measuring some 95 by 90 ft and 70 ft high, is also normally attributed to Henry I (1100–1135) like the keep at Falaise which it resembles. It is generally supposed with good reason that the Albini keep at Castle Rising (**15**), also in Norfolk and dating from *c.*1138, was closely modelled upon it, yet recent detailed study of the fabric shows clearly two phases of building with a marked change of plan between the (externally plain) basement and the (externally very ornate) upper stages, in which case the first phase must go further back and perhaps to the late eleventh century.[51] The eccentric tower, whose lower levels alone remain, at Pevensey may also go back to that period, with its curious bastions or projections being later additions.[52]

Amongst tower keeps which certainly belong to the earlier twelfth century, pride of place may go to Rochester (**14, VII**),[53] both because it is a splendid example of its type, surviving complete save for its roof, floors and a small part of its forebuilding, and because it is securely dated by documentary evidence to the years following 1127. In that year Henry I granted the custody of the castle to William de Corbeil, archbishop of Canterbury, and his successors, together with permission to build 'a fortification or tower' within it. Contemporary chroniclers subsequently tell us that archbishop William duly built 'a noble tower' in the castle and there is no doubt that this was and is the present keep. It stands 70 ft square and rises to a height of 113 ft from ground level to parapet, with its corner turrets rising a further 12 ft. Its walls, built of Kentish ragstone with ashlar dressings and quoins from Caen in Normandy, are 12 ft thick at the base narrowing to 10 ft at their summit. The entrance, as usual, is at first-floor level, but now, in the twelfth century, covered and defended by a forebuilding or lesser tower built on to the north face of the great tower. The latter contains very obviously what must have been the best residential accommodation in the castle on three floors above the basement, the grandest suite, presumably for the archbishop, on the second floor and rising through two stages with a mural gallery about it. There was also, as befits a donjon made over to a prince of the church, a splendid chapel in the south-east quarter of the top floor, rivalling the chapels of the Tower of London and Colchester though entirely different in its structural arrangement within the keep. Yet with all this, the great tower at Rochester from the time when it was built was also the principal military strength of the castle, as is amply demonstrated by the two sieges of 1215 (below) and 1264. It is the first of those sieges that explains the cylindrical south-east angle of an otherwise four-square tower (**14**), for this is the rebuilding and reparation in the early thirteenth century of the extensive damage done by king John's miners on that occasion.

Rochester has close affinities with the great tower at Castle Hedingham[54] in Essex which must therefore be of similar date and is usually attributed to Aubrey de Vere, who was created earl of Oxford by the empress Maud in 1141, and may have built his splendid donjon to mark his elevation. It measures 54 ft by 53 ft externally, with walls 11 ft thick at ground level and rising to a height of 73 ft without the turrets. The forebuilding which, as at Rochester, covered its entrance at first-floor level, is almost entirely gone. Another stone donjon which can be pretty securely dated to this period is at Castle Rising in Norfolk (**15**),[55] built by William of Albini II, together with the whole of the then new castle, to mark his marriage in 1138 to 'Alice the queen', i.e. the young widow of Henry I, and his subsequent creation as an earl, first of Lincoln, then of Sussex or Arundel (1141). Perhaps through Alice's influence, Rising is closely modelled on the second and completed phase of Norwich, and *via* Norwich therefore has affinities also with Falaise in Normandy. It is thus of the oblong type, some $78\frac{1}{2}$ ft by $68\frac{1}{2}$, excluding the elaborate and unusually decorated forebuilding, but has a height of only some 50 ft comprising one residential floor (hall, great chamber, chapel, kitchen and garderobes) above the basement, and originally only one isolated chamber, presumably for the chaplain, above that level and over the chapel. Kenilworth, of the same basic type (though much altered by Robert Dudley, earl of Leicester, in the sixteenth century, and 'slighted' by Parliament in 1649), may well go back to the reign of Henry I, when the castle was certainly founded by Geoffrey de Clinton I, chamberlain and treasurer of the king, in the 1120's.[56] The shattered fragment of the keep at Corfe (43 ft x 48 ft),[57] a tower proper with two storeys above the basement, its forebuilding perhaps a slightly later addition, is generally attributed to Henry I (**XXII**), as is the former great tower at nearby Wareham (some 80 ft square) of which only the foundations remain.[58] The great tower at Gloucester built by Henry I and known to have been in existence before 1112 has entirely vanished,[59] and so has that of Bristol, traditionally raised by Robert earl of Gloucester in the time of Stephen, described in the thirteenth century as the flower of English keeps and with dimensions estimated to be 90 ft by 75 ft, which is about the size of the keep at Canterbury.[60] At Carlisle the existing keep, though now much altered, is most probably another instance of a great tower built in Stephen's time, in this case by David king of Scots.[61] The towers at Guildford (see also below) and Portchester (as first built before subsequent heightening also of unknown date) are similarly to be listed among rectangular tower keeps probably of the first half of the twelfth century.

In the second half of the twelfth century, and more precisely from the first years of the reign of Henry II, we move into a clearer architectural light, at least as far as royal buildings are concerned, because of the continuous survival of the Pipe Rolls, the great annual account rolls of the Exchequer, which, together with other annual rolls of the king's government, and notably of the Chancery which survive regularly from John's reign, often provide documentary evidence of date more precise than the fallible evidence of style and eye. In this way it is known for a fact that Henry II himself was responsible (and in that chronological order) for the rectangular tower keeps at his castles of Scarborough, Bridgenorth and the Peak, Newcastle and Dover, and partly responsible in that he completed the towers at Bamburgh, Bowes and Richmond. He also built at Orford, Chilham and Tickhill great towers of a different form and style from the rectangular, and with them we shall deal separately together with John's Odiham and Richard's Château-Gaillard (below). As for the king's barons, we have no better direct evidence than we had before (though the increasing survival in general of written records from an increasingly literate society in theory provides a better chance of stray documentary references), but the rectangular keeps of Bungay (Bigod Earl of Norfolk), Middleham (held of the Honour of Richmond by Robert fitz Ralph) and Norham (the bishop of Durham) are firmly attributed to the second half of the twelfth century.

VII Rochester, the keep, floor plans.

Begun 1127

Rebuilt 1226–7

Later

GROUND FLOOR (BASEMENT)   FIRST FLOOR

SECOND (PRINCIPAL) FLOOR   THIRD (TOP) FLOOR

Of all these, Dover (**1, VIII**) is the finest, though it is to be noted that Henry II's keep at Newcastle-upon-Tyne[62] built a few years before it in 1172–7, albeit smaller (62ft by 56), is otherwise very similar to it and was built in fact by the same master mason, Maurice the 'Engineer'. Dover[63] was raised in the 1180s, principally between 1181 and 1185, and is almost comparable to Colchester and the Tower of London as a palatial stone donjon, though now with the additional sophistications of an elaborate forebuilding to cover the entrances at both first and second-floor level, a multiplicity of subsidiary chambers in the vast thickness of its walls, and even a piped water supply. It measures 98 ft by 96 ft above the splayed plinth at its base and excluding the forebuilding and rises through two storeys above the basement to an overall height of 95 ft. Its walls, built of Kentish rag with ashlar dressings mainly of Caen stone, vary in their immense thickness from 17 to 21 ft. The keep which, it is important to note, continued to serve as a royal residence and part of the 'palace' buildings within the castle down to the seventeenth century, was extensively 'modernized' for Edward IV in the late fifteenth century, which has altered the appearance of most of its window openings externally, and its fireplaces and most of its doorways internally. The second and topmost floor, which rose through two stages with a mural gallery, was clearly the grandest, intended for the king himself, but the splendour of this has been ruined by the hideous brick 'bomb-proof arches' inserted in 1800 when the keep, together with the rest of the castle, was again modernized, though this time with exclusively military intent to make it a fortress against the threat of Napoleonic invasion. At this level, only the upper chapel, housed in the upper storey of the forebuilding, still gives some impression of late twelfth-century royal majesty. Amongst the other royal great towers mentioned in this section, Scarborough and Bridgenorth are now much ruined, and the Peak, at Castleton in Derbyshire, by contrast with Dover, is much smaller and less grand, some 40 ft square and 60 ft high, with no forebuilding and little sign of any residential splendour.[64] The keep at Richmond (Yorks) which Henry II is thought to have completed after 1171 is in reality, like the keep at the Lacy castle of Ludlow in Shropshire, the conversion of the early and eleventh-century gatehouse by heightening and strengthening, so that in both cases the former entrance passage at ground level can still be clearly seen.[65] Amongst the baronial keeps, Bungay, attributed to *c*.1165, was demolished by Henry II in 1176 and what little now remains of it was only quite recently revealed by excavations within the curtain wall or shell keep which is thought to represent the refortification of the castle in *c*.1294.[66] It measures 70 ft square with walls 18 ft thick, had a forebuilding covering the entrance on its south side, and is thought to have been some 90 ft high, all of which puts it in the class of Rochester. Norham in Northumberland[67] is stated on contemporary authority to have been built by Hugh du Puiset, bishop of Durham, on the order of Henry II. It is unusual among keeps of this date in having its basement vaulted: originally there were two residential floors above and the tower was heightened in the fifteenth century. Middleham, attributed to *c*.1170, is a magnificent specimen of the oblong type of keep with one main residential floor only, after the manner of Castle Rising which it exceeds in scale with measurements of 108 ft by 78.[68]

Something should be said in general about the rectangular stone tower keeps of the eleventh and twelfth centuries before we leave them, as an attempt to summarize their salient characteristics in spite of individual variations. That they were, in themselves and without counting the rest of the castle they dominate, the fortified residence *par excellence* is already sufficiently apparent. Their military strength seems mainly passive, dependant upon the immense thickness of their walls, the elevation and protection of their entrances, and their window openings small (externally – internally they are splayed or recessed) and few especially at the lower levels. This strength was increased by the splayed out base or battered plinth on which they generally stand, and to some extent by the pilaster buttresses which are another general feature, one or more on each face and others at the angles where they rise up above the roof line and parapet to form corner turrets. Recent work in France strongly suggests that these buttresses, their absence, presence and form, would repay closer study as evidence for typology,[69] while the relationship of the battered plinth to those few instances of great towers covered by earth at their lowest levels (Wareham, Bungay), or sunk in a motte (Farnham – **8**), or with a motte added to them (Lydford), would perhaps repay attention. There is a good deal of evidence to show that tower keeps (in common, indeed, with any other castle tower or wall) could be fitted with a war-head in time of need. This generally took the form of 'hoarding', i.e. a projecting timber gallery supported upon joists (the holes for which can still be sometimes seen, as at Rochester), enabling the base of the tower to be defended (**XXXI**). The more advanced 'machicolation' (**XXXII**), which is the same device in stone, appears on the keep at Niort (1170–5) in Aquitaine, though probably as a slightly later addition, and was evidently incorporated in Richard I's donjon at Château-Gaillard (1196–8, see below). Sizes, of course, vary considerably, but the distinction between the squatter type of oblong keep comprising a basement and one upper storey only (e.g. Chepstow, Castle Rising, Kenilworth, Middleham) and the more vertical towers has already been noted. A forebuilding to cover the entrance, absent in the earliest examples at the Tower of London, Colchester and Chepstow, is increasingly common thereafter, though both the Peak and Appleby are without them even in the later twelfth century. The forebuilding also affords additional accommodation, at least a basement and entrance vestibule in the low, oblong keeps (e.g. Castle Rising), and often a chapel above the vestibule in the higher forebuildings of the higher towers (e.g. Rochester, cf. Dover which has two).

Internally the larger rectangular keeps are usually divided by a cross-wall or spine-wall which gives greater rigidity to the whole structure and facilitates its roofing as well as providing a desirable partition. This could also have its advantages in defence in the last resort as is dramatically shown at the siege of Rochester in 1215.[70] The floors of the keeps of this period are almost invariably timber of joists and planks, though Norham is unusually vaulted at its lowest level and so, for example, is the basement of Newcastle-upon-Tyne. Communication between the various floors was commonly by a vice or spiral stairway in one of the angles, sometimes in each of two opposite angles (Rising, Dover). The residential arrangements of castles in all periods will be further discussed in a later chapter, but meanwhile we should envisage each main floor above the usual basement (or each pair of floors as at Castle Hedingham) serving as a self-contained suite of accommodation for an individual lord, or his lady, and his or her immediate household, each suite usually containing the two basic main apartments of hall and great chamber. Lesser chambers may be provided in the great thickness of the walls in the later keeps (e.g. Dover) or in the corner turrets

VIII Dover, plan of keep at 2nd floor level. The insets are (above) garderobes in the north wall, and (below) forebuilding at 1st floor level.

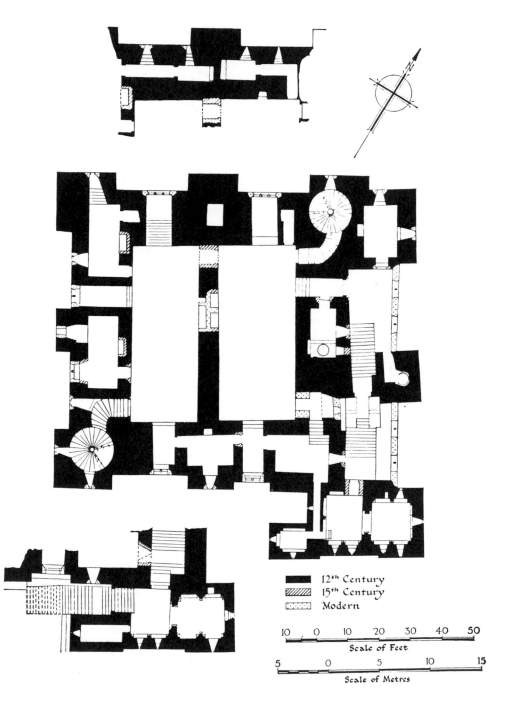

12th Century
15th Century
Modern

(e.g. Rochester). The trick of taking the principal residential floor up through two stages with a mural gallery in the upper stage to give more spaciousness and light has already been noticed at Dover and Rochester and is also found at Castle Hedingham. At Rochester the cross-wall is pierced at this level by a fine arcade, and at Hedingham, both at this level and the secondary residential level below, its place is taken by a great transverse arch. Identifiable kitchens are rare but exist at Norwich and Castle Rising (also at Orford, see below.) Window seats and fireplaces – the latter not invariably since Henry II's Peak has none, yet from the beginning since they are an original feature at the Conqueror's Tower of London – bear silent witness to the fact that these great buildings now stripped of all furniture and decoration were once lived in, and nobly so: so do the chapels (two at Rochester and Dover), and so also do the garderobes or privies, carefully planned and sited as a reproof to such 'modern' palaces as Louis XIV's vaunted Versailles (which had none) and to those who believe sanitation was an invention of Disraeli in the nineteenth century.[71] A well must have been a necessity in a building designed not only as a residence but also as a place of ultimate refuge and defence. At Rochester the well shaft is brought up through the cross-wall with a well-head on each floor for greater convenience, while at Dover it is also brought up to the top floor where the well chamber has a series of lead pipes running off to other parts of the keep.

Not all great towers of stone, however, are rectangular such as those we have so far discussed, but some are cylindrical, some polygonal, and a few others yet other shapes again. In this country received opinion tends to be that the cylindrical keep does not appear until about 1200, that anything which is neither rectangular nor round is 'transitional', and that when the cylindrical great tower does appear it is both an advance upon the rectangular, at least militarily speaking (having no sharp and blind angles difficult to defend), and is largely confined to the Welsh Marches (where, in a state of constant warfare, everyone had to be up-to-date). While it is true that all the earliest known stone tower keeps are of the rectangular pattern (which, it is sometimes suggested, is derived from timber construction), and while it is also true that the cylindrical form was in vogue at the turn of the twelfth and thirteenth centuries, especially in France, it is impossible to sustain the thesis further, since those keeps of whatever shape which are securely dated simply will not otherwise allow themselves to be arranged in any such logical sequence. It is much more likely to be a matter of fashion, and local fashion varying from region to region, of the wills and whims of individual lords and their master masons – and also sometimes of the building materials available, since one cannot build right-angles without dressed stone (a fact which surely explains, for example, the fashion for round church towers built chiefly of local flint in Norfolk and Suffolk, some of which date from the eleventh century). Thus with stone keeps we find, on the one hand, that the rectangular form stubbornly persists to the end of the Middle Ages and long after 1200 both in England (Tattershall – **34** and below) and in France (Vincennes), even though at about that date, in the France of the royal demesne and those provinces which he had acquired from John of England, Philip Augustus was raising cylindrical donjons in his castles like a trade-mark or a sign of royal lordship (Châteaudun, Gisors, Falaise, Chinon, Rouen, Lillebonne, Verneuil, Dourdan). On the other hand, in France we find the cylindrical form at least from the early twelfth century and from a date before some of the finest twelfth-century rectangular keeps were built. Thus Fréteval, near Vendôme and in the county of Blois, though it may not retain its traditional date of 1040, yet cannot be more than a century later.[72] Again, the round keep on the motte of Château-sur-Epte on the borders of Normandy is attributed to Henry I (duke of Normandy and king of England) and to a date of *c.*1130–35. The same Henry I is responsible for the great rectangular keeps of Caen, Falaise, Arques and Domfront in Normandy, and clearly cannot have regarded those as obsolescent when he built them. Further, the peculiarly shaped keeps at Houdan and Etampes, for example, which are not transitional between square and round but, rather, derivations from the latter – the one cylindrical with cylindrical buttresses, the other quadrilobe – are both currently given dates in the first half of the twelfth century (1100–1125 and 1130–50 respectively).[73]

In England, as in ducal Normandy (though there Conches is a further twelfth-century example), the cylindrical type of donjon seems never to have become very popular. Most examples are to be found in Wales and the Marches – Bronlyss (*c.*1176), Longtown (*c.*1180–85), Pembroke (*c.*1200), Tretower and Skenfrith (both early thirteenth-century) amongst others – but not all, for we have Conisborough (*c.*1180) in Yorkshire (**16, X**), Barnard Castle (*c.*1200) in County Durham and Launceston (**19** – early to mid-thirteenth-century) in Cornwall. The majority evidently belong to the late twelfth and early thirteenth century and are thus roughly contemporary with the cylindrical towers of Philip Augustus in France. Nevertheless there is no reason not to accept the truncated remains of the formidable round keep at New Buckenham in Norfolk as an original feature of a castle known from documentary evidence to have been constructed by William of Albini II in *c.*1146, in which case, of course, that tower becomes the oldest known cylindrical donjon in the country, antedating half its rectangular rivals. Further, the 'transitional' keep at Orford in Suffolk[74] – octagonal with three buttress-towers and a forebuilding (**17, IX**) – is known from the unimpeachable record of the Pipe Rolls to have been built between *c.*1165 and *c.*1167 by Henry II, who also probably built the somewhat similar keep at Chilham in Kent in *c.*1170–74 and the plain octagonal keep at Tickhill more certainly in *c.*1178–80 (**X–XI**). All three therefore antedate the same king's great but uncompromisingly rectangular keep at Dover built in the 1180s, yet Henry II, king of England, duke of Normandy and Aquitaine, count of Anjou, the most powerful prince, perhaps, in Latin Christendom, is not a man to be readily charged with obsolescence or out-of-date undertakings. To add, so to speak, to the confusion, and thus to emphasize again that there is no neat chronological sequence or logical development in terms of progress from square keeps to round keeps, in the very years when the classic cylindrical donjon at

Pembroke is assumed to have been built by William Marshal, earl of Pembroke, king John, who was nobody's fool when it came to fortification, preferred the octagonal form of keep (like Tickhill) at his new castle at Odiham (**XI**) in Hampshire (1207–12), and, similarly, there is nothing in England like the quadrilobe Etampes of *c.*1140 until Clifford's Tower at York (below) over a century later.

There is no doubt that the polygonal and cylindrical tower keeps of England and Wales would repay the close, comparative study more frequently given to the rectangular towers. Meanwhile it can be said that the polygonal donjons sometimes have a forebuilding (Orford, Chilham) and sometimes not (Tickhill, Odiham), but that this adjunct does not readily fit the cylindrical form although one is found at Barnard Castle. The internal cross-wall of the larger rectangular keeps is not to be expected, though one does unexpectedly occur in the cylindrical New Buckenham. In France the cylindrical form readily lent itself to vaulting, as witness the great towers of Philip Augustus, but little is found on this side of the Channel in this period (e.g. the basement at Barnard Castle; the top stage at Pembroke which had a domed roof). The buttresses, usually shallow, so characteristic of the rectangular keeps in this country lend themselves to the polygonal form (Tickhill: more pronounced at Odiham), and at Orford are developed, so to speak, into strong, rectangular turrets of which there are three, housing staircase and mural chambers (**IX**. At Chilham there is one, containing the staircase.). This use of buttress-turrets is sometimes found also in the cylindrical towers, after the manner of Houdan, as at Longtown (three), Skenfrith, Caldicot and Chartly (one each), and most notably at Conisborough where the elegant but formidable donjon of *c.*1180 (Warenne earl of Surrey) has six solid, slightly tapered (semi-hexagonal) buttresses projecting from its otherwise perfectly cylindrical shape (**16, X**).[75] Evidently at Conisborough, and perhaps in all cases, such projections facilitated flanking fire, and multiplied fire power, at any rate from the summit of the keep, though there is no known example in England or Wales of the stone machicolation, formed by arches thrown between such turrets or buttresses, which may be seen at Niort (above, p. 50) and which formerly crowned Richard I's keep at Château-Gaillard (1196–8). Nor is there any instance in this country of a great tower built in the shape of Richard's donjon at Château-Gaillard, though it had some vogue in France at the turn of the twelfth and thirteenth centuries, and is found in some of the early thirteenth-century mural towers on the outer curtain at Dover (the Norfolk Towers at the apex and the Fitzwilliam Gate on the east).[76] These towers in French terminology are *en bec*, that is to say, in the case of Château-Gaillard, round to the field (with a splayed out base or *glacis*) but on the other side, in the direction from which attack is expected, built out to a point in a solid prow or beak (**I, XII**). There is much that is dramatically sophisticated at Château-Gaillard (below), but a cruder and slightly earlier precursor for its great tower *en bec* is found at nearby La Roche Guyon, attributed to *c.*1190 and to Richard's rival, Philip Augustus, who built at least one other splendid example (albeit, like

La Roche Guyon, without machicolation) at Issoudun in Bas-Berry (La Tour Blanche, *c*.1202).

This long excursus on the great towers of stone is perhaps commensurate with their importance in the period covered by this chapter and their dominance of the castles which possessed them. We may move on by remarking that almost all those which have been mentioned were additions to castles already existing and thus point to two further considerations. The first, to be more fully discussed later,[77] is that, so great was the number of castles necessarily raised in England and Wales in the first century, and indeed in the first decades, after the Norman Conquest, new castles on new sites thereafter are comparatively rare especially in England (e.g. the castles as well as the keeps of Castle Rising and New Buckenham, Orford and Odiham, discussed above. In Wales expansion into new territory may somewhat alter the proportions). The second consideration is that the building of stone tower keeps, so widespread in the late eleventh and especially the twelfth century, is itself part of the steady increase in stone fortification in general which takes place during the period, the transition, indeed, from timber to stone fortification in so far as timber (and earthwork) was the norm in the generation of 1066. A writ of king John to the sheriff of Worcester in 1204, ordering the rebuilding at Worcester castle of the gateway 'which is now of timber, with good and fine stone',[78] may be taken as the text for the process, which was, however, piecemeal and not entirely complete by the end of our period. In the same year 1204 another writ of John orders the repair 'of our timber castles (*castrorum nostrorum ligneorum*)' in Shropshire,[79] the principal motte at York retained its timber stockade and tower until the present Clifford's Tower was built by Henry III between 1245 and *c*.1270,[80] and, indeed, timber palisades, like timber-framed buildings, will never be entirely obsolete as witness the peles of Edward I in Scotland.[81] It may be also, that the period of the so-called 'Anarchy' in Stephen's reign (1135–54) saw something of a regression in the otherwise steady progress of stone fortification, when, it will be remembered, 'they filled the land full of castles' and men said openly that 'Christ and his saints were asleep'.[82] The raising of castles, generally 'adulterine' i.e. unlicensed, is one of the best known features of the wars between Stephen and his rival the Empress Mathilda, and according to the chronicler Robert of Torigni (abbot of Mont St Michel) one thousand, one hundred and fifteen were destroyed after the peace treaty which settled the succession of the future Henry II in 1153.[83] Though, in spite of its curious precision, we do not have to believe Robert's figure, it is obvious (and confirmed by such evidence as exists) that a high proportion of so many castles can only have been of earthwork and timber, whether of the motte-and-bailey or simple enclosure type, and some were transitory like the castle raised by Mathilda 'in the village of Bampton [Oxon], on the tower of the church there'.[84] But too much should not be made of the case of Bampton, any more than too much should be made of 'the Anarchy', which can be a very misleading historical label if it is taken to mean more than a state of civil war waged over the succession to England and Normandy, neither

IX Orford, the keep, floor plans.

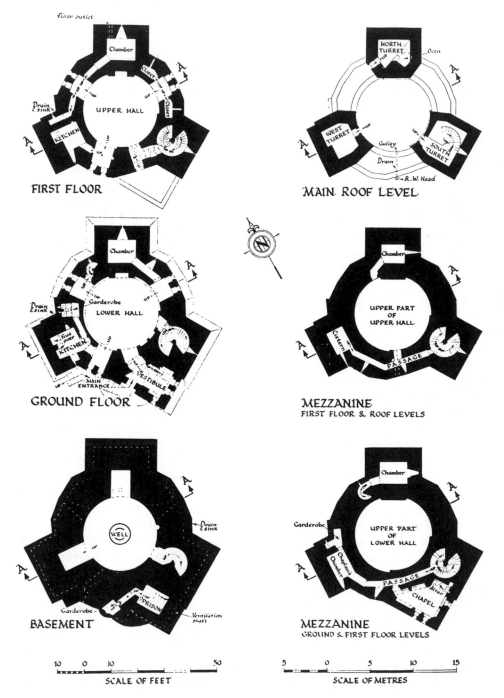

X Comparative plans of twelfth-century keeps, a.

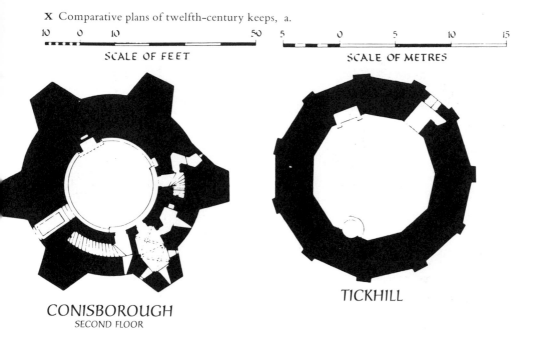

SCALE OF FEET   SCALE OF METRES

CONISBOROUGH
SECOND FLOOR

TICKHILL

continuous nor universal but in this country mainly confined to the south and west between Wallingford and Bristol. It certainly does not imply prolonged conditions in which no permanent or stone fortification could be carried out, as witness the castles of Rising and New Buckenham, the keeps of Carlisle, Castle Hedingham and Bristol itself, the elaborate construction of the timber tower and motte at South Mimms if, indeed, it belongs to this period, and many other instances.[85]

The castles of the 'Anarchy', therefore, do not form a separate category of castle – and in so far as they comprised hasty and illicit structures derived from the urgency of war, these will in any case occur again in the rebellion of 1173–4 and the civil war of 1215–16 – nor do they in themselves make any special contribution to the architectural history of the castle in this period which, as we have seen, is one of increasing stone fortification. As, within this process, we have already dealt both with the development of the enclosure and of the great tower of masonry, comparatively little more now remains to be said. But since, largely because of the circumstances of the Norman Conquest, the typical history of the typical castle in England and Wales is of an early foundation followed by continuous development on the same site, it follows that in very many instances motte-and-bailey castles which at first had only timber buildings and defences in addition to their earthworks must have later been converted into stone castles. A dramatic example is evidently provided by an aerial photograph of Windsor (**36**) where the Conqueror's motte and two baileys can be seen still to underlie the accumulated masonry of subsequent centuries, while another

XI Comparative plans of twelfth-century keeps, b.

ODIHAM   CHILHAM

extreme example of the conversion of an early motte-and-bailey site into a sumptuous castle of almost *Très Riches Heures* sophistication is afforded by Sandal in Yorkshire, now undergoing thorough excavation.[86] That 'conversion' is the appropriate word for this development of many early castles may be adequately shown by, for example, an aerial photograph of Berkhamstead (**18**), where it seems obvious that the existing stone walls of twelfth-century date have simply taken the place of former palisades about the bailey and the summit of the motte. One of the earliest known instances of such a straight-forward conversion occurs at Carisbrooke on the Isle of Wight, where the motte-and-bailey castle of William fitz Osbern established in the early years of the Norman settlement had received by 1136 a complete system of stone-built defences and buildings, comprising a curtain wall about the bailey (a former Roman fort) with a gatehouse and projecting mural towers (rectangular and open to the gorge), stone buildings within the bailey including chamber-blocks, kitchen, hall and chapel (the chapel already in existence by 1082), and a ring-wall encircling the summit of the motte.[87] Such a ring-wall upon a motte is known amongst English archaeologists (and also nowadays among the French, in flagrant defiance of the purity of their language) as the 'shell keep' (*'le shell keep'*), a term which tends to obscure the fact that very often it is simply the conversion into stone of the palisade upon the motte. The 'shell keep', however, may also take the alternative form, found at Berkeley and at Farnham (**8**), in which the ring-wall rises from the foot of the mound and thus revets it – though here it may perhaps be remarked that a timber palisade about the foot of an early motte may also occur, as at Hen Domen, while the South Mimms motte was revetted in timber.

It is possible that with the shell keep we may meet a certain problem – though it is also possible that the problem only arises from the historian's habit of trying to make a tidy pattern out of the untidy past. Nevertheless, while, as we have seen, the motte in the beginning is generally associated with both a timber tower and a palisade about it, the shell keep as we know it generally stands alone. Possibly 'as we know it' and 'generally' are here significant words, for there are, of course, surviving examples of both a stone shell keep and a stone tower keep combined upon a motte or its equivalent – Castle Acre (**10**), Clun, Farnham (**8**), Gisors, Guildford, Launceston (**19**), Lewes, Mitford, Norham, Tretower – and though such cases may now seem exceptional there are not a few of them and there may have once been more. It is possible, too, that the timber tower survived for some time within a shell keep, as may have been the case at Durham. In default of archaeological evidence we do not know – and thus it is worth remarking that no one knew there was a tower within the shell at Farnham until it was recently discovered by archaeological accident. It may be suggested also that in those many cases where no great tower in stone was ever added to a motte, this is likely to have been because of the danger of insecure foundations, as seems to be suggested at Guildford and at Clun where early-twelfth-century tower keeps stand half on but half off their mound in order to have their foundations on the natural *terra firma*. Nevertheless, there seems no doubt from surviving examples that the shell keep could and often does stand alone, without a great tower and as an alternative to it. The shell keep at Windsor (**36**) could in fact be called 'the great tower' by contemporaries as could that at Builth, and the shell keep at Pickering is the King's Tower.[88] Such a keep, no less than the tower keep, will be the donjon, at once the strong-point of the castle and the residence of its lord. 'Houses' for the king are known from the Pipe Rolls to have been under construction on the motte at Berkhamstead (**18**) in Henry II's time,[89] and no doubt such accommodation within a shell keep was often enough disposed about the inner face of the ring-wall as is the extant arrangement, for example, at Restormel (where the buildings are generally attributed to Richard earl of Cornwall in the earlier thirteenth century) and at Tamworth (there much altered and developed later). This, too, is the pattern at Windsor (**36**) where the shell keep, probably raised by Henry I, upon the Conqueror's motte, though heightened as well as restored in the early nineteenth century, still contains a range of timber-framed residential buildings constructed for Edward III in the mid-fourteenth century.[90] Though the keep at Edward I's Builth, built in the late thirteenth century, is thought to have been of this type also, the shell keep seems especially associated with the twelfth century, and is frequently found with the characteristic shallow pilaster buttresses of that period. Its ring-wall will also be crenellated and have a parapet for its better defence, as is the case at Restormel and Trematon, while at the former castle joist holes for an external 'hoarding' or over-hanging timber gallery can still be seen. The keep itself is frequently joined to the curtain of the bailey, and the whole castle thus bound together, by wing-walls up the sides of the motte, such as survive in whole or part at Tamworth, Berkhampstead, Tonbridge, Arundel, Pickering and elsewhere. There may be mural towers about the circuit of the ring-wall, as at Lewes (**VI**), Restormel or Tamworth, and one of these may be an entrance tower or fore-building such as is found at Arundel, Carisbrooke and Berkhamstead. At Launceston (**19**) there is a thirteenth-century mantlet wall about the edge of the motte top and surrounding the twelfth-century shell keep, while the narrow space between the shell and the thirteenth-century great tower within it was roofed over, so that what we may regard as three distinct elements upon the motte, which itself makes a fourth, formed in reality one complex structure. That the shell keep, or, rather, the motte and its superstructure, could indeed be developed into a towering complex is evidently shown especially at Sandal, where what seems to have been an elaborate shell keep (or a cylindrical structure open in the centre), with flanking towers, a projecting gatehouse and a great barbican tower thrust out in front of that again, had one of its towers rebuilt in polygonal fashion as late as *c.*1485. With Sandal we may surely compare the 'seven towers of the Percies' at Alnwick. Again, it is difficult to call the towered inner enclosure and core of Clifford, though built in the late thirteenth century, anything but an elaborate shell keep upon a mound, while for that matter the common arrangement of the shell keep, with its accommodation arranged in a circle about a central courtyard, finds a close analogy in the central 'rotunda' of Edward III's Queenborough in the later fourteenth century (**XXIV** and below) – and that too on one occasion is referred to as 'the great tower'.[91]

When a motte-and-bailey castle is provided with masonry buildings and defences and thus converted into a stone castle, the defences of the bailey will be the same as those of any other castle enclosure and thus need no further comment. What we do need to notice, however, are what contemporary records often call the 'houses in the castle', the accommodation other than that provided by the keep, shell or tower, where there is one, within the castle bailey or enclosure. These will comprise the essential domestic units of hall, chambers and chapel, as well as kitchens, storehouses and stabling. Some of them sometimes of stone from the beginning, they are increasingly so as our period proceeds, and some survive. Pride of place here should probably go to the breath-taking chapel at Durham dated to the 1070s, while the hall (Scolland's hall) at Richmond in Yorkshire also dates from the eleventh century and, evidently, the first phase of the castle. There is a twelfth-century chapel, with circular nave in Templar fashion, free-standing in the bailey at Ludlow, and twelfth-century halls at Christchurch in Hampshire and Oakham in Rutlandshire. Particular interest also attaches to the appearance, as early as the twelfth century, of articulated ranges of residential accommodation disposed in a quadrangular fashion more usually associated with the later Middle Ages. Thus the (old) castle at Sherborne in Dorset is attributed to Roger, bishop of Salisbury, between 1107 and 1139. It contained, and still partly contains, within its more or less rectangular walled enclosure with projecting mural towers, quadrangular ranges of residential buildings about a courtyard, with a small tower keep at the south-west angle. A similar disposition of accommodation, also attributable to bishop Roger, is to be found at Old Sarum, another of the same period at Wolvesey, the palace-cum-castle of Henry of Blois, bishop of Winchester, and the royal lodgings of Henry II and his queen at Windsor in the upper bailey were also built on the quadrangular plan. Our present period ends with the elegant hall-block added by king John to his favoured castle of Corfe (**XXII**), suitably called 'la Gloriette' and as sophisticated and beautiful as anything to be found in the castles and other lordly dwellings of the later thirteenth century.

How far the castle had developed by the end of the period covered by this chapter is best seen in two of the finest examples built in the last decades of the twelfth century, Dover in Kent (**I**) and Château-Gaillard (**20, XII**) on the borders of Normandy. Henry II's works at Dover,[92] mainly concentrated in the 1180s, represent the beginning of the rebuilding and expansion of the castle to take in the whole of the former Old English borough and Iron Age fortress which was not to be completed until the middle of the next century. It was, however, a very substantial beginning, and one of very high quality, and most of the work survives. It comprised the present great tower or donjon, the inner bailey about it, and a section of the outer *enceinte* to north and east. The keep, amongst the finest in the land, has already been sufficiently described (above). The inner bailey is particularly distinguished by its systematic use of mural or flanking towers of which there are fourteen, rectangular in shape, open to the gorge (and now sadly cut down in height). It is also distinguished by its gateways, of which there are two, as a mark of confidence, one to the north (the King's Gate) and one to the south (the Palace Gate). Each had a barbican or outwork in front of it further to defend it, that to the north still surviving, and the design of the gateways themselves is especially worthy of note. No longer in the form, first found at Exeter in *c*.1068 and which will continue throughout the Middle Ages, of a single tower pierced by the entrance passage, they fundamentally consist of a pair of flanking towers brought close together on either side of the entrance, and are thus, in terms of surviving examples of the type, the precursors of all the greatest gatehouses in English castles of the thirteenth century and later (below, p. 66). How much of the outer curtain at Dover was completed by Henry II before his death in 1189 is uncertain, but his work certainly includes the section on the north-east from a point just north of the FitzWilliam Gate (a thirteenth-century insertion) to Avranches and thence southwards to the almost vanished Penchester Tower, and it may have continued thence along the east flank of the castle to the cliff's edge though this has now vanished. The surviving section is again marked by the characteristic rectangular and open mural towers (two between FitzWilliam and Avranches) and by the formidable sophistication of the polygonal Avranches tower with its double tier of firing loops (without counting the vanished battlements), built effectively to block the potentially dangerous re-entrant of the Iron Age earthworks at this point. Further, and perhaps most important of all, the fact that Henry II at least began the outer curtain at Dover in the 1180s means that we have here already the principle of concentric fortification, one line within another, a century before Edward I who is popularly supposed to have invented it.

Yet with all this one may still feel that Château-Gaillard (**20, XII**) above the Seine at Les Andelys is another world.[93] This, of course, is not strictly an 'English' castle, but it was built by the king of England as duke of Normandy, and cannot be omitted from any history of the development of medieval military architecture in this country. It has, of course, the advantage of being an entirely new work on a virgin site, raised in a single operation in the urgency of war with no thought for the cost. The amazing speed with which Richard Coeur de Lion completed the project, the castle itself being only the *pièce maitresse* of the whole system of fortifications including a new town, between 1196 and 1198 at a cost even exceeding the cost of his father's more leisurely (but uncompleted) Dover, will be more fully discussed in a later chapter. Meanwhile it seems impossible not to attribute the advanced techniques of Château-Gaillard, which make it one of the finest castles in Europe though built a century before its rivals, to the military genius of Richard I, by repute the greatest soldier of the age – though to attribute any of its particular features to the king's crusading experience is another matter. Again, we find, surely, the principles of concentric fortification, the keep of unusual and advanced design (containing accommodation for the king and adjacent to the main residential range of the castle) within the inner bailey which is itself more or less surrounded by the middle bailey. A dry rock-cut ditch separates the inner bailey from the middle bailey, and another divides the latter from the outer bailey which is thrust out to the scarped point of the promontory upon which the castle stands. All these defences are disposed, one after the other and interlocked, in the only direction from which attack can come. The tailoring of the masonry to fit the living rock, and the scarping of the rock to fit the masonry, is a feature to be found again at a Conway or Caernarvon a century later. The mural towers set about the outer curtains at Château-Gaillard are mostly cylindrical in the latest fashion and stronger than those at Henry II's Dover. The extraordinary construction of the wall of the inner bailey, into which the inner gateway is ingeniously set, must also have been conceived to give the maximum effect of flanking and enfilading fire (the effect upon the visitor now is rather like those portraits whose eyes look at you wherever you may stand), as well as to strengthen the structure and turn the force of missiles to a glancing blow, and has no known parallel elsewhere. Richard himself was so pleased with the design of his new castle at Les Andelys that he is reported to have boasted his ability to hold it even if its walls were made of butter, and it became the favourite residence of his last years and from it writs and charters were proudly dated *apud Bellum Castrum de Rupe* – 'at the Fair Castle of the Rock'.

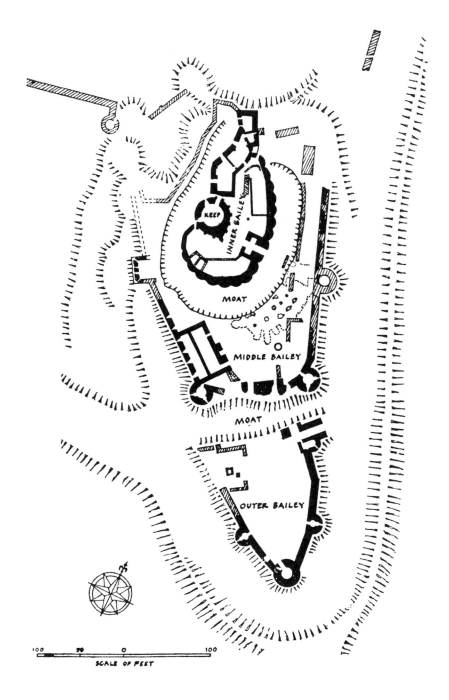

XII Château-Gaillard, ground plan. (*Redrawn from Malencon's plan, by courtesy of Monuments Historiques, Paris.*)

Chapter 4

Apogee

In the course of the thirteenth century, especially towards its end and notably, as it happened, in the reign of Edward I (1272–1307), the castle in England and Wales achieved in architectural terms its apogee. That there could be particular reasons beyond mere architectural logic for these developments will be noted later as appropriate, but meanwhile it is beyond dispute that a concurrence of circumstances produced, at the turn of the thirteenth and fourteenth centuries, the castles, for example, of Caernarvon (**21, XIII**) and Conway (**22, XIV**), Harlech (**23, XV**), Beaumaris (**24, XVI**) and Caerphilly (**26, XX**), which are not only the finest and noblest in Britain but also amongst the finest and noblest in Western Europe and Latin Christendom. The principles of their construction, above all the flanking tower and gate-tower, were not new but manifest a century earlier at Dover or Château-Gaillard, and going back, whether in stone or timber, far beyond and probably to the beginning. But they are applied and developed in this period with a sophistication and ruthless confidence that beggars all description. By these means the castle is now bound, as it were, into an integrated unit, its whole *enceinte* adequately, and aggressively, defended, sometimes tailored to the living rock on which it stands (Goodrich, Conway), or, when the chosen site has no such natural advantages, doubly secured by concentric fortification (Beaumaris, Caerphilly), and/or set within a great expanse of water (Leeds in Kent, Kenilworth, or Caerphilly again, which has both the last named defences).

The result, in many of the new or redeveloped castles of the age, which opens, so to speak, with Beeston and Bolingbroke, both new castles built by Ranulf de Blundeville, earl of Chester, in the 1220s,[1] and ends with Edward's Beaumaris, is often the enclosure type of castle with no keep or great tower as *pièce maîtresse* to provide both ultimate military strong-point and the best residential accommodation. Since also such castles are, perhaps misleadingly, commonly regarded as particularly characteristic of the period, it may seem that the keep has gone out of fashion, rendered unnecessary by the developed strength of the enclosure and the increasingly sumptuous residential accommodation within it. So it is often argued, and, indeed, at Goodrich the small, twelfth-century rectangular tower keep appears almost to be made redundant by the later curtain wall, with its great angle towers and gatehouse, wrapped about it, and by the elaborate residential apartments placed within the enclosure thus defended[2] (all this by Aymer de

Valence, earl of Pembroke, in *c.*1300), while at White Castle (Llantilio) a similar keep of mid-twelfth-century date was entirely demolished in the third quarter of the thirteenth century so as not to impede the flanking fire of the towers then added to the curtain.[3] Nevertheless the train of thought is false which concludes that the tower keep is obsolete from about the year 1200. On the one hand, we have seen the enclosure type of castle with no keep to be a basic type from the beginning, and Caernarvon is nothing else but a sophisticated version of it (Caernarvon, in short, is a 'ring-work' if that term must be used). On the other hand, not only were innumerable keeps of an earlier generation maintained at castles up and down the land, including those at major fortresses like Dover and the Tower of London, both of which were extensively developed and 'modernized' in the thirteenth century, but also new ones were built, as we shall see, and the great tower remains (as it will to the end) a prominent form of fortified residence, the donjon *par excellence*, and a potent symbol of lordship.

The essential function of the mural tower – which, like much else, was inherited by the so-called Middle Ages from the Roman past (e.g. Portchester) – was to provide flanking fire, and especially, by projecting forward from it, to enable the defenders to cover the exposed outer face of the wall without exposing themselves to the slings and arrows of outrageous fortune. In addition, such towers also command with superior fire-power the wall head which they rise above, should the enemy seek to gain it by escalade (p. 131 below), and they divide the wall up into sealed sections against any such event or other breach. They are also, of course, themselves a series of strong-points round the circumference of the castle and, being regularly and systematically placed, cover each other as well as the wall between them. To all these vital functions, it will be observed, the actual shape of the tower externally matters little, and while the cylindrical, or semi-circular, or 'D'-shaped, tower seems undoubtedly the favourite form in this period, it is doubtful if any inherent superiority should be argued for it in the case of mural towers any more than in the case of tower keeps (p. 52 above). The twelfth-century rectangular pattern (e.g. Dover, Framlingham) returns in the fourteenth, for example at Pickering (the Barbican, 1323–6), and meanwhile there were variants in the thirteenth. Polygonal towers, though rare in this country, were preferred at Henry III's ill-fated new castle on the rock at Dyserth in Flintshire[4] (begun in 1241 and demolished by Llewelyn ap Gruffydd in 1263 so that 'not one stone was left upon another'), as they were also, albeit for particular reasons, at Caernarvon (below) – and as they will be again, for no particular reason, at Raglan in the fifteenth century (**31**). The beaked towers (*en bec*) fashionable in France in the early thirteenth century also appear in Henry III's work at Dover, in the splendid trinity of the Norfolk Towers (**1**) at the northern apex of the castle and in the adjacent FitzWilliam Gate of *c.*1227, though we have met this form before in the donjon of Richard I's Château-Gaillard (above). That donjon, like Norfolk and FitzWilliam at Dover, shows the feature of a splayed out or battered base common to mural towers and tower keeps alike, and sometimes in the thirteenth century on rock

XIII Caernarvon, ground plan.

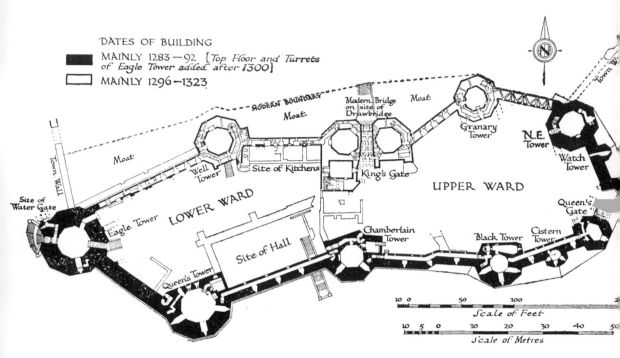

sites especially this develops into dramatic batters and spurs revetting the towers to the ground, as at Goodrich. In this period also additional defence may be provided for towers and walls alike by stone machicolation rather than by the temporary war-head of timber hoarding (**XXXI–II**), though on the whole this feature is less common in England and Wales than France and, when used, tends to be confined to gateways (e.g. Conway).

The gateway itself undergoes considerable development in this period, to produce in the fully developed gatehouse of the later thirteenth and earlier fourteenth centuries, as at Beaumaris (**24, XVI**) or Harlech (**23, XV**), Caerphilly (**26, XX**) or Tonbridge, Dunstanburgh or Kidwelly (**25, XIX**), one of the finest individual features of English medieval military architecture. While the older and seemingly original form of a single tower pierced by the entrance passage, first found at Exeter in 1068 (above), may still be used, as it is in the gatehouse remodelled by Edward I at Leeds in Kent, the most usual form of the most powerful specimens is now that of two mural or flanking towers, one on either side of the entrance passage. The earliest surviving examples of the type, in its simplest form, appear to be the two gateways, the King's Gate and the Palace Gate, to Henry II's inner bailey at Dover (above). King John's gateway at the northern apex of Dover (blocked and converted into the present Norfolk Towers in the early thirteenth century, after the siege of 1216)[5] was of the same

XIV Conway, ground plan.

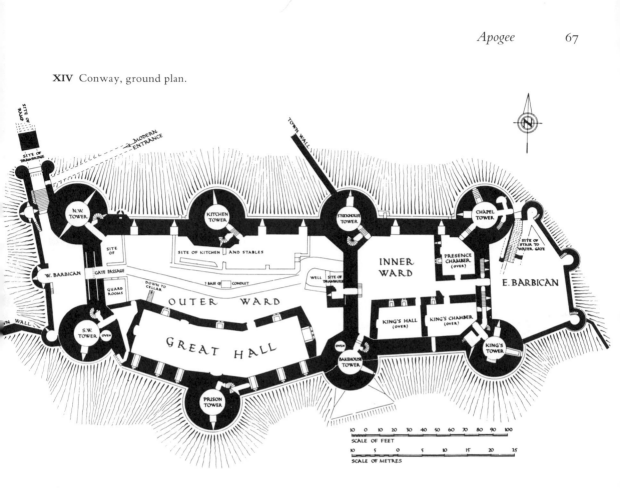

type but with round towers, and so was the gateway at Skipton in the West Riding, of roughly contemporary date.[6] At Beeston in the 1220s the twin towers are again the drum towers of contemporary fashion but, being bound together, so to speak, at the rear and also above the entrance passage, a true gatehouse has appeared, with residential accommodation in its upper storey. From Beeston the way is straight, via e.g. Rockingham and St Briavel's (both *temp.* Edward I), to the splendours of Harlech and Beaumaris, Caerphilly and Tonbridge (the latter much like the former, both pertaining to the same Clare lords), and the rest, all of which, however grand and formidable, are in principal two projecting mural towers on either side of an entrance passage. What has happened is that by these means, combined with such detailed devices, it may be, as machicolation and murder-holes (*meurtrières*, and probably intended more for the quenching of fires at the wooden gates than the slaughtering of foes), drawbridge and portcullis, the gateway, a potential weak spot simply because it is an entrance, has become in many cases the strongest point in the whole circuit of defence. It is not thereby a good idea to refer to such gateways as 'keep-gatehouses' (as is sometimes done), though it is a fact that in its security the great gatehouse from the later thirteenth century onwards may contain some of the best residential accommodation in the castle, as is certainly the case at Caerphilly and Tonbridge, for example, and most notably at Beaumaris, where each of the two gatehouses contained two very grand residential suites.

An added defence of the gateway increasingly found in this period (though found also, e.g., at Henry II's Dover) is the barbican or outwork, designed to keep the enemy at his distance or, by dictating the only possible approach to the gate, to pin and mow him down by withering fire if he advances none the less. In its simplest form it may consist of two parallel walls projecting forward on either side of the entrance to form a narrow and defended passage, though something more complex was devised by Edward I's masons for the main landward entrance of the Tower of London in 1275–6, and subsequently copied by Aymer de Valence at Goodrich.[7] At the Tower there were two gates of twin-towered pattern which still remain on either side of Edward's ditch, namely the Byward Tower and the Middle Tower, but beyond the latter (as its name suggests) was a further defence, in the form of a half-moon barbican (later known as the Lion's Tower and now almost vanished) with its own spur-moat about it. The similar half-moon barbican still survives at Goodrich, and in both cases one could only reach it by another narrow bridge or drawbridge across its moat, and another gate, while upon it one turned at right angles, covered all the time by fire-power, to reach the main gate or gates by further bridges (**XXI**).

The culmination of the advancing techniques of English medieval military architecture is found by common consent in the best of the castles built in the time of Edward I in Wales, notably in the six major royal castles of that king himself in the north, Flint and Rhuddlan, Conway and Caernarvon, Harlech and Beaumaris, and most notably in the last-named four. All these were merely part, albeit the greatest part, of a huge castle-building programme which was itself part and parcel of the conquest of Wales and the Welsh wars of 1277, 1282–3 and 1294–5, and they were concentrated in the north because this, the principality of Gwynedd and the mountain fortress of Snowdonia, was the main centre of Welsh resistance. On this castle-building programme, how it was done and at what cost, we shall concentrate again in a later chapter,[8] but we should certainly note here that it was carried out with all the resources of the most powerful prince in Latin Christendom, with little concern, at least in the beginning, for expense, and that it comprised in all ten new royal castles (including Aberystwyth and Builth in the south), four new seigneurial or 'lordship' castles for the king's marcher lords (Hawarden, Denbigh, Holt and Chirk), and the substantial strengthening and improvement of many existing castles in Wales and the Marches from Chester to St Briavel's. In addition, the new Lacy castle of Denbigh and five of the new royal castles (Aberystwyth, Flint, Rhuddlan, Caernarvon and Conway) were planned and built from the beginning in association with their respective fortified towns.

We may begin with Caernarvon (**21**),[9] for though it was among the last to be begun – with Conway and Harlech in the spring and summer of 1283 in the second Welsh war – it was intended from the beginning to be the finest of them all, the centre and seat of royal government in the north, and the particular symbol of the newly imposed royal and quasi-imperial authority. A glance at a plan of the great castle (**XIII**) will reveal its overall form and design almost without further description – a narrow waisted enclosure whose shape is determined partly by the rock upon which it was sited and, to a lesser extent, by the motte of an earlier castle of the eleventh century which was deliberately retained in the Inner or Upper Bailey to the east (below). The whole is bound together into one integrated and defensible unit by the great and splendid series of polygonal mural towers, so disposed about the circumference as to lay flanking fire upon all of it, and reinforced along the south front by two firing galleries, one above the other, in the thickness of the wall (intended also, but never provided, along the north front), which, combined with the crenellated summits of walls and towers alike, must have provided one of the most formidable concentrations of fire-power to be found in the Middle Ages. The most majestic of the mural towers is the Eagle Tower at the west end, singled out by the further architectural distinction of its three turrets each of which originally had a stone eagle upon it, almost the donjon of the castle since it also contained some of the best residential accommodation (intended at first for Otto de Grandison, the king's vice-regent in north Wales, and perhaps ultimately for the prince of Wales), and containing a watergate leading into an entrance vestibule in its basement (above which were three storeys). The whole castle, of course, is replete with ample and sumptuous accommodation, fit to house not only the resident constable and justiciar with his own household, but also the king, the queen, the prince of Wales, should they come each with their households and aristocratic companions and retainers. As at Conway, the inner sanctum to contain the apartments of the king and queen, which were never completed, was intended to be the Inner or Upper Bailey, to be cut off from the Outer or Lower Bailey by fortified buildings, never completed either, running from the King's Gate to the Chamberlain Tower. There were, in addition to the water-gate in the Eagle Tower, two main gateways to the castle, each in the almost standard form of two flanking towers on either side of the entrance passage, though this is more obvious on plan than when one views them from the ground outside the fortress. The Queen's Gate at the east end, still unfinished, leads into the royal inner bailey and was approached up a ramp and across a drawbridge. The lofty level of the actual entrance and its towering arch is due to the ancient motte retained within the bailey. Of the King's Gate on the north front, which is the main and state entrance from the fortified town built at the same time as the castle, it has been said that 'no building in Britain exhibits more strikingly the immense strength of medieval fortification'.[10] First a drawbridge across the northern moat, then five great doors and six portcullises bar the way, together with an intended right-angle turn and a further drawbridge beyond (never completed), and one is covered all the way by firing loops and spy-holes at various levels, with no less than nine surviving meurtrières or murder-holes above.

Work on this great castle, perhaps the finest in the realm, which began in June 1283, ceased to all intents and purposes in 1330 still not finished. There was the serious set-back of the Welsh revolt of 1294 when the less than half completed castle was over-run and badly damaged, but still more serious for its long-term effects was the increasing diversion, after 1295, of the king's resources to his wars in Scotland and in France, so that the work was never continued quite as originally planned[11] and in the end was never completed. Yet more than enough was done to show king Edward's intentions which at least were nearly realized by the time of his death, still at war with the Scots, in 1307. Moreover, Caernarvon castle as originally conceived is now known to be even more impressive than appears at first sight. For the royal fortress was, amongst other things, a conscious architectural exercise in symbolism and propaganda. The careful albeit inconvenient retention in the Upper Bailey of the motte of the former castle of earl Hugh of Chester, dating back to the first Norman penetration of north Wales in the late eleventh century, was meant to emphasize that Edward's campaigns in Wales were no new conquest but the reassertion of ancient right. And there were also more elevated claims than this proclaimed by the new castle. In this period of the formation of national monarchies in France and England, imperial ideas derived from Roman Law were current. In France the lawyers of Edward's rival, Philip the Fair, were to proclaim that 'the king of France is emperor in his kingdom', and in England also the law-giving king had notions of imperial hegemony over all Britain. It was no accident that the site selected for the principal castle in north Wales and the seat of royal administration was that of the former Roman city of Segontium, with its legendary imperial past. In 1283, the very year of the castle's foundation, what was believed to be the body of the Emperor Magnus Maximus (383–8), allegedly 'father of the noble emperor Constantine', had been found there and reburied in the church by the king's command.[12] There was current in Wales at this time, moreover, and presumably known to Edward, the romance of Maxen Wledig, i.e. of Magnus Maximus, still preserved for us in the *Mabinogion*,[13] which told how, long ago, this same emperor had dreamed of journeying from Rome to a land of high mountains and of coming to a river flowing into the sea, and of seeing opposite the land an island; of how in his dream he had seen a great fortified city at the mouth of the river, and a great fort in the city, the fairest that man ever saw, and great towers of many colours on the fortress, and in its hall a chair of ivory with the image of two eagles in gold thereon. 'To all this the castle which Edward . . . began to build at the mouth of the river Seiont and opposite the island of Anglesey was plainly intended to give substance, to be both the fulfilment of the tradition and the interpretation of the dream'.[14] This, then, is why Caernarvon castle looks to this day different from the other castles of the king in Wales, its polygonal towers and banded masonry a deliberate evocation of the Theodosian wall at Constantinople, Constantine's own city, and hence the Eagle Tower, and hence the eagles. There is something immensely impressive, still after 700 years, in the concentration of effort which Edward I brought to bear upon his wars in Wales, and the focussing of so much resource, not only skill and men and money, but also history and legend and romance, upon Caernarvon in particular. With all this in mind one cannot suppose that it was accident, either, which brought Eleanor, his queen, to Caernarvon to bear their first-born son in April, 1284 – the future Edward II, but also Edward of Caernarvon and the first English prince of Wales.

Conway,[15] built and completed with prodigious speed between 1283 and 1287, is very similar in overall plan (**22, XIV**) to Caernarvon, a long enclosure irregularly shaped to fit a rock site upon which it stands more dramatically than the latter. It, too, is divided longitudinally into an Inner and an Outer Ward, and, also like Caernarvon, was combined from the beginning with a walled town built *pari passu* with it. Like Caernarvon and, indeed, in common with all Edward I's major new castles in north Wales, it also stood upon tidal waters, and could thus be provisioned, maintained, and if necessary relieved, by the sea which the king's fleet commanded. The smaller, Inner Ward, as was the intention at Caernarvon, was an independent and heavily defended inner sanctum containing a grand suite of residential accommodation for the king and queen – hall, privy chamber and presence chamber, each at first-floor level to south and east, with a chapel in the north-east angle tower – and the four great flanking towers which stood about it were accordingly distinguished from the other towers of the castle by turrets as a sign of regality. The Outer Ward contains, amongst other accommodation, the communal great hall, impressive albeit of irregular shape to fit the south curtain which is its outer wall, and what is thought to have been the constable's lodging in and between the two great towers at the west end. All eight flanking towers at Conway are cylindrical drum towers, all gently, almost imperceptibly, battered towards the base in highly sophisticated masoncraft, and all had accommodation worked into them, thus emphasizing again the castle's dual rôle as residence and fortress. The two main gates of Conway east and west (a third lies between the two wards) give access respectively to the royal inner bailey (by water up a vanished flight of steps) and to the outer bailey from the town. They are unusual for this period in not technically being gatehouses but simply entrances through the main curtain wall, though this is no weakness since the adjacent drum towers of the curtain are close enough to serve the purpose of the twin flanking towers of the usual gatehouse, while the entrances themselves are further defended by machicolation above, arrow slits and, in each case, a towered barbican. The whole *enceinte* of the castle, walls and towers, was provided with square sockets below the battlements for the fitting of timber hoarding (p. 50 above). Though Conway of course lacked the particular, symbolic, architectural distinctions of Caernarvon's polygonal towers and banded masonry and eagles, it was, is, and was meant to be deeply impressive, plastered white originally from base to battlements, and with the purely decorative feature (now, like the lime wash, almost vanished) of finials or pinnacles upon the merlons of its crenellation. Nor was symbolism absent from it, whether in its inescapable impression of royal power, or when, before the work upon the new town and castle could properly begin, the Cistercian abbey of St Mary which occupied the ground under the patronage of the Welsh princes of Gwynedd (many of whom were buried there) was moved lock, stock and barrel to a new site at Maenan, as a sure sign that the native ruling house had fallen and a new order come to stay.

Harlech (**23**) is the most dramatically sited of all Edward I's new major castles in north Wales, high on its rock above what was the estuary of the River Dwyryd – hard as it is now to imagine water at the foot of the rock where the outer 'Gate next the Sea' still stands, and shipping in the dock whose place has now been taken by the railway goods yard. The castle was begun, with Conway and Caernarvon, in the spring or early summer of 1283, in the course of the second Welsh war, and was finished some seven years later in 1290.[16] A rock-cut ditch (1295) guards it on the only accessible sides to east and south, and within this the castle is, so to speak, notionally concentric, though the narrow outer ward on plan (**XV**) is more like a platform, its wall, without towers save for the outer gate to the east and the postern to the north, revetting the rock. A further wall runs off to the north to enclose the rock, and, on the west side, makes its way back up to the fortress from the Gate next the Sea. On this side of the castle there are also artificial platforms cut in the rock for the siting of stone-throwing engines. But most of Harlech's formidable strength is concentrated in its main inner enclosure, almost a rectangle, with great drum towers at each of the four angles and a majestic gatehouse in the centre of the east and longest wall, aggressively facing the only practical approach. This last is a classic instance of a late thirteenth-century English gatehouse, basically two D-shaped towers on either side of the entrance passage (originally equipped with three doors and three portcullises), boldly projecting to the field and brought back deep inside the inner ward where each is further strengthened by a projecting, cylindrical staircase turret at the angle. Truly the *pièce maîtresse* of the castle, this gatehouse, very like those at Beaumaris, contains some of the best residential accommodation including a chapel, though further lavish suites were provided against the curtain walls of the inner ward, where there is a great hall opposite the gatehouse with a chapel to the north-east of it.

Beaumaris[17] (**24, XVI**) was the last of Edward's castles in Wales to be begun and, like Caernarvon, was never completed, nor, in this case, were the defences of the fortified township planned to go with it to the south-east. Its immediate context was the Welsh rebellion and third Welsh war of 1294–5, when it was decided to plant in Anglesey a great new castle comparable to those set about Snowdonia on the mainland. Yet already, as early as 1296, with the rebellion crushed, the king's attention, and resources, were diverted towards Scotland: by 1300 the works at Beaumaris had ground to a halt; and though they were resumed again between 1306 and 1330 they were never finished, so that the castle in the latter year must have looked structurally much as it does now. Amongst other things, the great hall and domestic range planned to lie along the east side of the Inner Ward in association with the Chapel Tower were not built, none of the

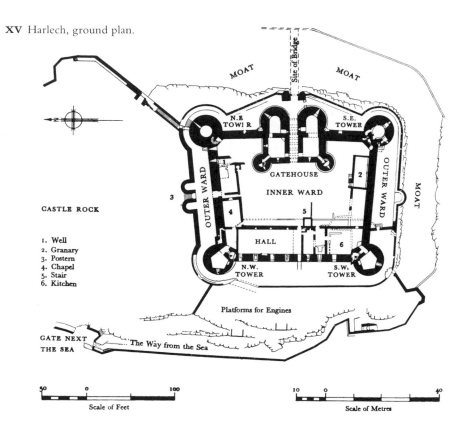

XV Harlech, ground plan.

CASTLE ROCK

1. Well
2. Granary
3. Postern
4. Chapel
5. Stair
6. Kitchen

Scale of Feet

Scale of Metres

great flanking towers of the inner curtain save the north-west angle tower, nor either of the great gatehouses, was ever carried to its full height, nor was the rear half of the southern gatehouse ever built above the foundations which may still be seen. Yet Beaumaris is scarcely to be thought of only in negative terms. Enough was done to make it effective, and more than enough to show the ambitious scale on which it was conceived by the king and Master James of St George, master of the works in Wales. For Beaumaris is the concentric castle *par excellence*, sited upon flat and marshy land which required the doubling up of defences, the inner overtopping the outer, while putting no impediments in the way of a logical and mathematical symmetry of design. The whole is surrounded by a broad and wet moat like that of Edward's Tower of London (below), the outer curtain is liberally supplied with crossbow slits and projecting, cylindrical mural towers, the largest at the four main angles, while the rectangular inner enclosure, its curtain wall of a minimum thickness of nearly 16ft throughout, has four drum towers at the angles, a D-shaped tower in the centre of each of the east and west sides, and not one but two gatehouses of the Harlech plan, respectively in the centre of the north and south walls, as a very aggressive defence. Again it is to be noted that these gatehouses were to contain much of the castle's best residential accommodation,

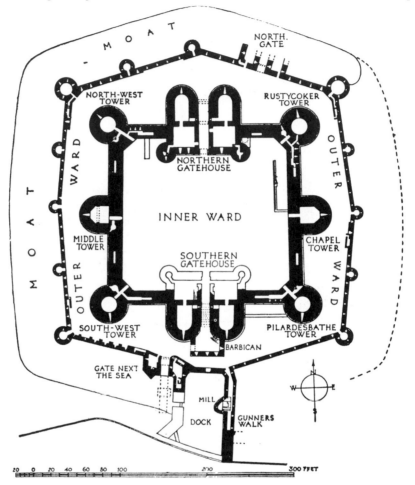

of which at least five separate suites were planned in all, two, one above the other, in each of the two gatehouses, and another on the east side of the courtyard. Again, also, sea–going vessels had access to the castle which had a dock immediately south of it, adjacent to its 'gate next the sea' and sheltered by its outer curtain, a spur wall (Gunners Walk), and the intended wall of the attached borough.

Only by comparison with Caernarvon and Conway, Harlech and Beaumaris, can Edward I's other two new royal castles in north Wales, Rhuddlan and Flint (**XVII–XVIII**), be regarded as of secondary importance. Both were products of the first Welsh war, begun in 1277 and built to secure the king's hold on the hitherto much disputed district of Englefield, now in Flintshire. Both were and are impressive achievements, both were combined with new fortified boroughs (defended in both cases, however, by ditch, bank and palisade, not by stone

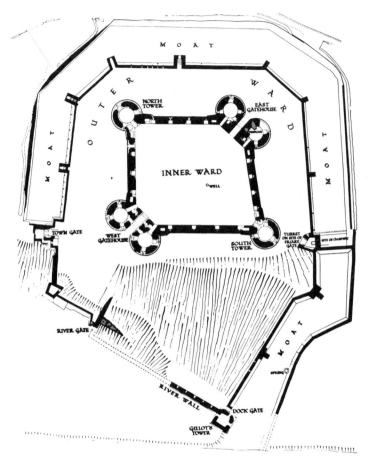

XVII Rhuddlan, ground plan.

walls), and both, as usual, had direct access to tidal waters and the sea, though in the case of Rhuddlan this could only be achieved by diverting the course of the river Clwyd into a deep-water channel, new dug for the purpose, between two and three miles long. The new castle of Rhuddlan (1277–82)[18] and its borough in fact replaced the old Norman borough and motte-and-bailey castle of Robert of Rhuddlan, planted to the south-east of it in the late eleventh century. Edward's castle was concentric in plan, with the waters of the diverted Clwyd originally washing the west wall of the outer curtain and entering the lower south-east arm of the moat where there was probably a dock defended by the present rectangular Gillot's Tower (**XVII**). The rest of the moat was dry, revetted in stone on both sides and closed by massive cross walls on a line with the south-west curtain of the inner ward and by the site of the two main landward entrances, the Town Gate and the Friary Gate. There were also two water gates into the outer bailey, the River Gate and the Dock Gate. The outer curtain, now much ruined and originally of no great height since it was commanded by the main inner curtain behind it, was strengthened throughout by a series of rectangular turrets and buttresses (the former all originally having steps down to form a series of sally-ports into the dry moat) and had also a regular system of arrow slits at alternate heights to rake the moat with fire power. The Outer Ward itself is irregular in shape in so far as it extended down the slope to the river on the south-west, but is entirely symmetrical in its upper section which envelops the perfect symmetry of the Inner Ward. Indeed it has been said of Rhuddlan that 'symmetry and uniformity are the keynotes of the whole design, and are present in a degree not seen in military *fortifications* in these islands since Roman times',[19] and one may add that such mathematical precision of *fortification* is scarcely exceeded before Beaumaris some twenty years later. The Inner Ward, which is, of course, the main strength of the castle, is in shape that of a square set diagonally to the points of the compass. The curtains, some nine foot thick and widened adjacent to the towers, were again equipped with arrow slits at ground level. There are two great drum towers diametrically opposite each other at the north and south angles (each of four storeys, plus a basement in the southern tower) and two massive gatehouses opposite each other at the remaining angles to east and west. The gatehouses are very obviously of the pattern of two cylindrical towers one on either side of the entrance passage (the towers are again of four storeys), though they originally had back quarters, after the manner of Harlech and Beaumaris, which here were timber-framed and have vanished. Both gatehouses and both mural towers contained residential accommodation, though the principal suites for the king and queen lay against the curtains of the inner ward and have largely gone.

Flint (1277–86), by contrast, is the most ruined of the Edwardian castles in north Wales, though by no means the least interesting.[20] Dismantled by Parliament after its final surrender in 1646, it was described as almost buried in its own ruins in 1652, and the site had been partly built over by the eighteenth and nineteenth centuries. It stands beside the River Dee and the Outer Ward is almost gone. The Inner Ward is a more or less rectangular enclosure and enough of the original curtain survives (chiefly to the south and north-west) to show that it was built after the manner of Rhuddlan, with arrow slits in wide embrasures at ground level and the walls mitred off behind the three angle towers (**XVIII**). There was no gatehouse of the usual sort, but three great drum towers at three of the four angles: the fourth angle, beside which is the gateway, was cut off by a curved wall on the same axis as the great tower or donjon which stands beyond it, like a vastly enlarged and detached fourth angle tower of which, indeed, it takes the place. The trick, so to speak, of enlarging one of the angle towers of the enclosure to form a donjon is found at certain thirteenth-century French castles like Dourdan and Yverdon, but the donjon at Flint has been more particularly compared with St Louis' Tour de Constance at Aigues-Mortes (from which new town and port Edward had embarked on his crusade in 1270). This resemblance,

XVIII Flint, ground plan.

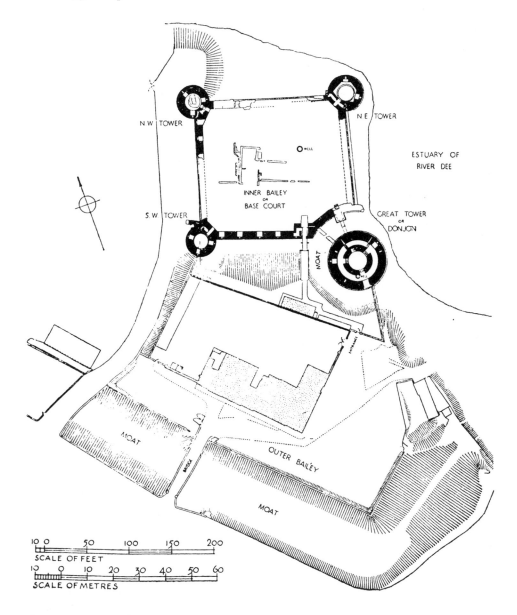

however, scarcely goes beyond the position and external appearance of the cylindrical great tower whose internal arrangements indeed, so far as its ruined state enable them now to be interpreted, seem to be unique. The basement consisted of a circular room surrounded by a broad mural gallery communicating by wide openings (**XVIII**) and was presumably used for storage, but above this in the residential floors, of which there were probably two, it appears that the apartments stood over the gallery and not in the central space, and were wedge-shaped about that central space which here formed an octagonal shaft bringing light into them from above. Such an arrangement has some affinities, not with any other known great tower, but with the castles of Castel del Monte in Apulia and Queenborough in Kent (p. 94 below), but in any event Flint, one of Edward I's new and major castles in Wales, thus had a tower keep, both affording some of the best residential accommodation within the fortress and standing as a defensive strong-point guarding in particular the main gate, the junction of the inner and outer wards, and the river approaches.

At least two other castles of the late thirteenth and early fourteenth centuries in Wales, Kidwelly (**25, XIX**) and Caerphilly (**26, XX**), both in the south, must be singled out for separate mention as representative of the best that the period could produce in military architecture. Both, also, are of particular interest in that while they are, at the least, in no obvious way inferior to the royal splendours we have been describing, yet they are not royal but baronial castles, raised by the ample resources of their respective lords, and thus reminding us of the type of society with which we are dealing. The existing Kidwelly[21] represents the entire rebuilding on the same site of a twelfth-century castle planted here with its fortified town by Roger, bishop of Salisbury, in the time of Henry I, and was begun by Payn de Chaworth (who had accompanied the future Edward I on crusade) in *c.*1275, to be completed by the great house of Lancaster who, in the person of Henry of Lancaster, had married the Chaworth heiress in 1298. It is, one may say, a concentric castle with a difference, adequately defended on the east beyond its walls by the steep drop to the river, but on the other three sides the quadrangular Inner Ward, with bold drum towers at the angles, is defended by the sweeping arc of the Outer Ward whose towered curtain, with two gatehouses, follows the line of the earthworks of the original castle. The grand residential apartments on the east side of the Inner Ward–hall, solar, kitchens, and a chapel projecting out on a spurred base towards the river – are attributed to *c.*1300 and the outer curtain to the first quarter of the fourteenth century, though it is now known that the great southern gatehouse (including its machicolation), the most impressive single feature of the castle, is the result of a substantial reconstruction between 1399 and 1422.

Kidwelly is very fine, but Caerphilly has been claimed to be 'the greatest of Welsh castles',[22] and may be thought even to exceed in strength and excellence the greatest of Edward I's own castles in north Wales, which at least in conception it also ante-dates (**26, XX**). All this befits its lords, the house of Clare, the greatest in the land, by the late thirteenth-century lords of Glamorgan, earls of Gloucester and earls of Hertford, now extinct in the male line since Bannockburn in 1314 yet their name echoing across six and half centuries in Clare College, Cambridge, and County Clare in Ireland. It is known that the present castle at Caerphilly was begun at the second attempt in 1271 (the first beginning in 1268, probably on the site to the north-west, having been

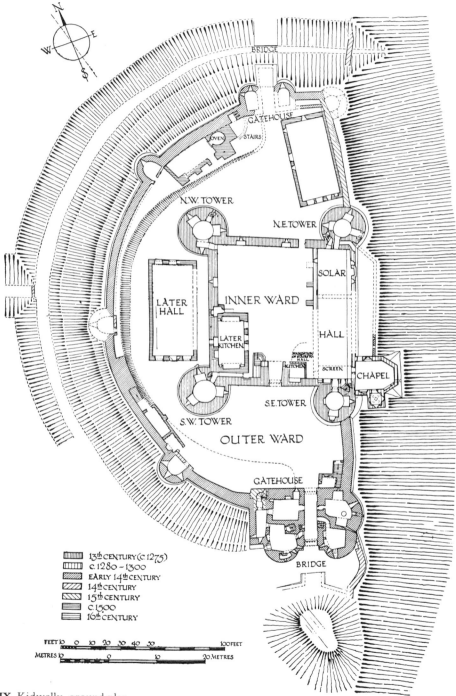

XIX Kidwelly, ground plan.

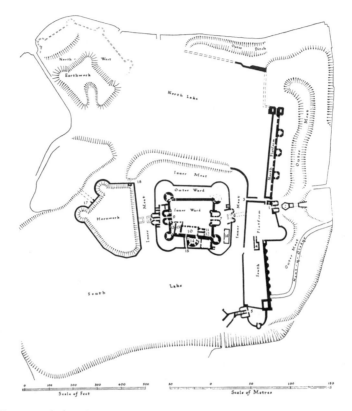

XX Caerphilly, ground plan.

destroyed by Llewelyn ap Gruffydd) but thereafter the absence of any surviving building accounts or documentation makes it impossible to know the sequence of the work or the time taken to complete it – though completed it certainly was, unlike either Caernarvon or Beaumaris. The castle proper is a concentric fortress fully worthy to be compared with Edward I's Beaumaris, the outer ward forming little more than a surrounding platform revetted by the low crenellated outer curtain which has no towers save the twin towers of its two gatehouses to east and west (there is also a water gate in the south front, adjacent to the hugely projecting Kitchen Tower of the inner bailey, and there may have been another to the north). The Inner Ward, the main strength of the castle, is an irregular rectangular enclosure bound together by two great gatehouses east and west (the former the greater), the Kitchen Tower and four massive drum towers at the four angles, each designed as a separately defensible unit. The hall (slightly later and also much restored) and principal residential accommodation line the south side of the court, though there was further accommodation in the towers and gatehouses, that in the east gatehouse being, it is thought, for the constable. Yet in addition to all this, Caerphilly has the unique feature of its Eastern Front, a long screen of curtain walls and platforms, strengthened by projecting turrets and buttresses, the magnificent series of flanking buttresses at its southern end almost reminiscent of the inner curtain of Richard I's Château-Gaillard. The purpose of this outer defence, traversed by the outer entrance, is to bar the main approach from the east, and also to dam the waters of the marsh in which the castle stands, to form and control the great lakes which entirely surrounded the inner fortress and gave Caerphilly the most elaborate water defences in all Britain (cf. Kenilworth and Leeds). In addition to this again, there was the Hornwork barring the western approach, an outwork consisting of a scarped and revetted island, its entrance from the west by a drawbridge guarded by two boldly projecting bastions and connected with the main castle by another drawbridge which led to the outer western gate.

It is to be noted, however, that all the castles so far individually described, whether of Edward I or his magnates, are in a sense exceptional, and that not only because they are amongst the finest in the land (or, indeed, anywhere) but also because every one of them is a new castle (Kidwelly is a total reconstruction as, technically, is Caernarvon) which had the good fortune, so to speak, to be built at this time with seemingly unlimited resources, all of them save Kidwelly and Caernarvon on new and virgin sites, and all of them save Kidwelly intended as new or renewed assertions of lordship and the means of controlling new territory. Outstandingly, Edward I's own six new royal castles in north Wales were the direct result of his Welsh wars and the means whereby the conquest of Wales was both achieved and rendered permanent. By contrast, as we have seen, the typical architectural history of the typical English castle is of a long and continuous development on the same site after an early foundation, and simply because so many castles had been planted in England and the Marches as part and parcel of the Norman Conquest and settlement in the later eleventh and earlier twelfth centuries, new castles upon new sites at any time after, say, 1150 are the exception rather than the norm. Our present period of c.1215 to c.1330, in consequence, saw more improvement and development than building of new castles, and this, too, at its best produced an apogee of medieval fortification.

Here pride of place must go, no doubt, to the Tower of London (**27, XXI**) as it evolved in the thirteenth century and more especially, once again, at the hands of Edward I, his masons and other craftsmen. The small and perhaps the original enclosure of 1066–7 within which, it is now known, the Conqueror had subsequently placed his great tower, i.e. the White Tower, the Tower of London,[23] was enlarged in the next century, probably in the time of Richard I (1189–99) and his chancellor, William Longchamp, to which date the present Bell Tower belongs and presumably marks its south-west corner. In the course of Henry III's long reign (1216–72) this enclosure was enlarged again to the line of the present inner curtain which, with its mural towers, is in the main Henry's work. In his day, however, the principal landward gate of the Tower was on the site of the present Beauchamp Tower (still pointing down Great Tower Street, as the main approach to the fortress) and the present Bloody Tower was a water-

XXI The Tower of London, ground plan.

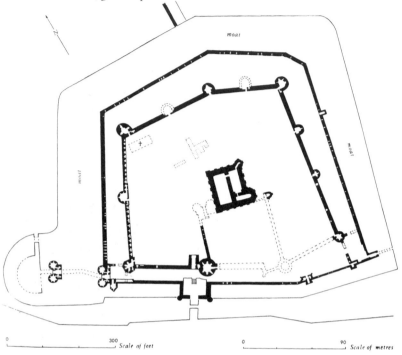

gate to the Thames which then flowed at its foot and washed what is now the south inner curtain. This enlargement of the castle, which involved breaking through the line of the former Roman city wall (marked by the Wardrobe Tower) to the east, and added an acre to the Tower's extent, was completed by a moat more or less on the site of the present outer ward. Within, the king built, rebuilt and improved the accommodation of this fortified royal residence in the city, most of it in an inner and more or less rectangular enclosure bounded by the White Tower to the north and the Wakefield and Lanthorn Towers, and thus adjacent and subsidiary to the accommodation in the Conqueror's great keep itself. Yet in spite of all this, Edward I further strengthened and enlarged the Tower to make of it the formidable concentric castle that it now is, and one of the strongest castles in his kingdom. His father's moat was filled in, a new outer curtain (now much restored and heightened) built on its outer line, and a new and broader moat dug round this, water-filled in Edward's day and until the nineteenth century. Henry's landward gate to the west was replaced by the present Beauchamp Tower which dominates the western inner curtain towards the city, and an elaborate new entrance made via the Byward and Middle Gatetowers and the hornwork barbican already mentioned (p. 68 above). Most impressive of all perhaps is Edward's southern extension of the area of the Tower, marked by his south outer curtain running from the Byward to the Well

Tower, for this involved the pushing back, so to speak, of the river itself by the distance of the present narrow southern outer ward – and hence the building of one of Edward's principal individual works at the Tower, i.e. St Thomas' Tower or the so-called Traitor's Gate, as a new water-gate in front of Henry III's Bloody Gatetower, now high and dry.

The Tower of London in this period thus achieved its ultimate development, only minor modifications (including the Tower Wharf and the Cradle Tower, a lesser water-gate, both in the fourteenth century) being thereafter necessary, and the same is true of other major castles in the kingdom, both royal and baronial. In the course of the thirteenth century, Dover[24] finally expanded to take in the whole of the lofty site of the former Iron Age fortress and Anglo-Saxon borough within which the Conqueror had placed his castle two centuries before (p. 27 above). The great works of Henry II here have already been discussed in the last chapter. King John evidently completed his father's towered outer curtain round the north end of the castle and back down its west side to Peveril's Tower, from which it ran east and south to sweep round the church and *pharos* and rejoin Henry II's wall in the vicinity of his powerful Avranches Tower (**1**). In the course of the long reign of Henry III the western outer curtain was extended southwards from Peveril to the cliff s edge towards the sea, thus incorporating the whole ancient site, the corresponding section of the vanished eastern curtain being built at the same time, unless, indeed, it had already been built by Henry II, which some evidence suggests. Within Henry II's inner bailey his grandson also built lavish residential accommodation which, together with the accommodation offered by the keep, formed the 'palace' buildings of the castle. All this, however, does not complete the thirteenth-century development of Dover. King John had placed the main gateway of the castle at the northern apex of his outer curtain, where the Norfolk Towers now stand and where, no doubt, Henry II had intended it to be, for it is lined up upon the northern barbican and the King's Gate of the inner bailey, and was linked thereto by an impressive causeway the remains of which can still be seen. In the siege of 1216 (p. 140 below) this gateway was attacked and the eastern of its twin towers brought down by undermining so that the castle was very nearly taken. When the war was over, the government of the young Henry III set about to remedy the weakness thus revealed in one of the most expensive exercises on record of locking the stable door after the horse has been stolen. John's gateway was blocked for all time by rebuilding its ruined tower solid and linking it to its western fellow by another solid tower, this time shaped *en bec* in the latest French fashion, and placed across the former entrance passage. In front of this, rising from the foot of the castle ditch, the cylindrical St John Tower was built, and in front of this again a great outwork was dug, still there but altered and cased in brick in Napoleonic times. Castle, St John Tower and outwork were linked (as they still are, though the arrangements are again altered) by underground passages, and the evident purpose is to deny to any future foe the ground from which the 1216 attack had been launched. At the same time the present

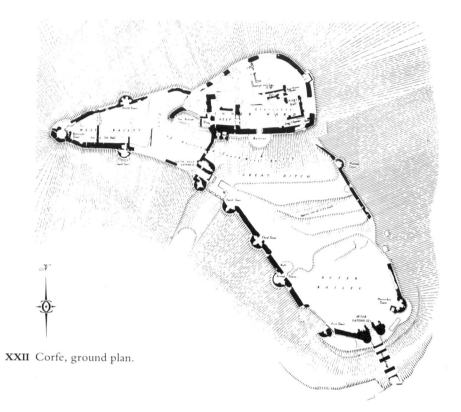

XXII Corfe, ground plan.

FitzWilliam Gate (its twin towers again *en bec*) was constructed in the outer curtain to the south-east, with a covered passageway across the ditch, so that here, too, sallies could be made as necessary towards the vital northern ground. Meanwhile the main gateway of the castle having been blocked, a new one had to be constructed, and the result was the splendid Constable's Gate in the western outer curtain. This, in common with most of the gatehouses of the period, is based upon the principle of flanking towers, but is so elaborate in its design that it would be unique were there not another very similar to it, also the work of Henry III, at the Black Gate at Newcastle-upon-Tyne.

The royal castle of Corfe, also, reached its final development in the course of the thirteenth century (**XXII**), and, like Dover, did so in terms of new towered curtains (about the two outer baileys to west and south) and new gatehouses (one inner and one outer).[25] King John, for whom Corfe was a favourite castle, is responsible for the curtain of the west bailey, with its two semi-circular mural towers opposite each other to north and south, and the polygonal Butavant Tower (cf. the Bell Tower at the Tower of London) at the western apex. John also built, in the inner sanctum of the inner bailey adjacent to the keep, the 'Gloriette', an elegant suite of residential apartments arranged about a courtyard and executed in very sophisticated masonry (viciously slighted none the less,

XXIII Chepstow, ground plan.

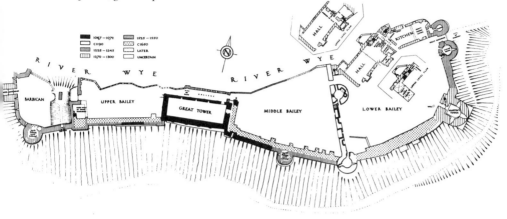

together with the castle's defences, by Parliament in the seventeenth century).
The walling-in of the outer bailey to the south was principally the work of
Henry III completed by Edward I, in whose reign, in the 1280's, it is known that
work was in hand upon the outer gatehouse. Similarly, and as another instance,
the baronial castle of Chepstow or 'Striguil',[26] where assuredly there is
something for every student of medieval military architecture, received in the
thirteenth century, during the lordship first of Marshal and then of Bigod, two
new enclosures to east and west, respectively the Lower Bailey and the Barbican
(**28, XXIII**). The latter, it is to be noted, has, in addition to a fine drum tower, a
gatehouse of the older but still continuing pattern, consisting of a single tower,
here rectangular, pierced by the entrance passage. The Lower Bailey, at the other
end of the castle, built out to the east and in front of the towered east curtain of
*c.*1190, has a Great Gatehouse which, though earlier in date than the Upper Gate
in the barbican, is of the more 'advanced' and at this time more normal pattern
consisting of two drum towers on either side. This bailey also has, to the south-
east, a mural tower to end all mural towers, the gigantic Marten's Tower (1270–
1300 in the Bigod period), a fitting rival to anything at Caerphilly or elsewhere.
Dating from the same period, there is also, along the north side of the Lower
Bailey, and thus both secure and monumental high above the river, a splendid
range of residential apartments, hall, chambers and kitchen. Nevertheless, it was
also during the thirteenth century, and in part at the same time, that the original
eleventh-century keep or donjon of William fitz Osbern (p. 45 above) was
heightened and otherwise altered to enlarge and improve its domestic
accommodation in accordance with contemporary taste.

The fact that the Marshal and Bigod lords of Striguil found it both necessary
and desirable not only to retain in use but also to bring up to date the keep at
Chepstow may serve to remind us again that the keep, and not least the great
tower, remained the *pièce maîtresse* of very many castles in this period no less than

formerly. And if in these cases it remained the ultimate military strong point, so also it retained its residential rôle, since to whatever extent domestic standards may have risen in the two centuries, more or less, after 1066 (and we may overdo this, assuming domestic standards to develop with architectural style), the facts of life and military lordship stayed very much the same, while the traditions of the latter were even more firmly entrenched. At Middleham in Yorkshire, or at Dover (**I**, **VIII**), or at the Tower of London (**27**, **XXI**), it is particularly evident that the keep remained an integral and dominant part of the palatial residential quarters within the castle, and it is instructive that for the last-named orders of Henry III survive both to whitewash the exterior of the great tower to make it look nice (a medieval custom not confined to his reign and which accounts for its name, the White Tower) and to equip it with a war-head of hoarding or projecting timber galleries to facilitate its defence. At Rochester much money and effort was spent in the earlier thirteenth century to rebuild that impressively large south-eastern section of the keep which king John's miners had brought down in the siege of 1215 (below, p. 140) though the rebuilding, while making some attempt to match the twelfth-century style inside, produced a south-east angle which was fashionably cylindrical externally, in marked contrast with the rest of the rectangular great tower (**14**, **VII**).

Yet it is not only a question of the maintenance and even restoration of tower keeps dating from earlier generations: new ones also were built in this period, as they will be later, and as they were in France. The continuation of the keep, the great tower, in France throughout the Middle Ages is generally recognized, but there is really no divergence in this matter between French and English practice, nor, surely, should we expect one. At York, on the motte of the principal castle, where a timber tower had continued to stand until 1228 (when it was blown down by the wind), a new tower keep, the present Clifford's Tower, was built by Henry III between 1245 and *c.*1270. Its quatrefoil or quadrilobe shape is unique in England, but finds an analogy in the French Etampes which itself dates from the twelfth century. The same king was also responsible for new great towers at Winchester, Cardigan and Castle Cornet at St Peter Port in Guernsey, all of them cylindrical and the first-named standing upon the motte of the castle like Clifford's Tower at York.[27] Edward I's major new castle of Flint had a great cylindrical donjon, as we have seen, and so also (though less well known since both have vanished) did his new castles at Builth and Cambridge. Each of these undertakings was the total rebuilding of a former castle, respectively destroyed and decayed. In the case of Builth the 'great tower' (*magna turris*) 'referred to in the building accounts may have been in fact a shell keep upon the pre-existing motte,[28] but at Cambridge the new keep, whose foundations were being dug in 1288, was evidently a cylindrical tower, again placed upon the ancient motte.[29] All the examples so far listed have been royal, but the splendid and trefoil tower keep which once rose at Pontefract, is attributed in its original form (it is also very relevant to note that it was subsequently 'modernized' and otherwise altered by John of Gaunt in the later fourteenth century) to the thirteenth century and the period of Lacy lordship,[30] while, on a smaller scale, the little rectangular thirteenth-century keep at Hopton in Shropshire is indistinguishable from its twelfth-century precursors save in details of mere architectural style.

Architectural historians and architectural histories are prone to concentrate mainly upon the best buildings of any particular type or period, but while this is no doubt inevitable, and also reasonable when achievement is to be measured, standards set, comparisons made, and the evolution of new styles dated, such concentration can nevertheless be misleading if one's interest is the whole history of castles or of churches or of houses. Certainly, just as not all churches were or were required to be cathedrals, so not all castles in the thirteenth and early fourteenth centuries – indeed, the great majority – whether new ones or old ones developed, were nor were meant to be in the class of Caernarvon or Caerphilly, the Tower of London or Corfe. Amongst the many which were not, we may mention Pickering in Yorkshire,[31] which received its stone buildings and defences for the most part in this period (strictly, *c.*1180 to 1326, though the Old Hall is earlier twelfth-century), including the King's Tower, i.e. the shell keep upon the motte, which is attributed in its present form to Henry III, and the curtain of the Barbican with its rectangular towers built by Edward II. Pickering, like Berkhamstead (**18**), stands as one of numerous examples of the straight conversion into stone of an early motte-and-bailey, and thus reminds us also of that continuity of development from an early foundation characteristic of so many English castles.

Finally we may end this chapter with particular reference to those places, so to speak, at the bottom of the scale, which were so lightly fortified as to be scarcely castles at all, but belong, rather to that hybrid type of lordly residence known to us as the fortified manor. The fortified manor is usually thought of as pertaining especially to the later Middle Ages and the fifteenth century, but in fact is found at any time after 1066. Domesday Book itself (1086) records 'defensible houses' (*domus defensabiles*). The castle is a fortified residence: it is the degree of fortification which distinguishes the castle from the house: that degree will always vary, and the borderline between the two was doubtless always hazy. In the medieval period as in any other, he who commissioned a building got (more or less) what he wanted and/or could afford, and not everyone wanted a castle fortified at every point to withstand the assault of armies, or had the resources or the prestige to make such a residence seem necessary to his status. 'Please God, I will build me such a house as thieves will need to knock at ere they enter' – thus Patrick Forbes, building Corse Castle in Aberdeenshire in *c.*1500,[32] and that sort of need and intention was not confined to that country and that time. Hence, one supposes, such a beautiful little thirteenth-century defensible house as still survives at Little Wenham in Suffolk,[33] or the not dissimilar Markenfield in Yorkshire which, unlike the former, still has its moated enclosure, gatehouse and courtyard of dependent service buildings. Two of the best known fortified manors in England in fact belong to the late thirteenth century and thus the very decades which could also produce a Harlech or Kidwelly. Stokesay[34] in

Shropshire (**29**), save for the lower two storeys of its northern tower (which date back to the Say period and *c*.1240) is the work of Lawrence of Ludlow, the richest wool merchant in the kingdom and a creditor of the king himself, between about 1285 and 1305 (Lawrence himself dying in 1296). Though, on the one hand, the present picturesque but ineffective timber gatehouse must be disallowed as of seventeenth-century date, and, on the other, the original crenellated curtain wall rose to a height of 34 ft from the bottom of the moat, here clearly is no major fortress, but basically a hall and chamber block with a tower at either end, the principal tower to the south being a kind of mini-keep. It would be easy enough to joke that Lawrence of Ludlow, being a merchant, was not quite a gentleman, and therefore his house was likewise not quite a castle, but one would be more justified in supposing that this *mercator notissimus* of the reign of Edward I could have done better than this in terms of fortification had he chosen. Certainly Robert Burnell could have done so at Acton Burnell[35] (**30**), built in the 1280s and also in Shropshire, for he was friend and Chancellor to the same Edward I, close counsellor in that king's legislation, and bishop of Bath and Wells. Yet Acton Burnell is so lightly defended that even its battlements have been held a mere matter of aesthetics and tradition as opposed to serious military purpose. It is, beyond doubt, a smart and sophisticated dwelling such as might befit a bishop, a rectangular block with rectangular angle turrets (that on the north-east originally projecting further east than now to house the chapel) and a rectangular projection in the middle of its west end, but a castle only by courtesy – 'an early example of the great country house of stone, planned to provide for the needs of a wealthy and powerful churchman'.[36]

Chapter 5

Decline

After the great achievements of the thirteenth and early fourteenth centuries it is difficult not to see much of what follows as an anti-climax, and impossible in any overall survey of the architectural history of the English castle not to label the next two centuries as the period of decline. Nevertheless we must not be in too great a hurry. The castle, like feudalism itself (and the two things go together), lasted long, and while, on the one hand, so-called 'Bastard Feudalism' in the so-called Later Middle Ages may seem remarkably like the real thing, on the other the castle in England had its sad Indian Summer of revived military importance in the seventeenth-century Civil War. With that exception, caused by special circumstance, what happens in England and Wales (Scotland, like Ireland, is another story) by, let us say, the earlier sixteenth century, is assuredly that the unique combination of fortress and personal, lordly residence, which is the castle, falls apart, and when it does so the history of the castle as a living and viable type of building is at an end. Tudor coastal forts – Deal, Walmer, Camber, St Mawes and the rest – being exclusively military buildings (and being also exclusively royal, i.e. national defences) are not castles, any more than Pitt's Martello Towers of a still later age are castles, though the former at least are often mistakenly said to be. And by the same token, great Elizabethan country houses are not castles (in France the word *châteaux* is still applied to their equivalents and thus the word changes its meaning *pari passu* with the residences to which it is applied), though some may have moats as a gesture to security, and others, it may be, crenellation as a decorative motif and a gesture to tradition and prestige.

The historian of castles, therefore, armed like all historians with hindsight, is prone to fall into the professional besetting sin of not only seeking, but even imposing, a pattern upon the past (in this case fourteenth- and fifteenth-century castle-building) which, being generally untidy, is impatient of it. Doubtless we shall find, as the fourteenth century is succeeded by the fifteenth, increasing signs of a lowering of the guard, of an increasing emphasis upon residential splendour and ostentation even at the expense of military strength, whereby the robust balance of the true castle as both fortress and residence is upset. But we must remember as we look at the military architecture of this period that the castle always was a residence, and that the residential accommodation within it always was as splendid as could be contrived and as befitted the lord who used it. We must also remember that at all periods there were lordly residences which were unfortified, as represented at the highest level of the king, for example, by Westminster or Clarendon – or Woodstock,[1] but found at all levels from the palace to the manor house. Similarly it is to be remembered that the hybrid type of comparatively lightly defended fortified house or manor existed at all times after 1066 (p. 87 above), and that if such buildings are indeed particularly characteristic of the fifteenth century they are certainly not confined to it, so that in this sense the balance between domesticity and fortification which is peculiar to the castle had been tipped before. Lastly, while the complex reasons, chiefly social, which brought about the decline of the castle will be separately discussed in a later chapter (p. 168 below), we should anticipate now by saying and insisting that the advent of gunpowder is scarcely to be numbered among them. By the time that cannon were sufficiently developed to be really effective in siege-craft and bring about substantial changes in the principles of fortification, the decline of the castle was already well advanced for other reasons, and the principal effect of 'foul, stinking bombards' upon late medieval military architecture was the introduction of gunports for the guns of the castles' own defences.[2]

This said, it will be well to begin this chapter devoted to the decline of the castle with exceptions, and thus emphasize how numerous for a long time they were. The biggest exception, in fact, is formed by a whole region of the kingdom, the far north towards Scotland, where the eventual failure of Edward I to conquer the Scots as he had conquered the Welsh resulted in the *damnosa hereditas* of three centuries of border forays and endemic warfare, made the new Scottish Marches more important than the Welsh Marches of old, and brought also the constant political danger of alliance between Scotland and France, northern invasion and war on two fronts, which lasted at least until 1603. In such circumstances we should expect to find, as we do find, an increase rather than a decline of serious fortification, and if the new castles here built in the fourteenth and fifteenth centuries cannot be numbered among the major fortresses of the realm, it is to be remembered that the major fortresses of the far north had already been long in existence, at Newcastle, Carlisle, Bamburgh, Alnwick, Durham and elsewhere. Nevertheless, Bywell in Northumberland, built *c*.1430 by the great Neville family, is of the advanced design evolved in the late thirteenth century, with its main strength in a powerful gatehouse which is now all that remains of it. This is of two storeys above the entrance, crenellated and machicolated, with the machicolation on the turrets of an unusual design, formed by placing octagonal parapets upon a rectangular structure.[3] Elsewhere the period produced relatively minor castles whose significance is not so much their lack of first-class status as the reason for it, namely that they are the work of relatively minor lords in need of fortified residences adequate to ward off the raids of the 'king's enemies, the Scots'. Thus Etal, also in Northumberland, thought to have taken its present form about the time of the 'licence to crenellate' (see p. 3 above), granted to one Robert Manners in 1341, consists simply of a rectangular tower keep, of four storeys in all, standing half in and half out of a simple walled enclosure or bailey with a rectangular gatehouse at the corner opposite the keep and a small square tower at the south-west angle. Edlingham (Northumberland again), dating from *c.*1350, consists of a simple, walled and rectangular enclosure with a rectangular tower keep at one end and perhaps a gatehouse at the other. Gleaston in Lancashire (*c.*1330) follows much the same plan, and so originally did Naworth in Cumberland, built at about the same time.

It is in fact very difficult to distinguish at all clearly between such lesser castles and the so-called 'pele towers of the north', dating from the fourteenth and fifteenth centuries or later, and forming a characteristic and well-known feature of the northern counties within reach of the Scots. The word 'pele' has become somewhat confusing by transference, chiefly by nineteenth-century antiquarians,[4] from its root meaning of a palisaded or stockaded enclosure (hence 'paling' and 'beyond the pale') to the thing enclosed, i.e. the tower. The pele tower thus defined is simply a tower, usually rectangular, forming the fortified residence of the owner – a lesser tower keep, in short – standing within what is commonly called the 'barmkin', usually a small and simple walled courtyard, lacking all elaborate niceties of flanking tower or gatehouse, and serving chiefly for the protection of animals and crops from marauders. The towers vary in size and elaboration from the almost insignificant proportions and extreme simplicity of the Vicar's Pele at Corbridge in Northumberland (*c.*1300), to the more imposing structures at Chipchase and Belsay (both also in Northumberland and dated to the early or mid-fourteenth century) with their crenellated and machicolated parapets. The internal arrangements are commonly of two residential floors, each comprising a main room with or without lesser chambers, above a basement. At Sizergh, Westmorland (*c.*1350) there is a projecting rectangular turret (the Deincourt Tower) incorporated in the middle of the south side and rising some 10 ft above the battlements of the main tower. Others of the more elaborate towers, like Chipchase and Belsay, have one or more short projecting wings containing the staircase, entrance and small chambers. Elsewhere the stairs were commonly in an angle of the tower, and the entrance, like that of tower keeps, is often at first-floor level. Whatever the architectural details it is clear that these peles are, so to speak, the lesser castles of lesser men, and the fact should not be allowed to be obscured by the use of different terminology. They, like the even more enigmatic 'bastles' (cf. *bastille, bastide*), were raised all over the northern counties (and on the other side of the border in southern Scotland) by gentry and others who had evidently not hitherto felt the need to live in castles or seriously to fortify their houses. For them there was no question, socially or economically, of an elaborate and vastly expensive castle of the first rank, nor was this necessary for the type of sporadic and raiding warfare in which they found themselves involved. It is, however, of particular interest that they often used, scaled to their own position and resources, the same fundamental type of fortified residence, i.e. the great tower, as had been used since the castle's beginning.

Meanwhile the Welsh Marches, where conditions were scarcely settled even after the Edwardian conquest of Wales, and where, in any case, the tradition of fortification was likely to remain strongest, saw the raising of at least one more castle on the grand scale at Raglan in Monmouthshire (**31**).[5] This stands partly upon the site of an early castle of motte-and-bailey form dating back to the twelfth century or beyond, but is now in effect a new castle of fifteenth-century date, save for possible traces of twelfth-century work at the foot of the South Gate, important alterations and improvements significantly to the main residential apartments in the sixteenth century (*c.*1550–90), and fragmentary remains of seventeenth-century outworks. The whole was deliberately destroyed as well as plundered by the victorious Parliamentarians in 1646, after its surrender which virtually marked the end of the Civil War, in which it was said that Raglan was the first castle to be fortified for the king and the last to be surrendered. It was begun by Sir William ap Thomas (d. 1445) in about 1430, and the work was carried on almost to completion by his son Sir William Herbert, later earl of Pembroke, until his execution in 1469. The former, 'the Blue Knight of Gwent', like others of his class (and other classes) did well out of the wars in France (cf. Sir John Fastolf at Caister, and Sir John de la Mare at Nunney, pp.96, 117 below), and also by marriage, and his son did even better, by commerce which made him one of the richest men in the kingdom, and by his prominent support of the Yorkist cause which triumphed at the accession of Edward of York as Edward IV in 1461. The Great Tower together with parts of the Fountain Court including the South Gate (in his time the main entrance) are the work of Sir William ap Thomas and the rest is his son's. The main enclosure is laid out in two courts which enabled the main residential range lying between them, including the great hall, to be planned and built with a spacious splendour which yet did not detract from the castle's outward strength (though again it is to be noted that much of this range, notably the hall and long gallery, is Elizabethan in its existing form). The Fountain Court was the court of honour surrounded by lordly accommodation, the Pitched Stone Court to the north being devoted domestically to service quarters. All the many towers of the castle's *enceinte*, except for the South Gate and an Elizabethan addition in the centre of the north face, are the work of William Herbert (*c.*1450 to 1469), and all are hexagonal in plan. There are gunports in the Kitchen Tower and the Closet Tower as there are also in the Great Gate, and this gatehouse (originally defended also by a drawbridge, two portcullises and three double doors) and the adjacent Closet Tower have a display of machicolation as good as any to be found in the kingdom (**XXXII**). Both the Great Gate and the South Gate, however, are further protected by the Great Tower which commands them, and which is by no means the least interesting feature of Raglan. Thrust out aggressively to the south-east, beyond the curtain of the main enclosure and on the line of the principal approach to the castle, it was raised between *c.*1430 and *c.*1435 upon the ancient motte which its footings now revet in stone. This is the 'Yellow Tower of Gwent', a majestic and very strong hexagonal tower, probably one storey

XXIV Queenborough, sixteenth-century ground plan.

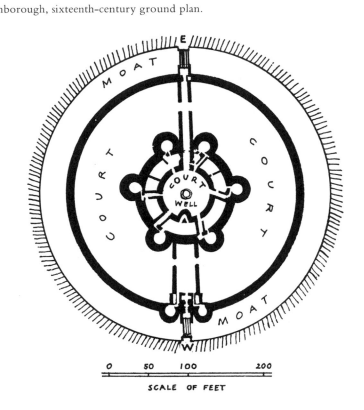

higher yet and crowned by machicolation before its slighting, and described in the seventeenth century as surpassing 'for height, strength and neatness ... most, if not every other tower of England and Wales'. It now has three residential floors above a basement, which probably served as the kitchen and was fitted also with gunports combined with arrow slits in embrasures of unusual construction. The whole is surrounded by a mantlet wall of slightly later date (i.e. William Herbert), which may have mounted guns on its turrets or bastions, and by its moat (also revetted in stone), and was connected with the rest of the castle only by a bridge which was originally a drawbridge.

In England and in the south (where, as indeed in Wales, it is again to be remembered that the previous centuries had long since produced all the major castles then necessary), the later fourteenth century produced at least two new castles, at Queenborough and Nunney, which show little evidence, in their very different ways, of any lowering of the guard: nor are they too easily to be connected with the new circumstance of French raids, as the 'Hundred Years War' began to go wrong, since the former was begun at the high-water mark of initial English triumph and the latter was built in a region unlikely to see much of French marauders.

Queenborough (**XXIV**),[6] on the Isle of Sheppey in Kent, has the distinction of being the only wholly new royal castle built in the later Middle Ages, and in plan it was unique in all England and Wales, though having some affinities with the thirteenth-century Castel del Monte in Apulia. Not one stone of it remains upon another after seventeenth-century Parliamentary demolition, but its form and appearance are known from the fortunate survival of a sixteenth-century ground plan and a seventeenth-century drawing, and its building, by Edward III between 1361 and 1377, is well documented. In plan it was both perfectly circular and perfectly concentric, and it has been said of it that 'it exemplifies the principles of cylindrical and concentric fortification carried to their logical conclusion with perfect symmetry'.[7] The outer *enceinte* was a strong, plain circular wall, surrounded by the moat and devoid of flanking towers save for the twin towers of the main outer gate to the west, directly opposite to which, facing east, was the postern. The loftier wall of the inner bailey, also circular, was strengthened by six cylindrical towers, two of which placed close together defended and formed the main inner gateway facing east in line with the postern. The principal residential apartments were disposed round the inner curtain, forming a continuous and articulated circular range, including hall, chambers and chapel (not unlike the shell keep at Restormel, p. 59 above, but more sophisticated), whose inner wall, again circular, thus enclosed a circular courtyard, in the centre of which, like the bull's eye of a target, was the castle well (now all that survives, albeit disguised by an ugly pumping shed). In the building accounts the outer ward is referred to as the barbican, and the main, towered central core of the castle is sometimes called 'the rotunda' and once 'the great tower', which, strictly speaking, it is not, though we may well call it the donjon. It is this which most closely resembled Frederick II's Castel del Monte in southern Italy in overall concept, though Frederick's building was octagonal with eight towers also octagonal,[8] while Edward III's Queenborough has entirely gone together with all architectural detail. Nevertheless, from what evidence we have we may see that the castle was further strengthened by devices which have all the simplicity of genius. Open walled passageways linked the outer gate and postern to the inner bailey and thus, working indeed like barbicans (p. 68 above), pinned down an enemy who should carry the outer gates or attack the inner one, while at the same time they divided and blocked the circuit of the inner ward. The sixteenth-century plan also shows that the inner gateway giving access to the 'rotunda' is placed on the east and as far as possible from the main outer gate to the west. Thus if the latter should be taken and the enemy gain the outer bailey, he is forced to proceed halfway round its circumference, exposed all the way to the fire power of the inner towers and walls, to reach the entrance of the inner bailey from which he is still cut off by its eastern walled passage. There is, in short, no doubt of the military potential of Queenborough, which served among other things for coastal defence and more particularly for the protection of the river Swale, between the Isle and the mainland, which was then the usual passage for shipping in the Thames estuary.

The castle, too, came to be well supplied with guns, though it is especially to the well-tried stone-throwing 'engines' and trebuchets (p. 126 below) that the building accounts refer as being both made and maintained within it, and it was these which were shot off before him when the old king made an inspection in September 1373.

Nevertheless, Queenborough, like any other castle, royal or otherwise, was also conceived in the context of residence. With the (unfortified) town founded at the same time (both dedicated to Edward's queen, Philippa of Hainault), it was a major item, costing over £25,000 in all, in a great programme of works carried out by Edward III to mark his victories in France, which largely paid for them, and especially concentrated in the Thames valley, from royal Windsor, the chief centre of his court and chivalry (p. 103 below), via Isleworth and Sheen (the medieval Richmond), Westminster Palace and the Tower of London, and so, via Gravesend and Rotherhithe, to Queenborough, and to Hadleigh castle on the opposite Essex shore. Some of these royal residences were castles and others not, and amongst them the king, as he aged, increasingly divided his time, travelling usually by water. His new castle of Queenborough was a particularly favoured residence in his later years, and a royal barge plied between it and Hadleigh with which it was closely connected, and which Edward had largely rebuilt between 1360 and 1370 to make of it a strong, irregular enclosure with great drum towers (some still standing) and a new range of residential apartments (now gone) on the south side above the river. *Sic transit gloria mundi* we must say, for the captains and the kings have all departed: little remains of Edward's Hadleigh and nothing at all of Queenborough, and the great clock which Edward set up in one of the towers of the latter (one of the earliest mechanical weight-driven clocks to which there is reference in England) has long since ceased to toll the passing of the hours.

If the design of Queenborough is so advanced as to be unique in England, at Nunney[9] in Somerset (**32**) we return to the lasting tradition of the great tower, though this particular example is French in its ancestry and usually compared to the Bastille in Paris (1370–82. Cf. also Pierrefonds and Tarascon). The castle was built *c.*1373 in pursuance of a licence to crenellate granted in that year to Sir John de la Mare, who, again, according to local tradition, had made his fortune in the French wars. There are still traces of a large embanked enclosure to north and west, but it is clear that ninety-nine per cent of the strength of the fortress was concentrated in the great donjon which contained within itself all the accommodation and service rooms required for lordly residence. In plan it is rectangular with a cylindrical tower at each angle, those on the shorter sides almost touching each other. Something similar occurs at the rather earlier (*c.*1320) keep at Dudley in Worcestershire, but that, though even stronger, was of only two storeys, whereas Nunney rises sheer through four, its towers surmounted by further turrets off-set from centre. At parapet level the whole building, projecting towers and straight sides, is heavily and impressively machicolated. Each floor consisted of a main room with lesser chambers in the corner towers, and the two upper floors certainly contained the best accommodation, their lavish decoration still discernible in spite of ruination and extending even into the garderobes. The donjon was surrounded by a moat whose waters originally lapped its walls (the present terrace is later). Access was by bridge and drawbridge to an entrance at ground level on the north side and otherwise undefended save by the adjacent flanking towers. Surprisingly in view of the date and builder, there are no gun-ports in the building. The whole north wall and entrance front fell out in 1910, having been breached and weakened by gunfire in the short and somewhat inglorious siege of September, 1645 (below).

After this notice of the fourteenth-century keep at Nunney and, before that, the notice of the fifteenth-century keep at Raglan, it is time to turn aside to the so-called 'tower-houses' of the later Middle Ages, amongst which both these buildings have sometimes been included. The truth is that this is a false category of English (and Scottish) medieval military architecture, entirely the invention of modern architectural historians and thus unknown to contemporaries (who would have called, and did call, these buildings by the time-honoured names of great tower or donjon), and its employment obscures the fundamental fact that the 'tower-house' is nothing but the continuation into the later medieval centuries of the ancient and constant principle of the great tower as the lordly fortified residence *par excellence*. The fault, one may add, is compounded when historians of the later castle in England, insisting that their 'tower-house' was neither a continuation nor yet a revival of the tower keep (obsolete, it is said, by the thirteenth century) but a new form, go on to associate it with an equally misinterpreted piece of social history labelled 'Bastard Feudalism', and write of lords perforce shutting themselves up in self-contained tower-houses out of fear of their own mercenary retainers – as though Henry II or Henry I or William the Conqueror, builders of tower keeps more self-sufficient than a Tattershall (below), had not used mercenary forces also in their time.[10]

That the great tower was one of the two basic principles of castle design from the beginning to the end has previously been stressed in an earlier chapter of this book, and we have also seen that in England and Wales it was not confined to the eleventh and twelfth centuries, when it was certainly both dominant and popular, but continued through the thirteenth century with new tower keeps, for example, at York and Pontefract, Flint and Cambridge, even though the techniques of fortifying an enclosure – the other basic principle of castle design – had by then been perfected.[11] If we now take up the tale from there, we find that Edward II, adding to the fortification and amenities of Knaresborough between 1307 and 1312, built principally a new great tower upon the site of the old one which he demolished, and spent upon the work the princely sum of £2,175.[12] The date of the tower at Dudley, as we have seen, is *c.*1320, and of that at Nunney *c.*1373. The principal work of the refortification of Southampton castle by the government of Richard II was a great cylindrical tower keep, built upon the ancient motte between 1378 and 1388, and described by Leland in the sixteenth century as 'the Glorie of the castelle'.[13] About 1380 John of Gaunt converted the splendid gatehouse of his castle at Dunstanburgh in Northumberland into a great tower by blocking its entrance passage amongst other alterations (rather as the gatehouses of Richmond, Yorkshire, and Ludlow had been converted into keeps centuries before), and the keep at Old Wardour in Wiltshire dates from the 1390s as does the remarkable great tower of unique design raised upon the motte in place of an earlier one at the Percy stronghold of Warkworth.[14] Elsewhere in the far north in the fourteenth and fifteenth centuries we have seen relatively minor castles built with tower keeps, and these shade off into the 'peles' which are simply tower keeps usually in miniature. The fifteenth century also produced in its middle decades, all of much the same date, the Yellow Tower of Gwent at Raglan, already noted (1430–35), and the well-known towers of Tattershall (**34**) in Lincolnshire,[15] built in brick by Ralph lord Cromwell between 1430 and 1450, and Caister-by-Yarmouth,[16] also in brick, begun by Sir John Fastolf in 1432 and perhaps finished by 1446; while the Hastings Tower at Ashby-de-la-Zouch[17] dates from 1474–83.

Of all these Caister (**33**) is certainly different from the rest in appearance, a tall and unusually slender cylindrical tower of five storeys, surmounted by a hexagonal turret carried up from the ground on the south side. It looks more like a watch-tower than a keep, and is in fact an immensely elongated angle tower of the main inner enclosure of a castle built on the two-courtyard plan. Unique in England, its affinities are with the *Wasserburgen* of the lower Rhineland (built in similarly marshy sites) and with Schloss Kempen in particular, which has a very similar tower at one corner of its brick-built structure. Nevertheless, Sir John Fastolf's tower was intended to have a residential function, all of its floors save the topmost having fireplaces, and was well defended, by the general standards of Caister castle, with walls four foot thick, a machicolated parapet, and gunports. In short, the tower served as a donjon albeit of unusual design, and was the principal strong point of a castle which evidently saw off the French in a raid in 1458, when 'many gonnes' were 'shotte'.

In all the other great towers, the so-called 'tower houses' of the fourteenth and fifteenth centuries now under discussion, it is impossible not to see even more clearly a living tradition going back in England to the Tower of London and beyond to still earlier towers of stone or wood in Normandy and in France. There is no doubt that all of them, from Knaresborough to Tattershall (**34**) and Ashby, contained grand residential suites presumably intended for the castle's lord. There can be no doubt (and if there were, a visit to Tattershall would cure it) that all of them were deliberately, indeed aggressively, symbolic of the proud territorial lordship of their day, and that not least when built by an *arriviste* like Ralph lord Cromwell or Sir William ap Thomas. It is deeply significant in this respect that amongst them Dudley, Warkworth and Raglan were (like the new keep at Southampton) built upon a pre-existing castle motte – one of the earliest symbols of feudal lordship – and it is certainly to be noted that Knaresborough, Dunstanburgh and Tattershall are each referred to as 'donjon', 'dugeon' and 'dongeon' in fifteenth-century records which happen to survive.[18] The only difference, surely, between these great towers and their predecessors of the eleventh to the thirteenth centuries, apart from stylistic differences of architectural detail and the contemporary military devices of gunports and machicolation, is that they mostly lack the formidable defensive strength of their precursors. Abbot Suger, in his 'Life of Louis the Fat', tells how the young man and future king of the French was once advised by his father, Philip I (1060–1108), about a certain donjon at Montlhéry: 'Look, my son, make sure you never let the Tower of Montlhery out of your keeping. It has caused me untold trouble. Frankly, that tower has made me old before my time.'[19] In those days and for long after, we may say, the great tower was much of the substance, as well as the symbol, of lordship, but no-one in the fifteenth century would ever have need to speak thus of Tattershall. We may probably exempt Raglan from any charge of weakness, but even Nunney had its entrance at ground level defended only by the moat and the adjacent flanking towers, while the north wall above it was less strong than it looked (as the seventeenth-century gunners discovered – or did they know before?) because of the stairs and vestibule within it. A Tudor survey describes Edward II's tower at Knaresborough as 'a marvelous hous of strength ... strongly fortified with worke and man's ingyne to abide all assaults',[20] but however strong it may have been externally to the field, where it was evidently three-sided or demi-hexagonal, with a cylindrical buttress rising up the centre of the middle face to form a surmounting turret, the straight façade facing into the inner ward had large and handsome window and door openings of very unmilitary quality. At Tattershall (**34**) all, or most, caution seems to be thrown to the winds, for the front to the field is the display front (protected to some extent, it is true, by the moat and a, here very narrow, outer ward), with splendid windows from top to bottom wide open to projectiles; on the other side the entrances are at ground level, and while the machicolation about the head of the tower itself is real, that upon the summits of the turrets is bogus and purely decorative. The compilers of the Official Guide to Warkworth remark that at first-floor level 'all pretence of military character is abandoned, the rooms having large windows and the walls, though apparently eight feet thick, being really two quite thin walls separated by ingeniously planned closets, cupboards and stairs'.[21] (For the latter point, therefore, cf. the north front of Nunney.) Finally, the Hastings Tower at Ashby-de-la-Zouch may serve as our end, seemingly raised by William lord Hastings in response not to need but to fashion, for he added it to a residence previously and otherwise unfortified, never a castle before nor, in reality, since, save by courtesy.

Considerable interest attaches to the quadrangular castles which are evolved in the second half of the fourteenth century and continue into and through the fifteenth to merge at length with the great, but unfortified, houses built on the same plan. Though we have had before, and as early as the twelfth century, residential accommodation arranged on the quadrangular plan even within castles (as at Sherborne, Old Sarum, Henry II's Windsor[22] and the 'Gloriette' at Corfe), such groups of buildings remained, like all other early 'houses in the castle' (as the documents call them), individual domestic units placed arbitrarily within the bailey without any particular reference to the military pattern of the curtain walls.[23] By contrast, the quadrangular castles of the fourteenth and fifteenth centuries succeeded in uniting almost for the first time the residential and military roles of the castle into one integrated architectural form, the articulated and elaborate accommodation disposed quadrangularly and of one build with the quadrangular enclosure of the castle's walls and towers – though we may notice the same achievement at Queenborough (above p. 94) albeit in a circular plan. Of course there have been castles in the form of rectangular enclosures before, not least in the classic concentric fortresses of Beaumaris and Caerphilly, but their domestic apartments were not an integral part of the whole structure in the manner of, say, Bolton-in-Wensleydale. This castle (**XXV**), built by Richard lord Scrope in association with a licence granted to him in 1379, contains eight distinct suites of accommodation for individual households (the invariable medieval social unit, and not at all the same as the modern family unit), together with twelve single-chamber apartments for lesser men (esquires and priests), a great hall and a communal chapel, as well as a common kitchen and all other service quarters, all of it dovetailed into one quadrangular building conceived as a whole, three storeys high with four rectangular corner towers five storeys high, and lesser rectangular turrets in the centre of the two longest sides (north and south). Bodiam in Sussex (**35**, **XXVI**), of much the same date (*c.*1385), is very similar in concept and basic plan to serve the same kind of lordly life and obligation, though here the four angle towers are boldly projecting cylinders, and there is an impressive twin-towered gatehouse in the centre of the north front and a postern tower opposite in the centre of the south, both machicolated and both features not found at Bolton. The main building at Bodiam is of only two storeys with its angle towers rising to three, and this, plus the generous fenestration within, gave its rather larger courtyard a more open and spacious appearance than the confines of Bolton, while the whole castle, whether by accident or design, and largely due to its wide moat and water defences, has a rare beauty – almost, one may say, grace and charm – denied to its grimmer northern counterpart.

The point may be relevant, for although in fact Bodiam appears in many ways stronger than Bolton, and the licence for it granted to Sir Edward Dalyngrigge in October 1385 empowers him 'to make a castle … in defence of the adjacent country against the king's enemies' (i.e. the French), it cannot be placed in the first rank of fortresses. However logically satisfying the plan as potentially combining to perfection the twin rôles of residence and fortress, the same is true of the many other quadrangular castles of the fourteenth and fifteenth centuries – respectively Maxstoke, Warwickshire (*c.*1345 and thus earlier than the others), Sheriff Hutton (*c.*1382, a neighbour to Bolton and built by the powerful Nevilles, responsible also for the rambling and ill-fortified Raby), Lumley (co. Durham, *c.*1389), Shirburn in Oxfordshire (*c.*1380) and Wingfield in Suffolk (*c.*1384), Caister-by-Yarmouth (see above, *c.*1432, built in brick and with two

XXV Bolton-in-Wensleydale, floor plans showing accommodation.

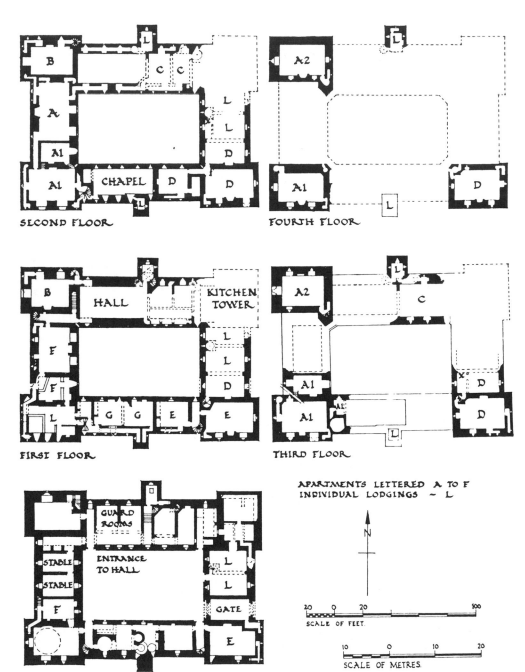

XXVI Bodiam, floor plans showing accommodation.

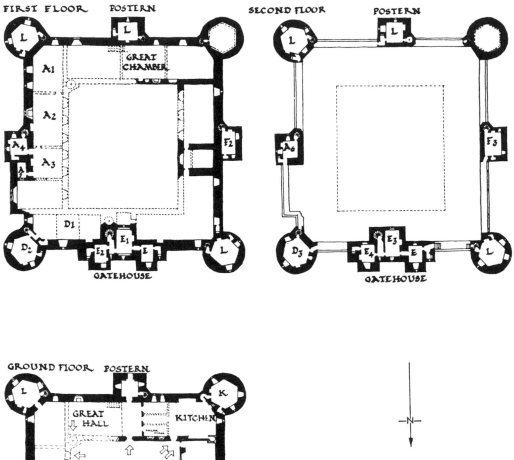

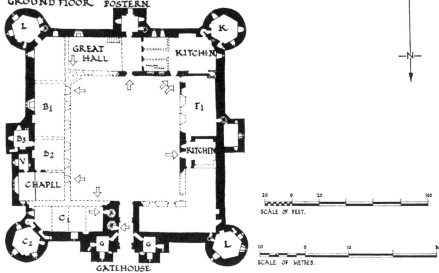

now with the gatehouse in the centre and a flanking tower at either end. The gatehouse is a fine example of the now perfected type, with a pair of towers one on either side of the gateway itself, bound together into a solid building above the entrance passage. In this instance there are three storeys above the level of the entrance, and lofty and embattled turrets rise at each corner above the embattled parapet of the roof. In front of this a barbican projects, consisting of two parallel embattled walls with a lesser tower at the end of each. While the long, narrow and hazardous entrance passage thus formed was further defended by its gates, portcullises, two drawbridges and the meurtrières in the vaults above it at either end, the most striking feature of the whole structure is that the approach and entrance are covered by scientifically disposed triple battlements – those of the barbican, those of the parapets of the gatehouse, and those of the latter's turrets which, commanding the whole, were joined together by flying bridges for intercommunication. There is not, thus, much lowering of the guard here, nor is there in the two towers, Caesar's Tower and Guy's Tower, which stand one at either end of the new work. Both are strong, lofty and machicolated, both are also residential, and both are rightly considered among the masterpieces of fourteenth-century military architecture. Guy's Tower, to the north, is polygonal; Caesar's Tower is tri-lobed like a clover leaf. Perhaps the latter is the finer of the two, standing upon a massive plinth and rising to a height of 133 ft, capped by the double system of battlements provided by its topmost parapet and the machicolated gallery beneath.

Of course elsewhere also there are evident exceptions to any obvious decline of military strength. The machicolated barbican or outer gateway at Lewes was added to the castle in the first half of the fourteenth century, and the present gatehouse at Lancaster was built between 1402 and 1422. Nevertheless, it is easier to point to improvements in the residential buildings of castles as the period advances than to improvements in their military capacity. On the grand scale, the virtual rebuilding (save for the keep) by John of Gaunt in the late fourteenth century of the inner core of Kenilworth was, like Edward III's work at Windsor, almost entirely devoted to the construction of the magnificent ranges of domestic apartments to west and south, not least the great hall, whose ruins still evocatively remain, though to some extent these are defended by their projecting mural towers, the outer curtain and the mere, and one has to wait for the time of Elizabeth I for Leicester's Buildings to break through the confines of the inner ward (he also 'modernized' the twelfth-century keep to make a mockery of its former massive strength). At the episcopal castle of Durham, to take another instance, bishop Hatfield (1345–81) enlarged the hall, his successor, bishop Fox (1494–1500) built the present enormous kitchen, and bishop Tunstall (1530–59) added the existing chapel. At Farnham, another episcopal castle, bishop Waynflete added to the accommodation by building, between 1470 and 1475, the present 'Foxe's Tower', in brick with bogus machicolation as an ornament.[28] At Baconsthorpe in Norfolk, at best a fortified manor rather than a castle, built in the troubled times of the later fifteenth century by a local, rising

and grasping family called Heydon, Sir John Heydon II in the first half of the
sixteenth century not only added the completely unfortified outer court and
outer gatehouse, but also established a kind of woollen textile factory in the east
range of the inner court.[29]

The development of the residential quarters of the castle, however, to the
point where they may break through any military restriction in the end, is
seldom better shown than at Carew (**38**) in Pembrokeshire. There what was
once a very strong castle, roughly quadrangular with angle towers, principally of
the thirteenth and early fourteenth centuries though dating back to the early
twelfth, was transformed and weakened by Sir Rhys ap Thomas between about
1480 and 1507. Of his work it has been said that it was 'entirely directed to
increasing the castle's magnificence and capacity as a residence, at the expense, if
necessary, of its military strength',[30] and it included the replacement of every
major medieval window by one of his own, the rebuilding of most of the
battlements as dummies, and the building of a great domestic range on the north
side of the castle, outside the curtain there which was demolished for the
purpose. This range in turn was replaced in the Elizabethan period by the present
one, with its fashionable and entirely unmilitary long gallery at second-floor
level, built by Sir John Perrott. To this day the juxtaposition of these buildings,
with their long line of graceful but civilian mullioned windows, and the great,
spurred, thirteenth-century drum tower which they join on the west (**38**), seems
eloquent enough of the vanishing military importance of the castle and its
resultant transformation into a splendid country mansion – though, as things
turned out Carew was to be besieged, breached, stormed and slighted in the
seventeenth-century Civil War. The same point is made by the fine range of
'Renaissance' buildings raised in the bailey at Dudley by the earl of
Northumberland in the reign of Mary Tudor, but for what may be thought
the *reductio ad absurdum* of the expansion of the residential buildings within a
castle we may turn to Berry Pomeroy in Devon. There, incongruously placed
within, but otherwise independent and entirely indifferent to the fortifications of
the medieval castle which surrounds it, stands a complete Tudor mansion, begun
by Protector Somerset in the reign of Edward VI. It is sad irony of history that
this of all buildings should have been in the event, like Carew, shattered by war
which it seemingly ignored, yet it was severely damaged in the Civil War in the
seventeenth century, was soon after abandoned, and stands now an empty shell.

1 Dover

2 Langeais

3 Doué-la-Fontaine

4 Rennes, from the Bayeux Tapestry

5 Dinan, from the Bayeux Tapestry

6 Bayeux, from the Bayeux Tapestry

7 Hastings, from the Bayeux Tapestry

8 Farnham

9 Pleshey

10 Castle Acre

11 Ludlow, showing the early mural towers above the river

12 Framlingham

13 Colchester, the keep. The apsidal projection, like that of the Tower of London, contains the apse of the chapel

14 Rochester, the keep, showing the rebuilt and cylindrical south-east angle

15 Castle Rising, the keep

16 Conisborough, the keep

17 Orford, the keep

18 Berkhamstead

19 Launceston

20 Château-Gaillard

21 Caernarvon

22 Conway

23 Harlech

24 Beaumaris

25 Kidwelly

26 Caerphilly

27 The Tower of London

28 Chepstow, Marten's Tower

29 Stokesay

30 Acton Burnell

31 Raglan, Gate house and Closet tower

32 Nunney

33 Caister-by-Yarmouth

34 Tattershall

35 Bodiam, the north front with gatehouse

36 Windsor

37 Warwick, the gatehouse and barbican with Caesar's Tower to the left

38 Carew

39 Rochester across the Medway

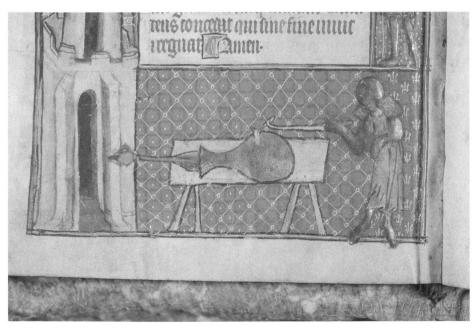

40 The earliest known illustration of a cannon, 1326

Chapter 6

Castle-building

In the preceding five chapters of this book the physical development of the English castle has been traced from its Norman and French origins in the mid-eleventh century to the triumphant culmination of the late thirteenth and early fourteenth centuries, and we have dealt also with the slow decline of the castle thereafter as an architectural form. Such architectural history raises, or should raise, the question of how these things were done, and by what sort of men. In recent years, in fact, historians have paid increasing attention to the practical side of architecture, including medieval architecture, that is to say to the actual process of construction as opposed to the mere description of those buildings which survive. The method used has for the most part been the very desirable one of combining with the examination of the structures themselves the study of the documents and other written sources relating to their building. In consequence something of the gap between architectural history and real history has been closed, and, though much work remains to be done, we are beginning to know something of the cost of medieval building in terms of money, labour, materials and time, to see something of the complex organisation which lay behind it all, to learn something of the methods used, and to appreciate more fully both the finished results as we see them and the high degree of skill, both scientific and artistic, which produced them. The study of the relevant written evidence also has the immediate value of enabling surviving buildings in many cases to be dated with more precision than is possible by structural evidence alone, and especially is this the case with castles which have far less decoration, such as carvings and mouldings susceptible to stylistic dating, than, say, churches. Finally, not the least satisfying result of these studies has been to dispel a good deal of the hitherto cherished anonymity of the so-called Middle Ages, to establish in some measure who built what as well as when, and thus to add to the roll of English architects, which too commonly began with Wren, some of the names of the consummate masters of the medieval past.[1]

Here our concern is only with castle-building. Yet it could be argued that castles are particularly characteristic of the Middle Ages since they are unique to that period, and while most architectural history concentrates most on churches, yet castles yield little to them either in interest or social significance, and the deliberate worldly magnificence of a Caerphilly (**26**) or a Caernarvon (**21**), Richard I's Château-Gaillard (**20**) or Edward III's Windsor (**36**), makes scarcely less impact upon the sensibilities than the ecclesiastical splendours of Durham or Ely, Salisbury or Norwich, York or Canterbury. The castle is a functional building but so is a church, and the impression made by the one is quite as deliberate as that made by the other. Sometimes the two stand significantly side by side, and it has been pointed out before now that the intended view of Rochester seen from across the Medway (**39**) is entirely evocative of the two pillars of order and authority in contemporary society, king and bishop, church and state, *regnum et sacerdotium*, God and Caesar. In a book of this kind no comprehensive account of castle-building could be attempted even if all the information were readily available, which it is not (literally miles of parchment, mostly unprinted), but some comment upon what is already known, and some examples of works carried out for which written evidence survives, may suffice to take us behind the façade of medieval military architecture, and do something towards answering the questions of how much castles cost, how long they took to build, what amount and sort of labour was employed, and who were the master craftsmen who planned and directed their construction.

Though the fact must not be allowed to detract from their formidable strength and worth, it is obvious that those many early castles in England and subsequently Wales which were of earthwork and timber only, without masonry buildings and defences, were relatively cheap, quick and even easy to construct by comparison with the stone-built fortresses of their own time and, especially, later. For this reason, indeed, they were the perfect instruments of conquest and of the rapid occupation of territory – in which respect it is significant that castles of earthwork and timber, and not least motte-and-bailey castles, were the marks of the Angevin invasion and settlement of Ireland in the second half of the twelfth century though by then such fortifications were becoming obsolete in England and in France. A quite small force of semi-skilled and unskilled labour would suffice, directed by some new Norman lord who, having skilfully chosen the site, could adequately control the work. The Bayeux Tapestry thus vividly portrays a scene that must have been enacted and repeated all over England in and after 1066 in its representation of the raising of Hastings Castle (**7**). A number of labourers are busily at work digging and throwing up a motte, under the direction of a Norman magnate who is probably Robert, count of Mortain and half-brother to the Conqueror. (Two of the labourers there depicted are apparently settling a difference with their shovels behind count Robert's back.) Even when they had mottes, the time required to make such castles at least militarily effective was short, though no doubt at some subsequent stage more skilled and time-consuming carpentry would be required to build suitable residential accommodation or anything like the elaborate timber tower described as standing upon the motte at Ardres (p. 18 above). As it happens, eight days is implied in two reputable chronicles to have been the time taken both for the planting of the castle within the existing fortifications at Dover in 1066 and for the raising of the second castle at York in 1069,[2] in each case by the Conqueror himself. Whether or not this figure is taken as literally true in either case, nothing emerges more strikingly from a reading of contemporary chroniclers than the speed and seeming ease with which castles, usually, no doubt of earthwork and timber, were raised by king and barons alike in the first generation of the Norman Conquest. Nor can this type of castle-building have been very expensive. Indeed, in the early days we can be reasonably certain that what in effect was forced labour supplied much of the necessary manpower, even though for the most part it was constitutionally respectable in being derived from the pre-Conquest royal right to take labour for fortifications (*burghwork*), now applied by the Norman king and his delegates to their new type of fortification which was the castle; so that the unfortunate English were constrained to raise the instrument and symbol of their own subjection. Certainly the juxtaposition of castles and oppression seems significant in the text of the Anglo-Saxon Chronicle after the Conquest – 'Castles he [William] caused to be made, and poor men to be greatly oppressed' – and the same association comes from the same source in a famous passage relating to the 'Anarchy' of Stephen's reign in the earlier twelfth century – 'they filled the land full of castles. They grievously oppressed the wretched men of the land with castle-works.'[3] Certainly also the beneficiaries of charters in the first century after the Conquest thought it worthwhile to include exemption from 'castle-works' among the liberties they sought and bought from the king. Later in the twelfth century this royal right and public burden, ancient in origin, may have given way to special local taxation for local fortification to which there are references in the records. Later still, as we shall see, the king acquired the right of pre-empting and directing labour for his works, both military and civil, though he paid the appropriate wages for the services thus obtained.

By contrast to the raising of relatively simple fortifications in earthwork and timber, castle-building in stone was a much more complex undertaking, and increasingly so as the castle became more elaborate and sophisticated, demanding not only skilful planning and siting but also more specialized workmanship and craftsmanship. There is a modern ring to a contemporary chronicler's description of building going forward at the Tower of London in the earlier years of Henry II's reign, when he writes that the work was carried out 'with so many smiths, carpenters and other workmen, working so vehemently with bustle and noise that a man could hardly hear the one next to him speak'. Elaborate building in stone was also necessarily slower and vastly more expensive. The reduction in the overall number of English castles which evidently took place in the twelfth century (p. 163 below), though it owed something to the established security of the Norman conquest and settlement, and something also to the control of fortification which (save in Stephen's reign) the Anglo-Norman and Angevin kings were able to exercise, was probably caused above all by the brute economic fact of increased costs exacerbated by inflation at the end of the century. Stone castles *à la mode* simply could not be raised with the gay abandon of the first, fine, careless rapture of the early decades of Norman hegemony, nor could all the castles then founded be kept up to date by the addition of stone walls and buildings, and many thus became obsolete and were abandoned.

Though the paucity of written, and more especially documentary, evidence relating to it must not be allowed to detract from our appreciation of the considerable amount of stone building carried out in the first century of the Norman Conquest, it is fortunate that the later twelfth and earlier thirteenth centuries, perhaps the most concentrated period of stone fortification in this country and when so many castles primarily of earthwork and timber were converted into stone, is also the period in which the king's ever expanding government increasingly adopted the habit of keeping written records – a habit largely acquired from the Church and in due course adopted by the great lay magnates also, though their records have less frequently survived. The English medieval state, it may be noted, was amongst the first in the West systematically to compile and keep records of its transactions and to establish thus an efficient bureaucracy. The secular records which have been preserved from this period are thus for the most part royal, but the king possessed, maintained and built more castles than any other lord, and from the copious documentary evidence of his castle works we can establish also standards of reference for seigneurial building elsewhere. The earliest and most important royal records for our purposes are the Pipe Rolls, formally the Great Rolls of the Exchequer, which, beginning even earlier, survive in majestic and almost unbroken sequence from the second year of Henry II (1155–6) to their final abolition in 1832. These rolls, made up annually and in duplicate for each year by the Exchequer, the financial office of the king's government, contain the annual accounts of the sheriffs and certain other royal officials, and thus contain also, at least from the twelfth to the earlier fourteenth century, most of the king's receipts and most of his expenditure therefrom. Year after year upon the Pipe Rolls therefore we may see the king's works upon his castles up and down the realm, and see also that castle building and maintenance is in fact the largest single and continuous item of recorded royal expenditure.

Even in the reigns of Henry II and his sons, Richard I and John, for which the Pipe Rolls are now all in print and thus the figures can be comprehensively worked out,[4] such expenditure frequently reaches the formidable total of over £1000 a year, and sometimes doubles this and occasionally trebles and quadruples it. At first sight such figures may appear, perhaps, more quaint than impressive, but in fact they represent great sums by the monetary values of the age. It has been reckoned that the average annual income of king Henry II (1154–89), which means in practice the average annual revenue of the government of the realm, amounted to some, £10,000. An American scholar, the late Professor Sidney Painter,[5] calculated that the regular annual income of one of the richest vassals of the king in the early years of the thirteenth century, Roger de Lacy, constable of Chester (whose family were soon to obtain the earldom of Lincoln), was some £800. The same historian found only seven members of the English baronage, who formed the small but immensely powerful ruling class, to have been regularly in receipt of more than £400 a year about the year 1200. This was a period, also, in which a knight or country gentleman might live comfortably on £10 to £20 a year, and when the appropriate wages of a knight on active service were 8d. a day in *c.*1154, rising (as a sign of inflation) to 2s. and more by 1216. Abbot Samson of Bury St Edmunds, in the reign of Henry II, maintained, possibly with the exaggeration of maturity, that five or six marks a year (a mark was 13s. 4d. or two-thirds of a pound) would have sufficed to keep him at the University. The constable of one of the king's castles at that time might expect an annual stipend of £10 or £12 a year to maintain him in his office and considerable responsibility, while the stipend of the chaplain of the same castle (like that of the porter and the watchman) was likely to be 1d. a day.

Of the many castle works of that great castle-builder, Henry II, for which the Pipe Rolls provide us with information, we may turn first to Orford.[6] For at Orford on the Suffolk coast king Henry built an entirely new castle, that is to say one raised from its foundations in one operation upon a site previously unfortified, and therefore the work is more convenient to use as an example of castle-building than the more normal process at this date of adding piecemeal stone buildings and fortifications to an existing site. Moreover, the keep at least at Orford (**17, IX**) still stands to give point to the record of its building, and while this great tower is unusual in its design (p. 53 above) the whole castle as Henry left it must have been typical enough of the 'keep-and-bailey' castle of the period, moreover with (as we know from a drawing of *c.*1600 by John Norden) a series of rectangular flanking towers about its curtain remarkably similar to those of Henry II's Dover (and Caen and Chinon) and of neighbouring Framlingham (**12**). The king's works at Orford evidently began in 1165, for on the Pipe Roll of 1165–6, on the account of the sheriff of Norfolk and Suffolk, there occur for the first time entries 'in the work of the castle of Orford', and the total recorded for this in that year comes to over £660 – a very large sum, and in fact the largest recorded annual outlay upon a single castle since the beginning of the reign. The next year £323 was spent, and by this time, the autumn of 1167, after an outlay of nearly £1000 in two years, the building must have been well advanced, for the same roll records payments of some £2 for stocking the castle and 20 marks to Bartholomew de Glanville as custodian of it. Work, however, continued over the next six years until 1173, when completion is indicated by the entry on the roll of £58 2s. 8d. spent 'in the work of one great ditch round the castle of Orford with palisades and brattices and in the work of a stone bridge in the same castle.' The total recorded expenditure upon the building of Orford between 1165 and 1173 amounts to just over £1,400, and the work evidently occupied eight years – in significant contrast to the eight days implied to be the time taken to plant castles at Dover and York in the Conqueror's day a century before.

It is probably more accurate to express the time taken to build Orford as eight or nine seasons (the Exchequer year covered by the accounts upon the Pipe

Rolls running from Michaelmas to Michaelmas) rather than eight years, for medieval building (like much modern building) was necessarily seasonal, concentrated in spring, summer and autumn, and slacking off greatly in the winter months. The relevant entries on the rolls are very summarized ('In the work of the castle of Orford, *so much*') and provide at this date few details of how the work was done, but the reference in 1167–8 to finished timbers, possible for the joists and flooring of the keep, brought from as far away as Scarborough in Yorkshire, where another royal keep was building, together with the fact that some of the dressed stone used in the keep is Caen stone from Normandy, are indications of the complex organization lying behind such large-scale under-takings. Of the master mason, or architect in modern parlance, and of the other craftsmen and labourers responsible for the design and execution of the castle, the Pipe Rolls unfortunately tell us nothing, and though it has sometimes been attributed to a certain Master Alnoth, a well-known 'engineer' and master mason employed by Henry II, there is in fact no evidence that he was in any way associated with it.

Although the cost of any building work must vary in accordance with its scale, the nature of the site, the availability of materials and labour and so on, and though it would be hazardous to assume that the recorded figure of £1,413 10s. 10d. represents the complete total of expenditure upon Orford, that figure is nevertheless a useful indication of the cost of a powerful castle with a keep in the later twelfth century. Certainly it compares well enough with the known recorded cost of other royal castleworks of about the same time. Thus, a principal feature of Orford castle was its keep, and the keep at Newcastle-upon-Tyne, built between 1167 and 1178, evidently cost some £1000, while Henry II's completion of the smaller keep at Bowes in Yorkshire, *c*.1170 to 1187, cost just under £600. The recorded cost of another complete new castle at Odiham in Hampshire, built by King John a little later in a period of rapidly rising prices, amounts to about £1000, and this, too, had a keep of polygonal design (**XI**). But of all the royal castleworks in the later twelfth and early thirteenth centuries in England, one far outstrips all others in the amount of treasure and labour lavished upon it, and the scale and nature of that work is emphasized by the cost which soars far above the level of Odiham and Orford. A castle had existed at Dover (**I**) since literally the earliest days of the Norman Conquest, but the great work of Henry II in the later years of his reign represents not only the complete rebuilding of the fortress but the beginning of its development on an entirely new plan to take in and comprise the whole area of the former Iron Age fortress and Anglo-Saxon borough (p. 61 above). All this was not to be completed for a century, but meanwhile Henry II's work included the great rectangular tower keep, the towered inner bailey with its two twin-tower gateways, and at least a section of the towered outer curtain to the north-east. The work appears to have occupied the years between about 1180 and 1190 (the accounts, at least, not ending until after the old king's death in 1189) and upon it the Pipe Rolls record an expenditure hitherto unparalleled. In each of the three years 1183–6 sums of over £1000 are entered for this one castle alone, and the total figure by 1190 comes to little short of £7000.[7]

Amongst the summary entries upon the rolls relating to the king's works at Dover there are references once or twice to 'the work of the wall round the castle', i.e. presumably the outer curtain, and to the wall 'about the tower', i.e. presumably the inner curtain, but over and over again, and especially between 1181 and 1185, to 'the work of the tower of Dover', i.e. the keep, which was evidently nearing completion by 1185, certainly cost over £2000 recorded in these specific references to it, and may have cost as much as twice that amount. Though again the Pipe Rolls afford little detail of the precise way in which the work was carried out, they refer to timber and lead brought in from East Anglia, and, most interestingly of all, to the payment year by year of first 8d. and then 1s. a day to a certain Maurice the 'Engineer' (*Ingeniator*), who was evidently in charge of the work at any rate of the keep. This Maurice is probably to be identified with the Maurice the Mason who appears upon the Pipe Rolls between *c.*1172 and 1177 in association with the building of Henry II's keep at Newcastle-upon-Tyne, which has many close affinities with the great tower at Dover, and thus he seems to have been responsible for both. If so, the long-forgotten Master Maurice leaps at once to the fore-front of medieval architects in England, and at Dover especially could have no grander monument. Dover by about 1190, both by the evidence of the Pipe Rolls and the enduring strength of Henry II's works still standing there, must have been potentially amongst the finest castles in the land, albeit incomplete, and one can comprehend already the chronicler Matthew Paris's famous and later epithet, 'the key of England'.

One other royal castle of the late twelfth century, however, at least rivalled Dover both in its cost and in its finished strength. Though in France, at Les Andelys upon the Seine and the border of Normandy, Richard I's Château-Gaillard (**20, XII**) would demand our attention in any case, as perhaps the finest castle of its date in Latin Christendom and built by a king of England (p. 62 above), even if the amount of surviving written evidence concerning its construction, together with the majesty of its present remains, did not make it an outstanding example of a major work of military architecture carried out with all the resources of an early medieval state.[8] If we assume that Richard built it all, as seems to be the case, then even more impressive than the cost of the operation was the speed with which it was carried out. A necessary preliminary was the acquisition of the site, which the king took from the archbishop of Rouen in whose territory it lay. The result of this was an interdict upon the Norman duchy, i.e. the prohibition of all or most church services and offices, and the chronicler Roger of Howden writes of 'the unburied bodies of the dead lying in the streets and squares of the cities of Normandy.' Even before the archbishop had been pacified by rich gifts of land elsewhere, and the interdict thereby lifted, Richard had begun his building. Thereafter it was pressed on with ruthless but efficient speed. Another chronicler, William of Newburgh, tells the story of how, when in May 1198 the king, as was his custom, was inspecting and urging on the work, a shower of blood fell from the sky. The king's companions were much alarmed by what they took to be an evil portent. But, says the chronicler, 'the king was not moved by this to slacken one whit the pace of the work, in which he took such keen pleasure that, unless I am mistaken, even if an angel had descended from heaven to urge its abandonment he would have been roundly cursed'. In the event, not only the splendid castle high on its rock, but also the fortified town together with outworks on the adjacent island in the river, were evidently largely completed in the two years, or at the most three seasons, between 1196 and 1198, at a recorded total cost of about £11,500 in the English money of the day – a truly remarkable achievement whose urgent cause was the military necessity of the defence of Normandy against the growing power of Philip Augustus, king of the French.

One of the most interesting features of the operation from our point of view is that the record upon the Norman Pipe Roll is in the form of a separate building account (as opposed to piecemeal entries relating to a work upon the general account of a sheriff or bailiff, which is more usual at this date) and is sufficiently detailed to show us for the first time something of the organization and labour involved in such a work. There are references to the quarry-men and rough masons who worked the stone from the quarries, and to the freemasons who fashioned it for the walls and towers; to the wood-men who cut the timber, the carters who brought it to the site, and the carpenters who then worked it for joists and floors and roofs. There are references also to the miners who cut the fosses and hacked out the cellars in the living rock; to smiths at their forges, lime workers, hodmen, watchmen and soldiers to guard the works, and to clerks who checked materials and expenditure and drew up the accounts. No master mason or architect in overall charge is mentioned, and perhaps there was none, for all the evidence points to Richard's personal interest in and direction of the work, into which he poured the experience of a life-time's soldiering and the study at first hand of fortifications in both east and west. 'Behold, how fair is this year-old daughter of mine!' he is said to have exclaimed as the castle approached completion, and his pleasure in the sophistication of its design we have noted before (p. 62 above). It seems as well he never lived to hear of its capture, cut off and after a prolonged and heroic siege in 1204. With it the duchy fell; but had Richard lived it might have been that neither would have fallen.

Great as was the cost and great the finished strength of Dover and Château-Gaillard, both are surpassed in both respects by the formidable strength and soaring cost of the best of Edward I's castles in Wales a century later.[9] While the total cost of Harlech (**23**, **XV**) is reckoned to have been some £9,500, that of Conway (**22**, **XIV**), between 1283 and 1287 when the main work was accomplished, amounts to £14,000, that of Beaumaris (**24**, **XVI**) to some £14,400, and that of Caernarvon (**21**, **XIII**) to no less than £27,000. In all, it has been estimated that Edward I spent upon the building of his eight new royal castles in Wales some £80,000 in twenty-five years, and not even this figure represents the total cost since work went on at Caernarvon and Beaumaris into the reign of his grandson, Edward III, and neither in the event was ever finished. In part the high level of this expenditure, which, taken as a whole, far outstrips anything hitherto recorded in the whole history of the king's works (the cost of Henry III's Westminster Abbey falls between £40,000 and £50,000[10]), is no doubt due to rising prices and in part is explained by the fact that five of king Edward's castles, including Conway and Caernarvon, were combined with new fortified towns. But also it directly results from the scale on which they were conceived and the sophisticated application of all the advanced techniques of fortification previously evolved. So great an outlay of treasure and effort has been described as 'the premium that Edward paid to insure his Welsh conquests against the fire of rebellion', for the raising of these castles was an integral part of the conquest of Wales and the determination to perpetuate it. The urgency of military necessity, also, as at Château-Gaillard a century before, lies behind the speed with which the work in the main was carried through. Here Beaumaris (1295–c.1330) and Caernarvon (1283–c.1330) are the exceptions. Amongst the other six, Flint (**XVIII**) was raised in the eight and a half years from 1277 to 1286, Harlech in the seven and a half years 1283–90, Builth in the five and a half years 1277–82, and Rhuddlan (**XVII**) in four and a half years between the same dates. Most striking of all, perhaps, in its achievement was Conway, raised complete in the five years from 1283 to 1287. None of these times considered separately, it is true, can rival the record set by Richard I at Château-Gaillard, but the true measure of king Edward's achievement is that his tremendous effort was concentrated not just on one castle but on eight. Aberystwyth, Builth, Flint and Rhuddlan were going up together from 1277, Harlech, Conway and Caernarvon together from 1283, and long before the last of these was finished work upon Beaumaris had begun. The eight Edwardian royal castles in Wales, which include among them some of the finest castles ever raised, and five of which were combined with fortified towns, taken together form one defensive system and one comprehensive achievement unique in the history of English castle-building.

For the most part proper building accounts, like that for Château-Gaillard, survive on the Pipe Rolls for Edward's works in Wales, and by this date there also survive many of the detailed rolls of 'particulars' upon which the final accounts were based, as well as the originals or (more often) enrolled copies of writs, letters and other documents issued or received by the king's Chancery, Exchequer and household. These records, like most surviving medieval records, are not complete, but taken together they shed a flood of light upon the way in which this great operation was carried out. They show the personal interest and command taken by the king himself, who, with his master mason, is almost invariably present at the initiation of each work. They show clearly the seasonal character of medieval building, and they also show what we might expect from modern experience, namely that wages account for some two-thirds of total costs. Indeed the most impressive feature of the works, over and above their huge expense, is the size and composition of the labour force involved. At

Harlech in the summer of 1286 an average weekly number of nearly a thousand men were employed. The three castles of Conway, Caernarvon and Harlech employed between them an average of some two thousand five hundred workmen in each week of the seasons 1285–7. At Beaumaris alone in the summer of 1295 about three thousand five hundred were at work. Perhaps no other figures show more clearly the scale of these great works and the capacity of medieval enterprise and administrative ability. Further, impressive as these figures are by any standards, it has to be remembered that their context is an English population of perhaps three to four million persons.

To mobilize so great a force of labourers and craftsmen it is scarcely too much to say that the countryside was scoured and that there was no county however far away that did not make its contribution. They were drawn not only from the adjacent Welsh lands and the Marches, but also from Northumberland and Yorkshire in the north, Nottinghamshire and Northamptonshire in the Midlands, Norfolk and Suffolk and Essex in the east, Oxfordshire, Wiltshire, Somerset, Dorset in the south and west, and from other English shires besides, and also from overseas – and all of them assembled at Chester to work king Edward's will in Wales (**XXVII**). It was at this time, indeed, from the endless precedents of Edward's reign, that the right of late medieval English kings to the impressment of labour for their works was established, derived, it seems, not from the ancient right of their predecessors to burgh-work and castle-work (above p. 108) but from their equally or more ancient right to military service, such service now being taken from appropriate categories of the king's subjects in the form of labour. Once established, the right was applied in the fourteenth century to works both civil and military, in peace as well as war, and it is impressive, not least for those brought up to think that the powers of Caesar were dormant in the so-called 'Middle Ages', for this is the direction of labour. The proper rates were paid, however, and though an account of 1277 relating to the bringing of workmen from Yorkshire to Flint and Rhuddlan records the payment of three mounted sergeants (at $7\frac{1}{2}$d. a day each) for 'guarding the said workmen ... lest they flee on the way',[11] we hear little of any opposition or complaint – save sometimes from other lords to the effect that you could not find any craftsmen because the king had taken them all (p. 121 below). When we do hear of what may be one of the earliest recorded strikes in English history, it is because wages are in arrears, in Scotland towards the end of Edward's reign, when things were going wrong, the success of Wales could not be repeated, and money was running low. On 12 November 1303, the old king at Dunfermline ordered certain of his sheriffs to send him sixty carpenters and two hundred ditchers for his works there, only to be informed that none would come unless compelled by force, for the king owed them so much for their work at Linlithgow that they would rather leave the country than work again for him.[12]

Amongst the great companies of men assembled for the king's castleworks in Wales we see again the same categories familiar from the accounts for Château-Gaillard a century before – freemasons, roughmasons and quarriers, carpenters

XXVII Map showing the impressment of labour for the king's works in Wales, 1282–3. (From *The History of the King's Works*, H.M.S.O.)

and smiths, plumbers, glaziers, carters, boatmen and a host of unskilled labourers. Some worked on piece-work and others on time, a few, the most skilful, had salaries, and all were paid by the ubiquitous, ever scribbling and calculating clerks. Amongst the throng, the master craftsmen are distinguished, not least the master masons, the most important of whom had an overall charge of the works of masonry and thus combined the role of a modern architect with their pre-eminence in their craft. Most important of all was Master James of St George, mason and 'engineer', brought by the king from Savoy where he had built castles in many respects similar in detail to those he was to build in Wales, and now appointed 'master of the king's works in Wales'. In that rôle he had a general and a particular responsibility for all that was done, and how it was done, no less than that of the king, and the castles built under his direction are no less his monument than Edward's. Later he was to follow the same king on the abortive campaigns in Scotland, and he died in 1309, to be held, now that he is once more given credit for what he did, surely the greatest architect in the history of English castles.

The examples of castle-building so far given in this chapter have been necessarily few and, no less necessarily in the earlier medieval period (since we are dependent in this matter upon surviving documents), they have been exclusively royal works. They have also been for the most part exceptional in the sense that each individual instance chosen for detailed discussion has been of a new castle or of a complete rebuilding as opposed to the alteration or improvement of an existing one, which development is the more normal type of castlework. We should, therefore, before we end, turn to at least one such operation of development, if only to show that this too could be a work of formidable proportions and complexity. Further, since at any time after 1066 seigneurial or baronial castles commonly outnumbered royal (there being more other lords than the king), and since the finest baronial castles, as we have seen, are not markedly inferior to their royal counterparts in strength or style, it follows that other lords were scarcely less active than the king in castle-building. For the earlier centuries almost no documentary evidence records their works, but from the later Middle Ages some seigneurial building accounts do survive, and it is to three such fortunate survivals, in no way that matters to be distinguished from comparable royal accounts, that we must next turn as illustration of baronial castle-building at least in the fifteenth century, at Caister-by-Yarmouth, Tattershall and Kirby Muxloe.

Sir John Fastolf, a captain of Henry V's campaigns in France (and whose actual character bore no relation to the version later dramatized by Shakespeare to the anger and distress of the real warrior's descendants), 'exercised in the werres contynually about xliiij yeres' according to his secretary William Worcester. Out of his martial profits and as a mark of his success Caister-by-Yarmouth (**33**) in Norfolk was built. The castle later passed to the Pastons and its ruins still stand, partially inhabited, distinguished by their very fine, slender and cylindrical tower (p. 97 above). The date of its construction is thought to be 1432–46. The accounts which have survived, now in the British Museum and printed some years ago,[13] cover only the years 1432–5 and record a total expenditure of £1,480 5s. 9¼d. By contrast, according to the statement of William Worcester the works occupied thirty years and cost £6,000. As was often the case with the castles and fortified manors of the later Middle Ages, a house already stood upon the site and was now altered and rebuilt beyond all recognition. Of the new buildings and works, the accounts mention the west and north walls, the hall, the chapel and 'les deskes' therein, a horse-mill for the bakehouse, and a garden. There were evidently occasional set-backs and mistakes, incidents common to building in all ages, and the accountant, William Granour, who was in charge of the administrative side of the works, sought allowance for his expenses on a certain 'counterwall' which had fallen into the moat because of a defect in its foundation. A notable feature of Caister is, of course, that it is built of brick and is a particularly fine specimen of early and medieval brickwork. Accordingly, the accounts are full of references to the bricks which were made locally, and the categories of craftsmen mentioned include brickmakers and bricklayers as well as the usual masons and carpenters. No overall master or architect is named, and indeed the surviving accounts mention few craftsmen by name, apart from a certain Henry Wood, 'masoun', who failed in his claim to be allowed half a day's wages for his journeys between Norwich and his work – 'the gwiche [claim]', noted the careful accountant, 'l have disalowid til I have oder comaundement of yow'.

For Tattershall in Lincolnshire, built by Ralph lord Cromwell between 1430 and 1450 (**34**), the accounts which survive are again fragmentary, partially covering the years from 1432 to 1446.[14] As is generally the case, they are not particularly informative about the structure itself (the main concern of accountants in any period being to itemize the costs of wages, materials and transport and set them against receipts), though significantly enough they refer to the great tower, the surviving glory of Tattershall, as 'le Dongeon'. Their most impressive single feature is their record of the vast number of bricks required for this, another of the great brick buildings of the later Middle Ages, and again made locally, at Edlington Moor a few miles north of Tattershall, where the pits from which the clay came may still be seen. Thus in 1445–6, 384,000 large bricks and 84,000 smaller bricks were made, in addition to the 274,000 then in stock. Other materials required included freestone (brought from Willesford and elsewhere), iron (brought and wrought at Coningsby and Tattershall, or Spanish iron imported), timber, glass (also of local manufacture), lead, lime, plaster of Paris, and coal. Wages as always loom large, and it is thought that a certain Baldwin Dutchman, the highest paid and most prominent 'brickmason' or 'brickmaker' amongst the craftsmen, may have been the master and architect of the work. Not all the expenditure upon the accounts is directly related to the works, and amongst the items which are not are expenses incurred when lord Cromwell himself visited his manor and castle, as he did in August 1438.

The accounts for Kirby Muxloe in Leicestershire which survive are more complete and much more detailed, being the weekly record of 'particulars' from which the final and summarized account would later be drawn up, and covering the whole period of the works.[15] Tragedy attaches to them also, as we shall see, as well as architectural detail. Kirby Muxloe itself was a castle or fortified manor characteristic of its period, albeit never finished: a quadrangular enclosure within a (wet) moat, with four rectangular angle towers, an imposing twin-towered gatehouse in the centre of the north face, and a rectangular tower or turret in the centre of the other three (p. 99 above). Though it is now by common courtesy called a castle, it is worth noting that it is never so called upon these accounts. Again, and as it happens, it was built of brick, and again it was built on the site of an existing house, part of which was incorporated in the new work. This new work was begun in 1480 by order of William lord Hastings, the great Yorkist leader.

The accounts begin in October 1480 and thereafter we can follow from them week by week the progress of the works until the end. As might be expected, activity in the initial winter months was slight and principally directed to the clearing and preparation of the site and moat. With the coming of spring in 1481 the tempo quickens. Large quantities of stone were brought from neighbouring quarries, timber was cut and made ready, bricks made and stacked by the thousand, and more craftsmen and labourers drafted in. Throughout the summer work was in full swing, with bricklayers, masons and carpenters, carters and common labourers all busy on and about the site. The walls were rising under the brick-layers and work was begun upon the two angle towers at the north end of the enclosure. Amongst the stream of entries of payments at this time for wages and materials, one, the payment of 1s 8d to a certain Powel and four other men, who watched throughout one night at the end of May lest the water in the moat should rise and flood the site, suggests that the English summer has changed little in the course of centuries. In the autumn preparations were made for the coming slack winter season, many of the workmen were paid off, nine cartloads of stubble were brought in from the adjacent fields to cover the unfinished tops of walls and towers against frost damage, and at the end of October the accounts were cast up to show a total expenditure over the previous twelve months of £330 3s.

The pattern of work and organization shown by the accounts for the first twelve months at Kirby Muxloe remains much the same in the ensuing years. The great activity of summer is followed by a slack winter period lasting from about October to March, during which the labour force was much reduced and the remaining workmen have their wages cut to correspond with their shorter hours – though as the building nears completion the contrast between summer and winter becomes less marked, and in all seasons the freemasons could continue to fashion stone under cover. The workmen, who all appear by name in the columns of wages paid, were drawn from a wide area (the medieval building industry being itinerant with or without the king's impressment and direction of labour), some coming from Wales and some of the bricklayers, especially, coming from East Anglia, the centre of late-medieval brickwork. All or most were resident on the site, a chaplain being provided for their spiritual welfare. Amongst the company at Kirby Muxloe we may notice especially the master craftsmen, John Hornne and John Corbell, master bricklayers, and John Doyle, master carpenter, each of them paid 8d. a day in distinction to the 6d. of the ordinary craftsmen and the 4d. of the common labourers. The principal master mason, and thus in effect the architect, was John Couper, who had previously worked at Eton, Winchester and the church at Tattershall, in each case evidently under William Waynflete, bishop of Winchester and founder of Magdalen College, Oxford, responsible also for the mis-named and brick-built Foxe's Tower at Farnham. As befitted a man so eminent in his craft, John Couper was not permanently on the site but visited the work from time to time.

Then in the early summer of 1483, in the midst of all the bustle and activity of the third full season then beginning, and when the work was approaching completion tragedy struck, and is reflected even in the detached and matter-of-fact accounts. King Edward IV had died in April, and lord Hastings, his close supporter, was seized and executed by the new king, Richard III on 14 June. On the accounts the work comes almost to a stop, and though it was later resumed by the widowed lady Hastings it was not to be on the grand scale again, and the great building was never completed on the original plan. The total recorded cost from the accounts, which end in December 1484, amounts to just under £1,000, expended upon a noble dwelling which, like Thornbury in Gloucestershire or Hampton Court, was never to be enjoyed by the lord who first commissioned it.

If we turn, finally, to those many works devoted to the development and improvement of existing castles so typical of English medieval military architecture, none shows more vividly the scale they might assume than the building commissioned by Edward III at Windsor (**36**), his birthplace, between 1350 and 1377, to turn at vast expense what was already a major royal castle and favoured residence into the Versailles of the age (above, p. 103). The cost was prodigious – over £51,000 – the highest recorded for any single building operation in the whole history of the king's works in the Middle Ages.[16] To obtain the whole army of craftsmen and labourers required, the by now established royal right of impressment was utilized to the full, as also was the royal right of purveyance, the pre-emption of materials (a procedure which, unlike impressment, does frequently appear in 'constitutional' documents as a source of grievance right down to the seventeenth century). Letters patent dated 26 April 1350, for example, empower the king's beloved clerk, Richard Rotheley, surveyor of the king's works in the castle of Windsor, 'to take and provide masons, carpenters, and other workmen who may be needed for our works aforesaid, wherever they can be found ... the fee of the Church only excepted, and except the workmen already retained for our works at Westminster, our Tower of London and Dartford; also to take and provide stone, timber, and other necessaries for the works aforesaid, and carriage for the same timber and stone and other premises ...'. The continuator of Ranulf of

Higden's chronicle declared that 'almost all the masons and carpenters throughout the whole of England were brought to that building, so that hardly anyone could have any good mason or carpenter, except in secret, on account of the king's prohibition'.[17] In the great labour force at and about the castle for close on thirty years, the surviving accounts list freemasons and roughmasons, scapplers and quarriers, carpenters and surveyors, plumbers, plasterers and daubers, glaziers and paviers, coopers and tilers, carters and smiths. Amongst them all, all in receipt of the king's wages willy-nilly, we can distinguish some of the leading masters of the day. The master masons in charge of the work were John Sponle and William of Winford, the last-named thought also to have been responsible for the west towers of Wells, the existing gatehouse of Abingdon Abbey, and perhaps New College, Oxford. Amongst the carpenters were Master William of Hurley, known to have been associated with the stalls in the chapel at Windsor and whose other work included the wooden vault to the octagon at Ely; William of Wintringham, who was in charge of the construction of the roof of the great hall at Windsor, and Master William Herland, who had worked with Hurley on the lost splendours of St Stephen's Chapel, Westminster, and whose son, Hugh, perhaps the greatest of English medieval carpenters, was to create the magnificent timber roof which still spans Westminster Hall. Payments upon the accounts of 1352 to 'Master John Lincoln glazier engaged upon the ordering of the glazing of the windows of the king's chapel', and to 'Master John Athelard glazier working with the same upon the glazing of the said windows', remind us also of another category of medieval craftsmen whose skills are now largely lost. Amongst the constant entries on the accounts for the acquisition and transport of materials, the great quantities of timber are especially notable, used for the roof, stalls and other fittings of the chapel and the roof of the hall and chambers, the timber-framed buildings within the shell keep on the motte, and a hundred other purposes. Three thousand oaks 'from a certain wood at Cagham' are referred to on an account of 1354, and the felling of more than two thousand is entered on an account of 1361–2. In 1367 a reredos of carved alabaster for the chapel was brought ready-made from Nottingham in ten carts.

Not all works were so large-scale, elaborate and costly as Edward III's at Windsor, or Edward I's in Wales or at the Tower of London, Henry III's and Henry II's works at Dover, or Richard I's at Château-Gaillard. Yet the sight of Warwick or Kenilworth, Alnwick, Caerphilly or Kidwelly, emphasizes that the lay magnates lagged little if at all behind the king in castle-building, nor for that matter (Durham, Newark, Farnham) did some of the princes of the Church. The castles which still stand in whole or part throughout the kingdom represent the cumulative labours of close on five hundred years. The works with which we have been specifically concerned in this chapter were reproduced on a greater or lesser scale on countless occasions throughout those centuries, and the building and continuous improvement of the hundreds of castles in England and Wales after 1066 demanded not only creative thought and scientific planning but a highly competent and highly organized building industry as well. Even in terms of mere maintenance the task was formidable enough. To think upon these things broadens the cloistered view, seen through a stained-glass window darkly, of the Middle Ages as simply the 'Age of Faith', which an over-emphasis upon ecclesiastical architecture encourages, while the study of medieval building as a whole should drive from the mind of the most recalcitrant 'modernist' any lingering concept of the Middle Ages as the Dark Ages. These things simply were not achieved by simple men inferior in every way to us. Nothing perhaps can put us more directly in touch with our medieval past than its buildings, and certainly no age could desire a more imposing monument to its skill than this.

Chapter 7

The Castle in War

The military rôle of the castle is the most obvious, the most romantic, and basically the most important. Though the castle was always a residence no less than a fortress, and though from these two fundamental rôles others subsidiary followed, it was military necessity which first called the castle into being, whether at the time of its origin in ninth- or tenth-century France or whether in the England of the Norman Conquest, and military necessity which caused precisely that fusion of the lordly residence and the stronghold which is the peculiar characteristic of the castle. It is, after all, the degree of fortification which distinguishes a castle from a house. Warfare in the earlier centuries at least turned first and foremost upon the castle, and though from the later fourteenth century the military importance of the castle may have begun to decline, to read of wars in the chronicles of the eleventh, twelfth and thirteenth centuries is largely to read of sieges, while the surviving records of English royal government, for example, show beyond doubt that the maintenance of castles and their fortification and preparation for war were primary concerns of contemporary military organization. If we begin to ask why this was so, one fundamental answer – by no means widely understood since medieval warfare is a widely neglected subject – is that the military rôle of the castle was not just defensive but also offensive. Indeed we may argue that the latter is primary, for it was the offensive capacity of the castle, its function as a base, heavily defended, for active operations by means of which the surrounding countryside could be controlled, that gave it much of its value in war, made it the prized object of attack, and thus accounts for all those sieges. Only in this way, therefore, is the defensive role of the castle its most characteristic, though certainly it is the sieges which attracted the limelight of recorded events. Because the base and residence should be as impregnable as possible, it is defence also which, above all other considerations and requirements, dictated the castle's design and architectural form in the centuries of its supremacy in war, even though it had to fulfil as well its other functions as lordly and prestigious dwelling, centre of local government and administration, and, it might be, treasury, armoury or prison. If, therefore, we wish to see not only the castle in action but also to understand more fully its architecture and development, we had best begin with medieval siege-craft, whose machinations it was the first concern of castle-builders to counter and overcome.

Those early castles in England and Wales as elsewhere, whose defences were solely or mainly of earthwork and timber, and not least those with mottes, were already, in spite of their comparative simplicity, very effective strongholds, at once a sufficient answer to the heavy cavalry of mailed knights which then dominated warfare and a formidable obstacle also to those who attacked on foot. The account of the siege and capture of the motte-and-bailey castle of Le Puiset in France by king Louis VI, the Fat, in the year 1111, which is contained in that king's biography written by abbot Suger,[1] provides a vivid illustration of such a castle in action, while the need to attack and take it is sufficiently indicated by the statement that when it was in hostile hands one dared not approach within eight or ten miles of it. On this occasion, the garrison of the castle began the action by taking the offensive and attempting to drive off the king's forces by a sortie. Only when this failed did they withdraw behind the defences of their palisaded ramparts, from which they showered down missiles upon their opponents. The king's men concentrated their attention first upon the castle gate and sought to burn it down. They failed, but the attempt is significant both in being directed against the gate, always a potential weak point inviting attack, and in the use of fire. In the thirteenth-century romance of Fulk fitz Warin, as one example, we are told of a fierce assault upon a castle whose gates 'were burnt and destroyed by fire fed with bacon and grease'.[2] Fire was especially dangerous to timber defences, and we may note, as another example, that in the illustration on the Bayeux Tapestry of an attack upon the castle of Dinan, two Norman warriors are attempting to set fire to the palisade upon the motte (5). To revert, however, to the affairs of Louis the Fat at Le Puiset, the next phase of the attack took the form of a diversion by a section of the royal forces under Theobald, count of Chartres, who rode round to the other side of the castle and attempted by surprise to storm the defences there. This also failed, partly because of the difficulty of assaulting up the steep sides of the earthen banks, and finally because the garrison delivered a devastating mounted sortie against them, cutting them up and tumbling them into the ditch, before riding triumphantly back into the castle. At length the main body of the besiegers, inspired we are told by the example of a priest, made a determined assault across the ditch and up the ramparts, hacked and wrenched their way through the palisade, and carried the bailey. Hugh, lord of Le Puiset, and those of the garrison who survived, then withdrew to the separate and ultimate stronghold of the motte;[3] but, disheartened no doubt by the loss of the bailey and many of their comrades, they failed either long to defend it or to escape to the open country at their back, and soon after capitulated to the king.

Though it has no direct connection with the affair at Le Puiset, we may legitimately add an authentic colour to the account just given by quoting at this stage a well-known passage probably from the later twelfth-century poet, Bertran de Born, which is notable above all in portraying the love of war by the new warrior ruling class of knights who dominated society at this time, especially in France, as also in England after the Norman Conquest.[4]

'I love the gay Eastertide, which brings forth leaves and flowers; and I love the joyous songs of the birds, re-echoing through the copse. But also I love to see, amidst the meadows, tents and pavilions spread; and it gives me great joy to see, drawn up on the field, knights and horses in battle array; and it delights me when the scouts scatter people and herds in their path; and I love to see them followed by a great body of men-at-arms; and my heart is filled with gladness when I see strong castles besieged, and the stockades broken and overwhelmed, and the warriors on the bank, girt about by fosses, with a line of strong stakes interlaced . . . . Maces, swords, helms of different hues, shields that will be riven and shattered as soon as the fight begins; and many vassals struck down together; and the horses of the dead and wounded roving at random. And when battle is joined, let all men of good lineage think of nought but the breaking of heads and arms; for it is better to die than to be vanquished and live. I tell you, I find no such savour in food, or in wine, or in sleep, as in hearing the shout "On! On!" from both sides, and the neighing of steeds that have lost their riders, and the cries of "Help! Help!"; in seeing men great and small go down on the grass beyond the fosses; in seeing at last the dead, with the pennoned stumps of lances still in their sides.'

Neither in abbot Suger's account of the attack on Le Puiset in 1111, nor, for that matter, in the passage from Bertran de Born, is there any reference to the more advanced techniques of siege-craft, though many were already known and practised when they wrote, and certainly there is no doubt of the adequate strength of ditches and stockades, earthen ramparts and, especially, the motte, against assaults mounted without them. Above all, as has been pointed out, you could not take a castle by a cavalry charge. Yet also it is clear that stone defences were stronger than timber, and it is certain that to a great degree the increase and evolution of stone-built castles was the result, as well as the cause, of advancing methods of attack. These methods were generally not new in the historical sense but, rather, the techniques of the classical past now increasingly applied or reintroduced in the West. Taken together, they involved almost all that the wit of man could devise against prepared positions before the development of explosives, and they made up an art and science of siege-craft which remained largely unchanged from at least the twelfth century until almost the end of the Middle Ages, for the introduction of gunpowder into warfare in the fourteenth century had very little immediate effect (below). Yet the castle, which largely developed in response to medieval siege-craft, rapidly achieved and maintained a supremacy of defence over attack, within the inescapable limits of human endurance and the adequate provision of supplies, which goes far to explain the conduct of medieval warfare, too often abused by uncomprehending modern writers.

In the Middle Ages as in any other period, the methods of attack against a fortified position may be broadly divided under the two heads of bombardment and close assault, though in practice they too are usually complementary to each other. The artillery of the medieval centuries used for bombardment were the great stone-throwing 'engines', of which we hear a great deal both in chronicles and records. The main use was to batter a breach in the defences through which an assault could be made, and, in modern parlance, to soften up the target. Their study is somewhat complicated by the fact that none is known to have survived, and even more by the vague and imprecise terminology which contemporaries used to describe them. Briefly, we may limit them to three main types, each with its own method of propulsion, though it is possible that in practice composite machines were made employing more than one. First, then, was the *mangon* or *mangonel*, which worked on the principle of torsion. A long arm, with a cup or sling for the projectile at its free end, passed through a skein of ropes stretched between upright posts. The ropes were twisted towards the target by windlasses, the arm pulled down against the torsion, and a large, shaped rock or some other projectile placed in the cup or sling. When released, the free end of the arm was hauled up and over by the torsion of the ropes acting on its lower end, and the projectile was hurled towards the target. A more powerful type of stone-throwing engine was the *trebuchet* (**XXVII–IX**), brought into common use, it seems, in the later twelfth century. This was evidently not an inheritance from classical times, but a new invention, and worked on the principle of the counter-weight. Here again the shaped rock or other projectile was discharged from the free and longer end of a revolving arm pivoting between two uprights, but the motive power was provided by the great counterweight at the other and shorter end. In addition to its greater power, the trebuchet was more consistently efficient, being less affected by the weather and its range capable of regulation by moving the counter-weight along the arm or adjusting its mass.

Though most commonly used for hurling great stone balls, both mangonel and trebuchet could cast, of course, any projectile that came to hand. These might even include the dreaded 'Greek fire', a combustible mixture which brought to the Middle Ages something of the horrors of modern scientific warfare and which, though often said to have remained a closely guarded secret of the Eastern, Greek Empire of Byzantium, is in fact known to have been used by Richard I at the siege of Nottingham in 1194, i.e. on his return from the Third Crusade (where it was also used), on the unimpeachable authority of the Pipe Rolls, and by Edward I at the siege of Stirling in 1297.[5] A fourteenth-century illustration of a trebuchet loaded with a dead horse, on the other hand, may suggest the medieval employment of something very like germ warfare. Principally, however, both machines were stone-throwing engines for battering down defences, and hence the Latin name *petraria* commonly and unhelpfully applied indifferently to each. By contrast, the third type of engine, the *ballista* or, to use a later name for the same device, the *springald*, though occasionally adapted to shoot stones, was most suited to the discharge of iron shafts or javelins. This worked on the principle of tension, i.e. the principle of the bow, and was, indeed, like an enormous crossbow – though to say that is to put the case backwards since the hand-crossbow, of which more will be said later, was in

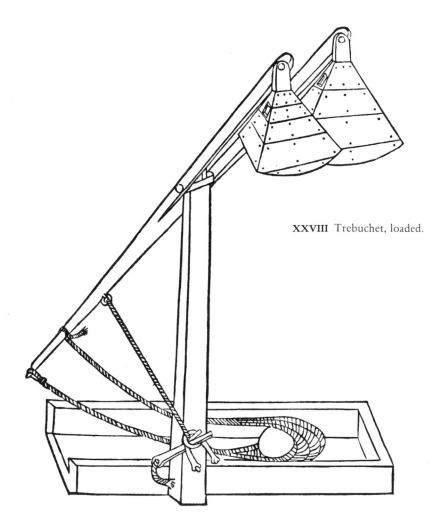

XXVIII Trebuchet, loaded.

fact a development from the *ballista*. Shooting thus formidable iron bolts specially manufactured, the *ballista* was generally used not for bombardment but for picking off adversaries who showed themselves at battlements or apertures, and with its flatter trajectory it could be aimed more accurately than either trebuchet or mangonel.

The lineal descendant of those bombarding siege-engines, performing the same function by a different and in the long run revolutionary method of propulsion, was the cannon, which, though not making its appearance until the later Middle Ages, is most conveniently dealt with at this stage. Gunpowder – the 'villainous salt petre' of Hotspur's mincing courtier – is generally said to have been introduced into English warfare in the first half of the fourteenth century, and more particularly by Edward III (1327–77) against the Scots in the first year of his reign, but may in fact have had its first recorded use by Edward I, also

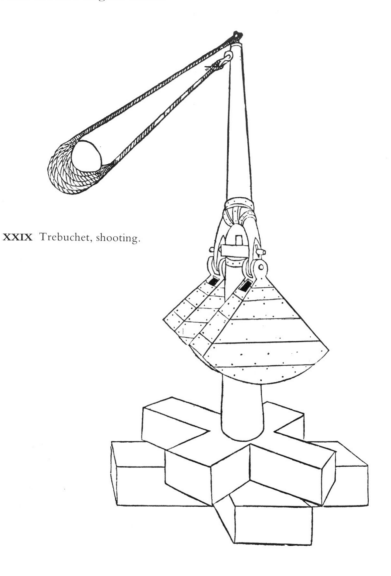

XXIX Trebuchet, shooting.

against the Scots, at the siege of Stirling in 1297.[6] Our particular concern is the use of ordnance in siege warfare, and here, as indeed with the use of cannon and hand-guns in the field, the essential thing about gunpowder in the Middle Ages is by no means to exaggerate its importance. A most interesting illustration in a manuscript of *c*.1326 belonging to Christ Church, Oxford (**40**), is the earliest known illustration of an English cannon. It shows a small device shaped like a bulbous bottle, loaded with an iron bolt like a large dart, mounted on a four-legged stand. A soldier, standing at a respectful distance as well he might, is in the act of firing it with a hot iron bar. Clearly this device at least is no threat to the strength and supremacy of the castle. In fact, early cannon were greatly inferior in every respect to the tried and powerful siege-engines (the word 'gun', 'gunne', 'gonne', is probably derived from an abbreviation of mangonel). They were slow; they were small; and in the fourteenth century at least they discharged principally only bolts or garrots (as in the Christ Church manuscript), for large pieces able to shoot stone balls were not yet cast and the iron cannon-ball lay even further in the future. For long after the introduction of guns, also, the ballistic force of the powder used was low – probably deliberately so, for fear of bursting the barrel. In all, early cannon were probably as dangerous to their users as to the foe (as late as 1460, James II of Scotland was killed by a bursting gun at the siege of Roxburgh),[7] and their chief value in the field seems to have been their effect upon the morale of the enemy (and upon his horses) rather than any damage they inflicted upon his person. In sieges they must have been for long even more ineffectual, and their use necessitated no response in military architecture and the design of castles in the fourteenth and fifteenth centuries save for the insertion of gunports for the guns of the castle's own defence. This suggests, indeed, that if they had any immediate effect upon the castle at all it was to add to, not detract from, its military supremacy.

In the fifteenth century, it is true, the development of guns and large ordnance was rapid, and the great Mons Meg, still at Edinburgh castle, dates from about 1450 (still effective as late as 1650, when she was referred to as 'the great iron murderer Muckle Meg'. She blew up, however, in 1680 and was restored to her present condition in 1829).[8] Such pieces as this, when available, were undoubtedly highly effective as bombards in siege warfare. With two such great guns, named 'Newcastle' and 'London', Warwick 'the King Maker', after the battle of Hexham in 1464, took Bamburgh castle which had hitherto been reckoned impregnable. Nevertheless it is to be remembered and emphasized that ordnance, in this country not least, were slow in development and adoption, remained vastly expensive, were by no means readily available where and when they were wanted (in 1497 Mons Meg was played out of Edinburgh castle by minstrels to take part in 'the great raid of Norham' by the Scots, but at once broke down in the suburbs of the city in spite of a hundred workmen and five carpenters in attendance),[9] and are not to be regarded as the immediate and easy explanation for the decline of the castle in the later Middle Ages. It is of considerable interest in this respect that the late fifteenth-century edition of the *De Re Militari* by Robert Valturius still gives detailed drawings and descriptions of the trebuchet as well as of cannon and bombards. Only perhaps in the mid-sixteenth century, when our interest ends, were guns both generally effective and extensively employed, and only then did they dictate fundamental changes in the design and construction of fortresses, which, however, had by then ceased to be castles for quite other reasons. And even so, a century later, in the seventeenth-century Civil War of King and Parliament, many English castles (and some houses as well) held out long and heroically against the pounding of Cromwellian guns.

In medieval siege-warfare, in addition to the long-range artillery of stone-throwing engines and cannon, there were other devices and techniques for breaching the defences at close quarters. The crudest but not the least effective was the battering-ram, usually the biggest tree-trunk that could be found, capped with iron, swung on ropes from strong supports, and crashed again and again against masonry or (especially) gates until successful. Counter-devices sometimes employed by the defenders were the lowering of some form of buffer between the ram and its point of impact, or the skilful dropping of a heavy forked appliance to catch and hold its head. A rather more subtle device than the ram, though probably slower in its effect, was the bore, which was a smaller instrument with an iron point, used especially on sharp angles to work away the stones of the masonry piecemeal. The same end could be gained, albeit with more labour and more dangerous exposure, by the use of picks and crowbars, and we are told that at the siege of Acre during the Third Crusade Richard I offered cash rewards to those of his soldiers who succeeded in wresting a stone from the walls of the doomed city.[10]

The most efficient method, however, of destroying a section of wall or tower to make a breach (though of less use against timber buildings and none against earthworks) was undermining, and the mine was, with good reason, the most dreaded device of siege-craft. Contrary to a popular belief, the technique did not have to await the advent of gunpowder before it was evolved, nor was it a new technique in the thirteenth century, and its first recorded use in England seems to be by William the Conqueror against the walls of Exeter in 1068.[11] The miners, usually well-paid professionals, dug and tunnelled their way beneath the foundations of their target area and shored them up with stout timber props. The excavated mine chamber was then filled with brushwood and other combustible material, and, when all was ready, fire was applied and the miners withdrew. The props having been burnt, the masonry above collapsed into the cavity, and the waiting assailants poured through the breach thus made. Only the castle built upon the living rock (e.g. Goodrich, Harlech, Conway), or one surrounded by the broadest water defences (e.g. Caerphilly, Kenilworth, Leeds, Bodiam), was proof against this deadly and most nerve-racking form of attack. Against it there was no remedy save the hazardous process of the counter-mine – an attempt by the besieged to tunnel down into the mine and capture and destroy it – which even if successfully directed could only result in a desperate, claustrophobic, hand-to-hand encounter in the dark. It is probable, indeed, that the effects of mining could be as devastating upon the morale of the castle's defenders as upon its structure, and we are told that at the siege of the great crusader castle of Margat in Outremer in 1285, the Hospitaller garrison, on being shown the extent of the Sultan's mine beneath their majestic keep, yielded up the castle which could no longer be defended to any purpose. In this country, there are few more dramatic examples of the use of the mine than at the siege of Rochester castle by king John in the autumn and winter of 1215 (below). Having breached and taken the bailey, the king found himself faced by the massive rectangular keep, into which the defenders had withdrawn and which was impervious to the battering of his siege engines. Accordingly he put his miners to work, and in due course they brought down one whole corner and section of the great tower which is still one of the most impressive in the kingdom (p. 46 above). A royal writ enrolled upon the Close Roll of the king's Chancery, addressed to Hubert de Burgh and dated at Rochester on 25 November 1215, refers directly, after seven hundred years and more, to the technical details of the matter.[12] 'We command you', it runs, 'that with all speed, by day and night, you send to us forty bacon pigs of the fattest and least good for eating, to bring fire beneath the tower' – i.e. to fire the mine. In fact, today the monument to those forty pigs yet stands as the one rounded corner and cylindrical angle turret of the keep at Rochester, built in the post-war reparations of the next reign in the latest fashion and thus in marked contrast to the rectangular plan of the rest of this early twelfth-century great tower (**14, VII**).

Breaching the defences of the castle, by whatever means, was always a long, skilled and laborious process, and to the end assault by escalade, i.e. by the simple but hazardous use of scaling ladders, remained a common method of forcible entry. An elaboration of this form of assault was the use of a great movable tower or belfry. Pushed up against the castle walls (though the ditch must first be filled in for the purpose), it enabled an attack to be launched upon their summit with a much greater concentration of force than the one-at-a-time effect of the ladder. The belfry also had other valuable uses, for in addition to being an elevated platform for launching attacks, it could serve as a look-out post and a firing platform, commanding even the interior of the beleaguered castle. Thus at the siege of Bedford in 1224, Henry III commanded such a wooden tower to be constructed and manned by archers and crossbowmen, and so effective was it that, according to the chronicler Roger of Wendover, no defender could remove his armour for fear of being mortally wounded.[13]

It has already been noted that broad (and well protected) water defences were almost the only artificial defence against the mine, and even the more normal ditch or moat was amongst the most vital defences of the castle, for a section at least had to be filled in with much labour and dangerous exposure, or adequately bridged, before ram, bore or belfry could be brought up to the walls, or indeed, before almost any form of assault could be launched – or boats had to be used, as they sometimes were. Even so, the ram and the bore and the men working them had to be protected from the defenders above them, and this was commonly supplied by large, movable penthouses, under cover of which they could move up to the walls or towers and operate upon them. The penthouse, too, was used as cover for the entrance to the mine if this was close to the castle. These penthouses themselves, and also the belfries and the *petrarie*, were often covered with raw hides, or sometimes metal plates, since otherwise, being made of timber, they were inflammable. Fire, indeed, played a large part in medieval sieges: the meurtrières or murder-holes found frequently in gate passages are there chiefly to quench fires at the gate, and the age-old phrase 'with fire and sword' echoes an age-old practice. Finally, it is worth noting that many of the engines and devices of medieval siege-craft were commonly given fanciful names, sometimes derived from classical antiquity and which, loosely used by contemporary chroniclers not always well versed in military matters, give to the subject a romantic sounding confusion. Thus the movable penthouse sheltering ram or bore may be called 'tortoise' or 'cat' from its slow or stealthy approach. The same word 'cat' seems also to be used of a belfry at Acre by one of the chroniclers of the Third Crusade, while a belfry filled with archers and crossbowmen at Kenilworth in 1266 was known as a 'bear'. The bore, picking holes in the masonry, is often called a 'mouse', and a common nickname for a prized stone-throwing engine is *Malvoisin* or 'Bad Neighbour', as prince Louis named the great *petraria* which he had sent from France for the siege of Dover in 1216.

The principle defence of the castle against the formidable resources of medieval siege-craft was, of course, the strength and ingenuity of its own fortifications, expressly designed and developed to resist and overcome them. The direct answer to the pounding of the *petrarie* was the breadth of masonry which is such a feature of medieval military architecture, and the massive strength in this respect of the tower keep in particular was almost impervious to them, as king John found at Rochester in 1215. The plinth upon which the great tower usually stands and the similar plinths, batters and spurs at the base of other towers and sometimes walls are sufficiently explained by the threat of the battering ram and the bore, though they may also have served to make stones and other missiles dropped from above bound, ricochet and perhaps splinter amongst the assailants. The advantages held to attach to polygonal or round towers as opposed to rectangular are similarly that they have no sharp angles for the bore and that their shape deflects and thus reduces the impact of projectiles. The fact that the besiegers so often concentrated their resources on the gate points to the necessity of that continuous elaboration of the gatehouse which is a particular feature of English castle-building, as it points also to the purpose of such details as the turning-bridge or draw-bridge, portcullis, *meurtrières*, and machicolation. The importance of the moat or ditch, wet or dry but preferably the former and as broad and deep as possible, is self-evident, and so are the advantages of building one's castle upon the rock. More than half the art of castle defence in an age of comparatively short-range weapons lay, indeed, in preventing the enemy from coming to close quarters, and the importance of many and well-placed loops and arrowslits, battlements and crenellation to give cover to those in action on the tops of walls and towers (**XXX**), barbicans in front of gateways, or the refinement of timber hoarding or stone machicolation (**XXXI–II**) which enabled the foot of wall and tower and gatehouse to be defended without exposure, again scarcely requires emphasis. Perhaps more than anything else, however, some consideration of siege-craft and the methods of attack upon the castle lays further stress upon the crucial importance of the flanking tower – thrust forward towards the field to cover the base of the wall between it and its neighbours to either side against all the machinations of ram and bore, over-topping the wall to guard against escalade and belfry, and

XXX Crenellation. (From Viollet-le-Duc, *Dictionnaire Raisonné de l'Architecture*.)

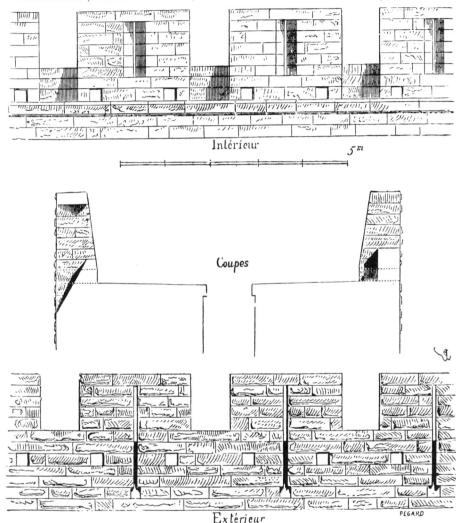

Intérieur   5ᵐ

Coupes

Extérieur   PEGARD

dividing up the wall into defensible sections should the enemy gain a footing or a breach be made.

The task of manning the castle's defences fell of course upon the garrison. In the early days of the Norman settlement some of the castles then planted in such large numbers were provided at least with the knights they needed by feudal means, that is to say the vassals and knight-tenants of the lord of the castle were required to do castle-guard service in return for the fiefs which they held of him, and it is known from later evidence that certain of the greater castles of that period had elaborate arrangements of this kind (e.g. Dover, Windsor,

Richmond). The provision of knights in this way, however, had its disadvantages, and in any case it is clear that many and probably most castles even of the first generation of the Norman Conquest were not so provided. It is also clear from the comparatively abundant record evidence of the later twelfth century, both that by then such feudal and knightly castle-guard services as there were were generally commuted for a money rent in lieu, and also that (though admittedly almost all the available evidence relates to castles in the king's hand) the normal method of providing castle garrisons was to hire all grades of personnel as and when required. Certain other general features of the manning of castles also then become apparent, and can almost certainly be assumed for later periods upon which little work has as yet been done. One is that the payment of garrisons was an expensive business and only undertaken in time of trouble – from which it usefully follows that the historians can use the evidence of garrisoning, as of other preparations to put the castle upon a war footing, as a kind of political barometer. It also follows that it is a mistake to imagine the castles always filled with men-at-arms, and it appears that in fact in time of peace, and in the frequent and prolonged absence of the castle's lord with his multitudinous household, only a skeleton staff, so to speak, of constable (perhaps with his lesser household if he was himself a man of consequence), porter, watchmen and chaplain might be in permanent residence.

It is also evident that even in time of war, the numbers of the garrison were frequently quite small, and thus one can begin to appreciate that the military value of the castle was out of all proportion to the number of men involved, while the high proportion of mounted men, knights and others, within that number points to the reality of that value, i.e. that the castle was a base for active operations whereby the surrounding countryside could be controlled. Lastly, it is a point very much worth making in this chapter that to speak thus of 'the garrison' as though it were something exceptional and outside the normal pattern of social life, and even to make too much distinction between peace and war, can be misleading and produce anachronistic assumptions. If one thinks about these things, there is no more striking negative fact than that we do not find any separate and distinct provision for a 'garrison' in the design and plan of castles[14] which, as we have seen in previous chapters devoted to their architectural history, are from first to last the fortified residences of lords. The domestic unit they were designed to accommodate is the household (cf. below, p. 151), and the several households of the lord himself, his lady, it may be, his guests of equal status, and of his constable and other senior officials if they themselves are men of rank. Such households will at all times contain a military element, and that element will be expanded in time of war. We should probably get nearer to the truth if we thought of castle garrisons, like other military forces of the day, as consisting of members of the expanded military household of the lord in whose name they served and fought. Further, these lords themselves were warriors (sometimes, too, their ladies) who knew how to fight. We are dealing with castles which are the symbols and the substance of their power. If warfare in the Middle Ages was not exclusively the sport of kings and magnates, they assuredly were born and bred to be its dominant participants. The castle is the setting for this military aristocracy, and in such a world there was no need of barrack-room accommodation for a separate class of soldiers. Certainly none was provided, and we must assume that the lesser men and lower ranks must have slept and eaten as and when they could, and doubtless still in close attendance on their masters.

The actual numbers of the garrison in time of war and in action will obviously vary with varying circumstances, not least the size of the castle concerned. Contemporary chronicles are more or less in agreement that the garrison of Rochester which put up such a determined resistance to king John in 1215 contained some hundred knights and men-at-arms apart from lesser men.[15] The garrison at Dover under Hubert de Burgh a year later, when the castle was held for the same king against the French prince Louis, is said by Roger of Wendover to have included a hundred and forty knights plus many men-at-arms.[16] On the other hand and by contrast, the heroic defence of Odiham for two weeks in the same wars is said to have been conducted by only three knights and ten men-at-arms.[17] The Pipe Roll of 1174 refers only to twenty knights at Orford and ten knights and forty men-at-arms at Wark in that year of rebellion against king Henry II by his son.[18] In the disturbances of 1193, when count John was in rebellion against Richard I, his brother, then a prisoner in Germany, the Pipe Roll gives a total of seventy-five at both Norwich and Canterbury castles, in each case made up of knights and men-at-arms both horsed and foot.[19] After the fall of Framlingham castle to king John in the spring of 1216, his Chancery rolls list fifty-seven members of the defeated garrison, including twenty-six knights, twenty men-at-arms, seven crossbowmen and a chaplain.[20] Figures derived from chroniclers may be inaccurate and those given by records may for divers reasons be incomplete, but nevertheless such instances confirm the points already made of the comparatively small size of castle garrisons and the comparatively small investment of men that the castle required to hold it.

The commanding officer of the castle was usually the constable in whose custody it was placed. On the whole it is uncommon to find the lord of a castle besieged in it, presumably because his political and military value was too great thus to be enclosed, while also his ransom might be crippling in the event of capture. After the constable himself, the leading members of the garrison would be the knights, whose social pre-eminence must have made of them a kind of officer corps, while their proficiency as mounted warriors *par excellence* made them also the leading members of the castle's strike force, which they formed with the mounted sergeants and mounted men-at-arms. After the men-at-arms both horsed and foot came the archers and crossbowmen, and such semi-combatants and individuals as smiths and farriers, carpenters and 'engineers', the cook, the chaplain, the porters and the watchmen. Amongst the names of those upon the Pipe Roll of 1176 fined for the surrender of Appleby to the Scots in the recent war, and whose names may indicate their occupation, are William the

XXXII Machicolation. (From Viollet-le-Duc, *Dictionnaire Raisonné de l'Architecture*.)

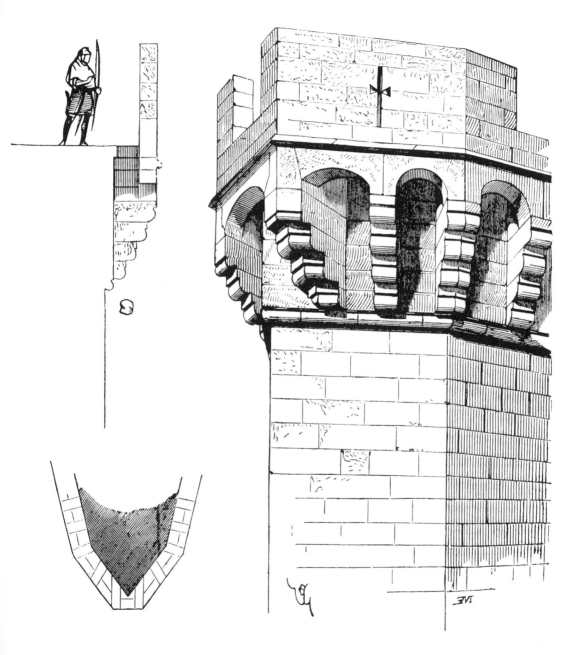

clerk (i.e. in Orders), Rankil the miller and Bernard the cook.[21] Probably the most valuable members of the castle's garrison for its defence were the crossbowmen. Condemned by the Second Lateran Council of the Church in 1139 as a weapon hateful to God, but in use long before and in England probably present for the first time at Hastings, on the Norman side, in 1066, much employed by the Angevin kings Richard I and John (though its prominence then may only reflect the increase in the number of records referring to it), it is likely that the crossbow never lost, even to the famed English longbow, its fitness as the paramount weapon for castle defence. The penetrative power and range of its iron bolts were formidable, and though its rate of shooting was slower than that of the bow and longbow it needed less space and less exposure for its discharge – and certainly neither weapon was ever seriously rivalled by the hand gun in the medieval period.

In addition to their personal arms of bow and crossbow, sword, spear and axe, and the miscellaneous missiles dropped upon assailants too close to the walls, the defenders of the castle also made use of the artillery of mangonel, trebuchet and *ballista*. Their targets were chiefly the siege-engines and devices of their assailants and their object to destroy them before damage could be done by them. Thus the Turks in the beleaguered city of Acre in 1191 succeeded in burning and destroying the engines of the French king Philip II, which, we are told, so angered him that he fell sick.[22] At Kenilworth in 1266 the garrison broke with their engines two great belfries which the king, Henry III, and his son, the lord Edward, had caused to be erected, and they answered each *petraria* of the royal forces with one of their own so that, according to one account of the siege, the hurtling stones frequently met and shattered in mid-air. Edward I's Harlech has platforms cut in the rock it stands on for its engines (p. 72 above). From the later twelfth century, it is thought, flat roofs covered with lead appear in castles on keeps and towers to serve as platforms for *petrarie*, though there was always a risk that their vibration would damage the masonry. Cannon in the later Middle Ages were an even greater danger in this respect, and had also the disadvantage that they could not be dipped to fire downwards at the enemy. Nevertheless, gunports make their appearance in English military architecture from the fourteenth century, as we have seen (above p. 129), guns being used as much for the defence of castles as for attack upon them. On the whole, however, the introduction of gunpowder and cannon has left little mark upon the castle in this country: the bastion gun-emplacements on the north side of the Tower of London's outer wall, for example, are Tudor additions to the castle, and it is not until about the middle of the sixteenth century, when our period and our subject ends, that Henry VIII's coastal forts appear especially designed for defence by and against heavy cannon.

The defenders of the castle, however, did not only rely upon missiles and artillery to carry the war into the enemy's camp. It is noteworthy that at the siege of Le Puiset in 1111 already referred to (above p. 124) the garrison made a highly successful mounted sortie against the men of count Theobald of Chartres. We have also noted in an earlier chapter, for example, the elaborate system of posterns and underground works which enabled sorties to be made from the redesigned Dover castle of the earlier thirteenth century, or the multiplication of even the main gate in some of the great new castles of the late thirteenth and early fourteenth centuries (Caerphilly, Beaumaris). Such developments made easier the tactic of active and aggressive defence. Nor were such sorties only the gallant last flings of desperate garrisons. At the siege of Kenilworth the defenders made repeatedly successful attacks upon the enemy's lines which caused much damage and loss of life among them. The medieval garrison, as we have seen, contained a substantial proportion of knights and men-at-arms capable of fighting on horseback as well as on foot, and this was one – though by no means the only – reason for their presence, while one may guess, also, that in a society and a warfare dominated by knighthood and the cult of chivalry the doctrine that attack can be the best form of defence would have a wider than usual currency.

Finally, in this analysis of the defence of castles we must not omit perhaps the most vital matter of all, the adequate supply of provisions. Without that the strongest castle, though fully manned, must fall. Conversely, an attacking force, if its resources were sufficient for a close, complete and prolonged investment, could always hope in the last resort to starve a garrison into yielding – as prince Louis swore, but failed, to do at Dover in 1216. The chroniclers tell us that when, in the autumn of 1215, the rebel barons decided to seize and hold Rochester against king John, those who undertook the defence (under William de Albini of Belvoir) were worried by their inability to stock the castle adequately, and some two months later, in the last desperate days, imminent starvation contributed in fact to their capitulation. They were reduced, the Barnwell annalist tells us, to a diet of horse-flesh and water, which, he adds 'bore hard on those brought up in luxury'.[23] In many another hard-pressed siege failure of supplies is listed high by contemporary writers among the causes of eventual surrender, as at Château-Gaillard in 1204 or Kenilworth in 1266. Surviving structural evidence shows vividly enough the care taken to ensure sufficient and safe supplies of water, often by wells which are themselves marvels of medieval engineering skill. Surviving records show no less the extensive buying up of supplies to stock the king's castles before the outbreak of hostilities. Corn is brought in in large quantities and hand-mills or horse-mills are supplied to grind it, while some greater castles have their own mechanical mills like the tower windmill built by Edward I at Dover or the tide-mills across the moat at the same king's Tower of London. Meat commonly takes the form of pork or bacon and much salt is brought to preserve it. Sometimes, however, the meat might be fresh, for eighty live cows (£16) and one hundred and thirty live sheep (£6 10s.) were brought into the castle at Lancaster in 1215,[24] perhaps to be slaughtered as required, and the garrison at Bedford were keeping livestock in the outer bailey of that castle when it fell in 1224. Cheese and also beans were evidently amongst the garrison's staple diet, and oats, at least partly for the horses, were supplied in large measure. Malt and barley, sometimes mentioned, may have been for beer, but the perusal of medieval military accounts leaves a lasting impression of huge quantities of wine. Arms are sometimes bought up together with provisions, but not as a rule on a large scale, presumably because they were more often the personal equipment of the garrison and/or were permanently kept in the castle. Miscellaneous stores appearing on the records and accounts include charcoal, firewood, iron, lead and tallow, and, above all, ropes, cords and cables needed especially for the engines of war.

To see the castle in action against the full concentrated resources of siege-craft, we can scarcely do better than turn to the extant accounts by well-informed contemporary chroniclers of the more important sieges and campaigns in the English kingdom of the twelfth and thirteenth centuries when the military importance of the castle was at its height. Upon some of those accounts we have, in fact, already drawn to supply examples for the analysis of besieging and defence attempted above. The siege of Rochester,[25] for example, in the autumn and early winter of 1215, conducted by king John, was the most important single event in the civil war which ended his reign and also produced Magna Carta as a kind of unsuccessful peace treaty. It is especially notable as a striking example of the technique of the mine, and also for the remarkable and possibly unique use which the gallant defenders made of the cross-wall by which the keep at Rochester, like most of the larger rectangular tower keeps, was strengthened and divided (p. 50 above). When the king's miners brought down one corner and more of the great tower (**VII**) and his forces poured into the breach, the garrison continued their resistance in the other half. 'For such was the construction of the tower', writes the knowledgeable Barnwell chronicler, 'that a strong wall separated the half that had fallen from the other'.[26] In all, the operation lasted for almost two months, from Sunday 11 October to the final surrender on 30 November, with the king present throughout, and was probably the greatest siege of a castle in England up to that date. The fall of Rochester had a severe effect upon the morale of the rebel party, and afterwards, wrote the same chronicler, 'few cared to put their trust in castles'.[27] At the siege of Dover in 1216,[28] held for John by Hubert de Burgh against prince Louis of France, the ally of the rebel barons, mining was again the principal method of making a breach and the most noteworthy feature of the engagement. The mine was sprung beneath the gatehouse recently constructed at the northern apex of the great castle, and brought down the eastern of its twin towers. In the event Dover did not fall, Hubert de Burgh and his men blocking the breach with timber and defending it with their strong right arms, but after the war the incident was the motive for the remodelling of the castle's outer defences and the alternative construction of the present Constable's Gate (**1** and above p. 83).

The siege of Bedford castle in 1224 we may describe in greater detail, for, while it provides a near-perfect example of a full-scale investment of a castle carried through to its completion, a wealth of contemporary written descriptions, supplemented by the evidence of official records, survive to provide ample and detailed information about it.[29] The unfortunate story of its lord, Fawkes de Bréauté, is one not unfamiliar in almost any age or place. A tried soldier, he had risen to great place chiefly by loyal and efficient service to king John in the civil wars that ended the reign (and witnessed the sieges of both Rochester and Dover). In the ensuing peace his power and high-handed habits accorded ill with the settled government which the new young king, Henry III, and his ministers sought to establish. Amongst the many rewards formerly showered upon Fawkes by his late royal master had been Bedford castle, previously confiscated from William de Beauchamp for his part in the rebellion against John. The tension created by Fawkes' persistent refusal to surrender Bedford at the order of the new government to its former Beauchamp lord was finally snapped when his castellans there seized and imprisoned in the castle a royal judge, Henry de Braybroke, proceeding on his very lawful occasions through the district – occasions which included the hearing of suits brought against Fawkes de Bréauté himself. The act was outrageous. The young king, personally affronted by this insult to the hard-won dignity of his Crown, marched upon Bedford and concentrated about the castle almost the entire military array of his kingdom, reinforced by the Church Militant in the persons of the archbishop of Canterbury and many of his clergy. The garrison, commanded by William de Bréauté, brother of the absent Fawkes, were excommunicated, and the secular arm of the state began the military operation by the raising of siege-engines. The chronicler of the nearby priory of Dunstable describes their number, type and disposition.[30] One *petraria* (probably a trebuchet) and two mangonels were set up on the east, two mangonels on the west which plied against the keep, and one mangonel on each of the north and south sides of the castle. In addition, two strong and lofty belfries were raised to overlook the beleaguered fortress and filled with crossbowmen and look-outs (*exploratores*). By day and night the besieged had no rest from the showers of bolts and the thunderous pounding of the great stones against their walls and towers. For their part, the defenders had no thought of surrender but, on the assumption that their lord Fawkes would relieve them, maintained a determined defence and inflicted considerable losses upon the royal forces. Ralph of Coggeshall tells us that a certain lord, Richard de Argentan, was severely wounded in the stomach by a crossbow bolt which pierced his armour, that six other knights of the king's army were killed, and over two hundred of the men-at-arms and the labourers manning the engines.[31] With the arduous necessity of a prolonged siege and the mounting losses, bitterness grew, and the king swore that the garrison should hang if the castle were taken by storm.

Although, as the direct result of these events, almost nothing of the castle now stands above the ground save for the truncated remains of its original motte,[32] we can still follow the various phases of the siege, conducted like a text-book operation. Bedford was taken, the Dunstable annalist tells us, in four main assaults.[33] First the assailants took the barbican or outwork, losing four or five men in the action. Next, with heavier losses, they stormed and took the outer bailey, and captured with it a great part of the defenders' equipment and provisions – horses and harness, hauberks and other armour, crossbows, livestock and corn. Then they were faced with the inner and ultimate defences, evidently the inner bailey, a section of whose stone revetted ditch has recently been discovered in the south-east section of the castle adjacent to the motte, and the tower keep upon the motte itself. For these the miners were brought in. First they breached 'the wall next the old tower', presumed to be the inner bailey wall near the tower keep. The subsequent capture of the inner bailey was achieved only with great difficulty and further losses, while ten of the assailants who attempted to press home too ardently their victory were captured by the defenders and carried off into the ultimate refuge of the keep. In the final act of the drama the miners again played the crucial role. On the vigil of the Assumption (14 August), towards Vespers, writes the chronicler, the mine beneath the keep was fired: smoke poured into the inner rooms where the defenders were gathered, the tower sank upon its foundations, great cracks appearing down its sides. Further resistance was impossible. The ladies, including Margaret, Fawkes' wife, and the prisoners, including Henry de Braybroke, the judge, were sent out, and the garrison ran up the royal standard in token of submission. The next morning, some eight weeks after the siege had begun, they were brought before the king and, having first been absolved from their excommunication, they, or the chief men among them, were hanged.

The surviving records also show us much of the organization and administrative effort which underlie the drama of the siege of Bedford as the king's government mobilized the resources of his kingdom against the castle. They tell us of siege-engines carted from Lincoln and from Northampton and across Oxfordshire, while others were made on the spot by the many carpenters assembled for the purpose. The constable of Windsor was ordered to provide horses for Master Thomas and his fellow carpenters, together with their gear, 'so that they shall be able to travel to us by day and night as swiftly as they can and not tarry'. Master Henry the carpenter came from Lincoln, and the sheriffs of London provided horses for Master Walter and Master Simon to ride to Bedford. Timber was sent from Northamptonshire, while the monks of Wardon complained of the losses they sustained when the king's men cut down trees in their woods. Ropes and cables for the engines came from London, Cambridge and Southampton; hides to protect them from fire and to make their slings were sent from Northampton; and tallow to lubricate them came from London again. To quarry, fetch and shape the stone balls for the engines' bombardment a small army of labour was required, and the sheriffs of Bedfordshire and Northamptonshire were ordered 'without delay to cause to come to us at Bedford ... all the quarriers and stone cutters of your jurisdiction, with levers, sledges, mallets, wedges and other necessary tools, to work stones for mangonels and *petrarie*'. Miners were sent from Herefordshire and the mining district of the Forest of Dean by Roger de Clifford, constable of St Briavel's, and amongst their company assembled at Bedford we can recognize in Master Arnulf and William son of Lambert two who had previously served king John. Amongst the crossbow-men, we hear specifically of those coming from London, and orders went out to supply by the thousand the bolts or quarells for their weapons. Fifteen thousand were ordered from the royal castle of Corfe, and the bailiffs of Northampton were commanded 'as you love us and our honour, that you cause to be made both by day and by night, by all the smiths of the town who are skilled in the art', four thousand quarells, well barbed and well flighted, to be sent with all speed to Bedford.

From the same records, too, we catch glimpses of the king's young majesty at war, his tents and pavilions spread (having been sent up from London in good and strong carts), and we can imagine them providing a colourful backcloth to the fighting, emblazoned with the royal arms, perhaps, and gay with pennants flying. His arms and his war gear also came from London, and his personal requirements during the siege included large quantities of wine together with almonds, pepper, saffron, ginger and cinnamon. At length, when all was over, the army was dismissed, the great engines dismantled and dispersed in storage, some to Northampton and some to the Tower of London, and the king's arms and baggage were also returned to London in the charge of Nicholas of the Chamber. The castle of Bedford was razed to the ground, and Fawkes de Bréauté, deserted even by his wife, went into exile, to die a few years later still angrily uncomprehending the seeming injustice which could turn loyal service to one king into rebellion against that king's successor.

Not the least remarkable feature of the siege of Bedford in 1224 is that the castle before it fell held out for some eight weeks against the concentrated military resources of the whole kingdom. It is even more remarkable that in 1266 the castle of Kenilworth[34] successfully withstood a similar concentration for no less than six months, and in the end was never taken but surrendered upon terms. No two facts could demonstrate more clearly the strength of the contemporary castle and the supremacy of defence over attack which it established. The siege of Kenilworth itself has all the romantic appeal of a lost cause. The castle was held by a gallant band of the surviving supporters of Simon de Montfort, earl of Leicester, after his defeat and death at Evesham – they were the 'Disinherited', and desperate men who had no more to lose. The action was begun in earnest by Henry III and his son, the lord Edward, in June 1266. Resistance was still unbroken six months later when, in mid-December, the gallant defenders dragged themselves out of the battered castle. Considerations of space prevent the full story of the siege from being told here, but one or two salient features must certainly be noted. First, the fact that the castle was never taken by force may be bracketed with the fact that its broad water defences made the use of the mine impossible. Secondly, the manner of its final surrender is instructive. By October, though the hope of relief which had borne them up throughout the summer was not entirely gone, the condition of the defenders was becoming serious especially through lack of food and other supplies. They therefore sought and obtained from the besieging army a truce, whereby if no help came within forty days they would surrender. On December 14, when the term was up and no help came, they yielded and were allowed to march out with the honours of war.

The surrender of Kenilworth upon terms is as least as important to us as any other feature of the siege. It is probable that, as in this instance, the majority of medieval sieges were abandoned on the iniative of one side or the other, and after a shorter investment than was the case at Kenilworth, and that sieges carried through to the bitter end, after the manner of Bedford, Rochester or Le Puiset, are the exception rather than the rule. This hypothesis finds some illustration in the metrical chronicle of Jordan Fantosme,[35] one of the most valuable sources relating to early medieval warfare in England, describing the campaigns waged by William the Lion, king of Scots, during the rebellion against Henry II in 1173–4. Certainly Jordan's account of the Scots' invasion of the north of England at this time is instructive for the study of castle warfare.

When William the Lion crossed the Border in 1173 he came first to the castle of Wark, and there he demanded of its constable, Roger de Stuteville,

'How he would act,
Whether he would hold it or surrender it – which course he would pursue'.

In the event the outcome was a compromise; Roger asked for, and was granted, a truce of forty days during which he would seek aid. Thus satisfied, the Scots moved off to Alnwick, the castle of Eustace de Vesci; but this again they did not take, though whether because they thought it too strong, or because another truce was obtained, we are not told. Next they marched against Warkworth and took it, though, it is to be noted, with little difficulty because the castle's defences were weak. From Warkworth the host proceeded to Newcastle-upon-Tyne, and here we are specifically told that no attack was launched because they lacked the necessary siege-train – even though we know that at this date the great keep at Newcastle had not yet been built (above p. 48).

'Well sees the king of Scotland that he will never complete
The conquest of Newcastle-on-Tyne without siege engines'.

From Newcastle William the Lion marched on Carlisle, held for the king of England by Robert de Vaux, and here the castle was invested.

'The swords resound and the steel clashes:
Scarcely a hauberk or helmet there remained whole'.

Before, however, the issue could be decided the siege was raised on the news that an English army under Richard de Luci, the royal justiciar, was advancing north, and the Scots withdrew behind the Border.

It was not until the spring and Easter of the next year, 1174, that the Scots marched south again. As before, they came first to Wark, but this time laid siege to it. Their first assault failed, and William the Lion applied his siege-engines – which, evidently benefiting from the experience of the previous year, he had brought with him – and ordered them to bombard the gate. They, too, failed, one of them mis-shooting and striking down a Scottish knight.

> 'Then said King William, "Let us leave this siege:
> I see my men destroyed, and evil which cuts us off.... .
> ... Roger d'Estuteville has proved our match".'

So the host moved off, to the joy, albeit discreet, of the defenders – for Roger de Stuteville forbad them to jeer ('Say nothing abusive: for God's sake let be!'). From Wark the Scots came again to Carlisle but, on the refusal of Robert de Vaux to surrender, they withdrew and took instead the two castles of Appleby and Brough, the first with ease and the second after a stiff but brief engagement. From there they marched back upon Carlisle, where this time Robert de Vaux, both alarmed by the fall of Appleby and Brough and encouraged by news that his lord and king Henry had now returned from France to England to deal personally with the situation, obtained a truce of fifteen days, at the end of which, if not relieved, he would yield up the castle. Thus leaving Carlisle, the Scottish host marched east to Prudhoe which they rigorously assaulted. Prudhoe, however, was well provisioned and stoutly manned, while Odinel de Umfraville, lord of the castle, rode through the countryside raising a force for its relief:

> 'On maned Bauçan ...
> ... spurring continually day and night'.

After three days of unsuccessful effort before Prudhoe the siege was raised and, having divided his army, William the Lion rode on to Alnwick with a force of his French and Flemish allies. It was there, at Alnwick, before the castle, that they were attacked by an English army (led by Odinel de Umfraville amongst others), who came upon them unawares while the king, so Jordan Fantosme tells us, was at dinner with his helmet off. After a stiff fight, they were defeated. William the Lion himself, pinned to the ground by his dead horse, was captured and led away to imprisonment in the castle of Richmond, and the two years campaigning by the Scots were over.

No doubt in his account of these events Jordan Fantosme may sacrifice some detail and even bend his tale in the interests of poetic diction and dramatic effect, and no doubt also the Scottish army was not one of the best in terms of organization and equipment (though William the Lion took his knighthood seriously). Yet making whatever allowances are necessary, there may seem to the modern reader of his poem a note of almost joyful irresponsibility and seeming casualness – echoes, one may add, of Bertran de Born (p. 124 above) heard also in other accounts of other wars of the period. Of this it may be worth attempting some explanation. First, however, we would do well not to exaggerate it. In Jordan's poem there is, in fact, little support for the view of medieval warfare as a chivalrous tournament between high-minded knights in which few got hurt. The Scots marched about the north with fire and sword. Richard de Luci, justiciar of the English king, was heavy of heart as he rode through the once rich county of Northumberland.

> 'He rides in the ravaged and wasted country –
> ... Now it is in extreme famine, it is reduced to nothing.'

In this we are reminded of the grim advice on the proper conduct of war, given in this same poem by his ally, Philip count of Flanders, to the king of France:

> 'Thus should war be begun: such is my advice.
> First destroy the land and then one's enemies.'

The joy in war certainly felt by the warrior class of knights born and bred to the purpose did not necessarily reduce the devastation in which, in certain moods, they rejoiced, and what has been called 'the cult of violence' formed one part of their cult of chivalry. Further, touching the defence and capture of castles on which the campaigns significantly so largely turn, and in which our present interest chiefly lies, it is well to remember that the aged constable, Gospatric son of Orm, and his garrison, were heavily amerced afterwards by the English king for their too facile surrender of Appleby to the Scots. Nevertheless, it does appear from these campaigns of 1173–4 that the full-scale investment of a strong castle, even if one had the equipment, was not something lightly to be undertaken: that the yielding of a castle without hope of eventual success or relief was not regarded as dishonourable; and that the honourable compromise of a truce, often in the form of a sworn agreement to yield within a certain time if no help came, was frequently acceptable to both sides. When the keep at Brough was fired and the defenders surrendered, Jordan insists that they act honourably, 'like knights':

> 'For they see very well that they will have no succour ...
> ... That is a right act which they do now.'

And before Roger de Stuteville at Wark decided to negotiate a truce with the Scots he had begged his knights to 'Give me such advice that I may preserve my honour'.

For all this there were sound reasons which readily appealed to the hardheaded and efficient as well as chivalrous warriors of the so-called Middle Ages. From the point of view of the assailants, the strong castle, well defended and supplied, could not be taken without a full-scale and prolonged investment, perhaps leading to the deadlock of enforced and awaited starvation. To undertake this was a serious matter. Armies were small, and once they were committed to such an affair all other activities were foregone. Meanwhile, who could tell what might be happening elsewhere, and what chances missed? Once committed also, the army remained sensitive to the possibility of attack from the rear by a relieving force (as happened notoriously at the great sieges of Antioch and Acre on the First and Third Crusade respectively), and news of the approach of such a force could often be the reason for the raising of a siege. Nor was it easy to keep the large force required for complete investment, or any medieval army, long in one place or even in the field. Feudal knight-service, which probably set the standard, seems to have been limited to forty days in the first instance, while paid troops were immensely expensive and liable to melt away if their payment was left in arrears. Expensive, too, and cumbersome, was all the paraphernalia of a siege-train. It might well thus seem better, if a castle failed to yield upon demand or first assault, to move on elsewhere and try again, and, as one went, to indulge in profitable looting and also destroy the land it was the castle's purpose to protect. The latter tactics also were a deliberate and public insult to one's opponent and his honour and prestige in addition to being a diminution of his resources. From the opposite point of view, of the castle's defenders and their commander, no fortress however strong and well defended could indefinitely hold out, and in the last resort the term of resistance depended upon supplies. Hence the reliance placed upon the advent of relief, and hence, meanwhile and not infrequently, the truce. For castle warfare in the high Middle Ages it may not be too fanciful to cull the analogy of a game of poker, bluff and counter-bluff; but it was a grim game, the stakes were high, the rules could be harsh in operation (e.g. the garrison of Bedford in 1224), and one might well need, like Roger de Stuteville at Wark, to consult with one's peers and fellow knights in order to ensure the preservation of one's honour.

Such reflections, which may be wide of the mark, may equally explain why so many sieges were not pressed to a fighting conclusion. Too little is known as yet about the neglected subject of early medieval warfare, and especially about the principles, conventions, customs and laws which underlay it and which, if known, would do much to explain intentions and motives.[36] To return once more to the sieges of Kenilworth and Bedford, we may compare again the manner of their ending. Bedford was finally taken by storm and the garrison were hanged. The defenders of Kenilworth, who had given far more trouble over a period of six months to the royal army besieging them, eventually agreed to a truce, and when the terms were up marched out with honour. It seems very probable that these contrasting events reflect contemporary practice, and that a garrison which refused all terms could then expect no quarter. (Listen to Jordan Fantosme again, as the Scots march on Brough, swearing that 'If it is not surrendered to them, no one shall go out of it alive'.) If so, then the fact becomes one of wider interest and application. Rochester, too, was taken by storm, in 1215, and some accounts tell us that king John intended to hang the garrison until he was dissuaded by some of his captains, on the grounds that the same practice might then be used against captured royal garrisons and eventually thus have harmful effects upon the defence of royal castles. The story has been used as one more nail in the coffin of John's reputation, yet, if later events at Kenilworth and Bedford are indeed significant, it seems the king's first thoughts were strictly in compliance with the laws and customs of contemporary war.

We have spent much time on sieges because defence was a basic role of castles and that which above all else dictated their design. But it is as important to end this chapter as it was to begin it with emphasis upon the fact that the castle was not merely a defensive stronghold but also a firm base for active operations, and that its military value thus sprang more from its offensive than its defensive capacity. It is this which explains those mounted men, knights and others, that we have seen to have been prominent in castle garrisons. Based upon the castle, and secure within it from all but a full-scale and prolonged investment, the small force of the mounted elements of the garrison could swiftly respond to danger and command the surrounding countryside, riding out at will to protect or enforce the loyalty of neighbouring districts, or to launch attacks on marauding hostile forces, or to devastate the lands of their enemies. The range of the castle in this way was the range of their horses, there and back, a radius of some eight to ten miles, let us say, if one wished to be back before nightfall.[37] Surviving narratives and written sources give us examples. Knights from the (rebel) garrison of Leicester in 1174 attacked and plundered the town of Northampton and did much damage before riding back in triumph to their castle.[38] In a letter dated 21 November 1215, given at Rochester during the siege,[39] king John commanded the lady Nichola de la Haye (hereditary custodian of Lincoln castle whose sex did not prevent her from heroically defending the castle at a later date) to receive into the castle a force under Fawkes de Bréauté and Geoffrey de Neville, sent by the king to harry his enemies in those parts. A little later in the same year the garrison of Rochester, now royal after its capture by the king, rode out and took the neighbouring castle of Tonbridge, then a rebel stronghold.[40] Again, when in 1216 prince Louis gave to Gilbert de Gant the earldom of Lincoln, he also gave him the especial task of suppressing the king's garrisons at Nottingham and Newark, because they were destroying baronial houses and property in their districts and seizing their lands for their own use.[41] And finally, as a majestic instance, when Edward I built his castles in Wales they were not conceived as defensive strongholds merely but as the means of holding down his conquests by active operations.

Castles had, of course, yet other military uses. They were valuable as havens and halting-places for field forces, and, in moments of crisis, their garrisons could be drawn off to raise armies for the field. Roger of Wendover writes that when in 1216 the king wished to make a diversion to relieve his castles of Dover and Windsor, both then besieged, he raised a large force from his garrisons and proceeded to devastate the lands of his enemies in East Anglia.[42] (The plan worked and the siege of Windsor at least was raised.) Royal letters probably referring to this occasion, dated 22 August and enrolled upon the Patent Roll,[43] are addressed to eleven royal constables commanding them to be ready 'from dusk to dawn', with horses and arms, to ride on the instant with a part of their garrisons to wherever Fawkes de Bréauté (once again) shall direct them on the king's behalf. The castle, too, could not infrequently be a storehouse of munitions of war, as quarells were drawn by the thousand from

Corfe for the siege of Bedford in 1224. The king's armouries, too, were long at the Tower of London, as they still are. Yet these are but secondary uses. It is the aggressive rôle of the castle, combined with its defensive strength, that explain its military importance. The two were complementary: the castle required its defensive strength to ward off the attacks which its value as a base invited. He who would control the countryside must first hold, or take, the castles, and the castle dominated medieval warfare because it dominated the land.

Chapter 8

The Castle in Peace

The castle was no less prominent in peace than war, above all, of course, because it was the residence of the great, the centre and the seat of lordship, and this in an age of lordship when a ruling class really ruled. From first to last, as we have seen, the castle was a fortified residence: the residential function was no less fundamental to it than the military; and it was, indeed, this unique duality of residence and fortress that, so to speak, made a castle, and made it different from the fortifications of earlier and later periods. One may say also that it made it feudal, for while it is a matter of historical fact that the castle, the fortified residence of a lord, is the peculiar manifestation of feudal society, it is also entirely appropriate that it should be so. Feudal society, we are told, is society organized for war. It is also most certainly a society dominated by a military and a militant aristocracy, and what more appropriate setting could there be for them than castles? That the seigneurial residence should also be a fortress fits perfectly, and makes manifest, the military ethos of the age, as also do the seals whereon these aristocratic warriors formally represented themselves, or the effigies they had placed upon their tombs, in both cases armed *cap à pie*. Of course not every lord in the feudal period lived in a castle all the time, and not all lordly residences were fortified, i.e. were castles; but also there is no doubt that the castle became the symbol as well as much of the substance of lordship, and thereby an architectural concept meant to impress. Those castles depicted as rising on the skyline of the *Très Riches Heures* are real. And meanwhile, also, the castle as the residence of the lord (or his official) became inevitably the centre of local government, as we shall see, and sometimes other things as well, arising from its strength and social eminence.

There is one general feature of this medieval high society which must be noticed before any further discussion of the castle as its characteristic residence. Its members were almost continually on the move. The king himself, especially in the earlier medieval centuries, moved ceaselessly about his realm, visiting every region, seldom lying more than a night or two in one place, riding day by day and year by year the great and favoured circuit of the southern and midland counties, but ever and again also riding into the far west and north. And with him went not only a small army of servants, huntsmen and armed retainers, but also many of his barons, turn and turn about, and many also of his great officers of state, barons and officers alike with their own households and/or clerks. For the king not only reigned but also ruled and governed, and where he was there also was his court and government. In process of time, as administration became more complex with the ever expanding activity of royal government, the greater departments of state (Exchequer, Chancery, some royal courts of law) went 'out of court' and settled permanently at Westminster, and eventually, towards the end of our period, the king almost came to rest there also. But the royal itinerary long remained an essential feature of royal government and kingly living, and lingered on, indeed, to provide one explanation, for example, of the notorious predilection of Elizabeth I for sleeping in strange beds. The medieval magnates of both church and state, when they were not with the king, were similarly on the move each within his own sphere, from manor to manor, or from castle to castle, conducting his own affairs. It is necessary to remember that medieval England, like other contemporary lands, was full of movement of this kind, its roads and rivers constantly bearing the traffic of great households. This peripatetic life of kings and princes made possible the personal kingship and personal lordship of the day. It also helps to account for the curious mixture (in modern eyes) of extreme formality and grandeur with informality and earthiness which seems to characterize contemporary high society. It also helps to explain the itinerant household, the lord and his immediate servants and retainers (both, it may well be, of gentle birth) which we have met before as the basic domestic unit of medieval life at least above a certain level. And further, the lordly itinerary and the lordly household between them can explain much about the castle in its peaceful rôle – why, for example, so many castles were more than half-empty more than half of the time, while at the same time offering a multiplicity of accommodation in the form of semi-autonomous suites or blocks or groups of apartments, each intended for a household, that of the lord and those of his guests or high officials – six or seven such suites in thirteenth-century Corfe, or nine or more at Caerphilly.[1]

Of the two fundamental rôles of the castle as residence and fortress, we have already seen that the former eventually triumphed as the military importance of the castle came at last to decline. Yet this 'domestication' of the castle in the later Middle Ages, which has already been examined in an earlier chapter from an architectural point of view, only emphasizes a residential character always present and now only becoming more obvious, and perhaps also more luxurious, as the defences are increasingly lowered. It is noteworthy, for example, that the twelfth-century description of Ardres already quoted (p. 18 above) concentrates much more upon the wonderful amenities of the timber tower upon the motte – with its chambers great and small, its private room where they sometimes had a fire, its kitchen, its *loggia* and its chapel 'which was like the tabernacle of Solomon in its ceiling and decoration' – than upon the military strength of the castle. In the same century, Gerald of Wales, churchman, courtier and man of letters, writing of his own family's castle of Manorbier in Pembrokeshire, describes it proudly in terms which sound much like a modern recommendation for a gentleman's country seat – which, indeed, in a contemporary sense it was.

'The castle called Maenor Pyrr', he writes, '... is distant about three miles from Penbrock. It is excellently well defended by turrets and bulwarks, and is situated on the summit of a hill extending on the western side towards the seaport, having on the northern and southern sides a fine fish-pond under its walls, as conspicuous for its grand appearance as for the depth of its waters, and a beautiful orchard on the same side, enclosed on one part by a vineyard, and on the other by a wood, remarkable for the projection of its rocks and the height of its hazel trees. On the right hand of the promontory, between the castle and the church, near the site of a very large lake and mill, a rivulet of never-failing water flows through a valley, rendered sandy by the violence of the winds. Towards the west, the Severn sea, bending its course to Ireland, enters a hollow bay at some distance from the castle.'[2]

Gerald's description of his beloved Manorbier thus sheds a calm light upon the castle even in the twelfth century, and when in the second half of that same century administrative records become sufficiently numerous we can see from them how much attention contemporaries, at least as represented by the king, paid to the domestic quarters of their castles, see something of what those residential apartments were like, and even catch glimpses of the life led within them. The Pipe Rolls show that even in the reign of Henry II (1154–89) some of the royal castles most favoured as residences were palaces within, however heavily fortified without. At Windsor[3] (36), for example, Henry II built in stone, on the north side of the upper bailey where the cliff behind them made them most secure from attack, new royal lodgings set about a quadrangle and herb-garden, as well as enclosing the same bailey with a new and towered stone wall. Within the shell keep on the mound, also, there were further residential buildings, including a hall and chambers, and others again within the lower bailey. Though the rolls provide few details, we hear in particular at Windsor of the king's hall and his chambers, of the kitchen, larder and almonry, of the repair of the seats of the king and queen in the chapel, of pictures sent from London to the castle, and of a garden within it. In all, so far as we are able to compute it, it is probable that about a third of the heavy building expenditure upon Windsor in Henry II's time was spent upon its residential amenities, and this, of course, at a period when castles were at the height of their military importance.

At Winchester[4] in the same reign the Pipe Rolls, amongst continuous entries of building expenditure, speak of the king's hall within the castle and of hedges set about it, of work upon the castle chapel of St Judoc, upon the kitchens and upon a 'house' for the king's falcons, of work in painting the king's chamber and in preparing a separate chapel for the 'Young Queen', i.e. the wife of Henry II's son and heir, the young Henry, who was crowned king in his father's lifetime. At Nottingham,[5] again, much of the heavy expenditure by Henry II was devoted to the residential apartments within the castle. A new great hall was built between 1180 and 1183, chambers were constructed, the tower keep itself was given new timber floors, and there are references to the almonry, a mews for the falcons, a garden and the castle park. Possibly this work at Nottingham was intended for the king's youngest son, John, to whom Roger of Howden tells us that he had granted the castle in 1174, but the Pipe Rolls in any case are full of references at this time to royal lodgings within the king's castles, built, repaired, maintained up and down the land, in places as far apart as Exeter and Carlisle, against the king's coming as he moved constantly about his realm. And life within the castle, after the day's journey and the chase, must have been pleasant enough and by no means devoid of comfort if our historical imagination can supply the colour, the rich hangings and the panelling now missing from the bare stone walls. Henry II in his last years caused a garden to be made before his chamber window at Arundel,[6] a castle then in his hands, and king John, who followed his father's example in providing in his castles dwellings fit for kings, commanded new kitchens to be built at Ludgershall and Marlborough with ovens big enough to roast two or three oxen in each,[7] and built at his favourite castle of Corfe the elegant 'Gloriette', an embryo courtyard house of sophisticated masonry in the inner bailey east of the keep.[8]

For the reign of Henry III (1216–72) which extends over much of the thirteenth century, it so happens that a new series of royal records, the Liberate Rolls,[9] survive to record, in far greater detail than the Pipe Rolls, much of the lavish expenditure of a fastidious king, by common consent one of the greatest royal patrons of the arts in an age generally taken as a high-water mark in medieval culture. Amongst the wealth of information relating to the king's castles which these invaluable rolls contain, we may concentrate first again upon Winchester as providing an outstanding example of the king's high standard of living in the middle years of his reign. A typical order to the sheriff of Hampshire, dated in December, 1250,[10] orders him to cause to be painted with the story of Joseph the king's new chapel in his castle of Winchester, and to floor the same chapel with tiles; to paint the 'table' by the king's bed with images of the guardians of Solomon's bed; to pave the chambers of the king and queen with tiles; to make wooden windows in the gallery of the queen's chapel; to repair the privy chamber before the door of the Jew's tower; and to repair the long chamber above the stables in the tower where the wardrobe is usually made. Elsewhere on the same rolls for these years we hear of the great hall – now almost all that remains of the castle, and built by the same king between *c.*1222 and *c.*1235[11] – in which the king's seat is to be repainted together with the doors and windows, while the pictures above the royal dais (i.e. where the high table was, at one end as in an Oxford or Cambridge college hall) are to be renewed. Tables, chairs and forms are ordered for the chambers of the king and queen, and the queen's chamber is to be painted with green paint, new candlesticks to be supplied, and a 'Majesty' provided with gilded images about it for her devotions. Amongst the many other chambers in the castle for others than the king and queen, we hear of one for the king's stewards, to be conveniently built between the hall and kitchens; of a vaulted chamber, to be wainscoted, for the king's knights; of chambers for the chaplain and priests; and of a new chamber to be made by the royal stables to contain three beds and the harness. At Winchester, also, spiritual welfare was as lavishly provided for as creature comfort. A new privy chapel (probably the new chapel ordered to be painted in the 1250 writ quoted above) is to be made by the king's bed, and for his main chapel a marble altar is installed (the queen's chamber had a marble chimney-piece in 1252[12]). In the queen's chapel, behind which stood the castle dovecote, a beam was to be set up across the width, bearing a cross in the centre and figures of St Mary and St John on either side. On the western gable within the same chapel an image of St Christopher carrying Our Lord in his arms was to be painted, together with another showing St Edward the king giving his ring to a pilgrim.

Though Winchester may possibly be exceptional in degree, the Liberate Rolls especially make it clear that in the course of the thirteenth century many other royal castles were provided with increasingly elaborate residential quarters within the increasingly safe circuit of their walls. At Windsor,[13] for example, this time in the lower bailey and to the east of an earlier hall now much improved, a new set of royal lodgings and a new chapel were built, with a cloister between them, surrounding a lawn, and with a stone bench near the king's chamber. Meanwhile the lodgings in the upper bailey built by Henry II were also extended and improved and made over to the queen. In 1236 the queen's chamber there was set in order for Henry III's bride, Eleanor of Provence. Glass was set in two of the windows overlooking the garden, with shutters to open and shut, and another glass window, set in the gable, was painted with the Tree of Jesse. The new queen, however, or possibly her husband, evidently remained dissatisfied, for the following year the chamber was rebuilt. In 1239 Eleanor gave birth to her first-born son, the future Edward I, and a nursery was built for him, and for his sister who soon followed him. These were evidently two-storied and timber-framed buildings arranged about a courtyard to the west of the queen's lodgings. In the same year, 1239, the bailiff of Windsor was commanded 'to cause the chamber of our son Edward to be wainscoted, and iron bars to be made to each of the windows of the same chamber'.

At Ludgershall, to choose another example of the many possible, the constable of the castle was ordered in May 1244,[14] to make a new hall there, sixty feet by forty, in place of the old one, with four windows and, at one end, a pantry and a buttery; to build two kitchens, one for the king himself and one for his household (king John's kitchens with their great oven for two or three oxen evidently now being no longer serviceable); to wainscote the chambers of the king and queen; to repair the outer chambers; and to enclose the castle park with ditch and hedge all round. At the neighbouring Marlborough, a writ of 1241 addressed to the constable[15] ordered, amongst other works, a new dovecote by the castle; a new glazed window before the door of the queen's chapel; a new fireplace in the cellar before her chamber, which cellar was to be wainscoted and whitened and provided with a window painted with a dove and barred with iron; a portico to be made between the queen's chamber and her chapel, and a new door at the entry of her chamber; a new wardrobe, good and large with stores, behind the chapel of St Nicholas; and a larder for the king in a suitable place. At Llantilio (White Castle, Monmouthshire, in the Marches) a new hall was built with buttery and pantry,[16] and a new chapel at neighbouring Skenfrith,[17] while at Salisbury (Old Sarum) a nurse's chamber was provided.[18] Everywhere, it seems, new fireplaces were fitted in, and chapels improved and given rich furnishings. Everywhere, too (though not only in this century), there was colour, and that not only in the hangings and painted glass of chapels, halls and chambers. The wainscoting of one of the queen's chambers at Windsor was to be painted 'of a green colour with gold stars', and in the same castle the cloister was to be decorated with pictures of the Apostles, under the supervision of Master William, the king's painter and a monk of Westminster.[19] Even externally it is known that castles might be rendered and white-washed – hence White Castle (Llantilio) and hence also the White Tower of London.

If all this sumptuous good living, housed so far as military necessity would permit in ostentatious architectural splendour, was possible in the castles of the twelfth and thirteenth centuries (and, we may be sure, *mutatis mutandis*, in those of the tenth and eleventh centuries also), when – it must be emphasized again – the great fortresses of Caernarvon or Caerphilly, Harlech or Beaumaris, the ultimate in medieval military architecture, contained their splendid suites of residential accommodation, we should not expect to find the castles of the later Middle Ages serving any less as the residences of the great. Indeed, what happens is, as we have seen, that the residential rôle of the castle continues if anything at the expense of the military, as its military importance declines and the standards of noble living if possible rise yet higher. And here we are bound to refer again to Edward III's great works at Windsor in the third quarter of the fourteenth century[20] as symbolic, a prodigious expenditure, the largest recorded in the whole history of royal building in the Middle Ages, yet almost all of it disbursed upon the college for his new Order of the Garter in the lower bailey, and suite upon suite of accommodation in the upper bailey for the king and queen and their courtiers. It was suggested in an earlier chapter that Edward's Windsor was the Versailles of the age: to abandon the analogy, it was, in the fourteenth century, a fitting castle for his royal majesty (king of both England and France, and by the Grace of God), an appropriate centre for his chivalry, a proper architectural expression of the triumph of his arms at Poitiers and Crecy. The details of the work need now concern us less, but the royal lodgings in the upper bailey, which still substantially underlie all subsequent alterations, and upon which almost all the leading craftsmen in the realm were brought to work, must then have seemed to beggar all description. There was a new hall and a new kitchen. The king's apartments comprised a very large great chamber, converted from the former hall and having twenty windows, a painted chamber, and five other chambers one of which was called 'la Rose'. The decoration of the painted chamber is not known, but 'the chamber called la Rose' was coloured with azure and gold, green and vermillion. The queen had a suite of four chambers, one with a privy chapel, one hung with mirrors, and one called 'la daunsyng chambre'. In addition to all this and more, the apartments in the shell keep upon the Conqueror's motte were also renovated and partly rebuilt at this time, and a great clock set up there, with a bell brought from Aldgate to toll the hours – the earliest mechanical, weight-driven clock to which there is reference in England.[21] Amongst the appurtenances of the castle (as of many other English castles and great houses in the Middle Ages) was a vineyard, the wine from which was good enough for the king to make gifts of it to Alice Perrers. It was in Edward's day also that the parks and forests pertaining to and surrounding the castle reached their widest extent, dotted with hunting lodges in case the huntsmen were too far afield by nightfall.

In discussing the residential rôle of the castle we have perforce, by the nature of the documentary evidence which survives, used chiefly royal examples. We may cite a final one, perhaps, by referring to the large sums which, towards the very end of our period and the castle's history, Edward IV (1461–83) is reported to have spent upon Dover, and which have left their mark chiefly in the 'modernization' of the domestic amenities of the keep, still evidently a royal lodging, in the present window openings, doorways, and fireplaces with the Yorkist emblem still in their spandrels.[22] As for the king's barons, the magnates of the realm, if there is far less documentary evidence for them, the abundant architectural evidence alone suffices to show that they lived like kings. Strictly speaking, perhaps, there may have been no baronial equivalent of fourteenth-century Windsor, yet the fact remains that, from start to finish, there is no obvious architectural distinction between a baronial and a royal castle. Indeed the Albini keep at Castle Rising has close affinities with royal Norwich, as the keep at Rochester has with Castle Hedingham, Caerphilly need fear no comparison with Beaumaris, and in the later medieval centuries the good life was not noticeably lived at a lower level at a Kenilworth or a Warwick, a Bolton or a Bodiam, than at any royal castle of the same period. Though constitutionally speaking it was never true in England (or indeed elsewhere) that politically in the feudal period the king was only *primus inter pares*, socially there remains a good deal of truth in the dictum. We began this section on the castle as a lordly residence by quoting the proud description by Gerald of Wales of the de Barri castle of Manorbier in its peaceful setting, and we may end it with a positively lyrical description by a fifteenth-century Welsh poet of the castle of Raglan in Monmouthshire, founded by 'the Blue Knight of Gwent', Sir William ap Thomas (p. 92 above), with its 'hundred rooms full of festive fare, its hundred towers, parlours and doors, its hundred heaped-up fires of long-dried fuel, its hundred chimnies for men of high degree'.[23]

We have spent some time upon the castle as the dwelling of the medieval aristocracy, not only because it was in point of fact from the beginning a residence no less than a fortress (and, towards the end, more the former than the latter), but also because this peaceful and domestic aspect of the castle may be less familiar to the general reader and thus harder to visualize. It may well require emphasis that in all periods of the so-called Middle Ages, and not only at their close, the castle was lived in far more than it was fought in – and, indeed, it may often be the paradoxical truth that the strongest castles have the least active military history as the measure of their success. It may come as some surprise to read, in contemporary chronicles and records of the eleventh and twelfth centuries no less than in those of the fourteenth or fifteenth, of gardens, cloisters and dovecotes within the castle, or of vineyards, fishponds and parks without. Nevertheless such amenities are scarcely less fundamental than arrow slits and crenellations. When, at an early stage in the construction of Conway castle and fortified town, a new chamber was built for queen Eleanor, a lawn was also made before it with turf shipped up the river: it was fenced with the staves of an empty wine tun and on a July evening in 1283 it was watered for the first time by Roger le Fykeys, one of the queen's esquires, who received 3d. for his task (*pro aspersione aque super herbarium regine apud Coneweye per j noctem, iijd.*).[24] Investigation of the castle's residential rôle may also cast some light, as here, on the kind of life lived within it, whether we contemplate the eleventh-century Scolland's Hall at Richmond or wander in the ruins of Bodiam. Lost splendours can equally be evoked by records, as when amongst his writs in preparation for Christmas to be spent at Winchester castle in 1206, king John commanded his sheriff of Hampshire to provide one thousand and five hundred chickens, five thousand eggs, twenty oxen, and one hundred each of pigs and sheep[25] – or when everywhere upon the rolls of Chancery and Exchequer we meet the convoys of good wine trundling towards the king's castles. Yet at the same time it must be emphasized that fine residential buildings and good living seldom before the end impaired the castle's military proficiency. Henry III's close and tasteful attention to the lodgings within his castles coincides in time with that sophisticated elaboration of defence in the thirteenth century that will produce a Caernarvon or a Caerphilly, themselves no less luxuriously appointed inside, and it is not until the later Middle Ages that domestic comfort took priority over military strength. Meanwhile at no period in its history was the castle filled only or always with the tramp and clatter of armed men: the sound of revelry in the hall, the rustle of ladies' dresses in the chambers of the queen, even the laughter of children in the garden, are as authentic a distant note for our ears to strain after as the shouts of battle and the clash of arms. Joinville in his thirteenth-century Memoirs of St Louis (i.e. Louis IX of France) strikes that note exactly in telling of his leaving home to go on Crusade with the king. He received his scarf and pilgrim's staff from the abbot of Cheminon, and immediately afterwards 'I quitted the castle of Joinville without ever re-entering it until my return from beyond the sea'. Before embarkation, however, the seigneur de Joinville made pilgrimages to local shrines in his own country, and on one such occasion passed within sight of the castle he had left. But, he tells us, 'I dared never turn my eyes that way for fear of feeling too great regret, and lest my courage should fail on leaving my two fine children and my fair castle of Joinville, which I loved in my heart'.[26]

The fact that the castle was lived in by no means exhausts the list of its non-military uses – though in making these distinctions we must constantly remind ourselves that any rigid division between things civil and things military accords ill with the warrior aristocracy of the feudal period, while also the castle had the quasi-military rôle of policing its district. Comparatively little study has been made of the castle in the institutional sense of what it was for (compare and contrast, as always, the study of religious houses), but something is known of its uses at least in the twelfth and thirteenth centuries and there is no good reason not to project this knowledge both backwards and forwards into earlier and later centuries, since the fundamental nature of society did not much change, and since these other uses follow naturally enough from the castle's two basic rôles as residence and fortress. Thus the fact that castles were the seats and residences of kings and princes, and more permanently of their officials, made many of them the centres of local government as well as of the power they symbolized. The seigneurial castle commonly stood as the focal point of widely scattered estates and franchises, the head or *caput*, as the contemporary phrase ran, of the lord's honour; while the king's castles either similarly stood as the head and centre of estates or districts, or were in the custody of sheriffs, the chief local officials of the Crown, and thus became the centres of county administration. The latter category includes, of course, castles in county towns but often others in the shire as well. The sheriff's office was thus frequently in the local castle, as was also the steward's office for a non-royal lordship. It was therefore in the castle, in the hall, that the local courts of shire, hundred or honour might be held, to the castle that a man might repair to plead his suit, present his services or pay his taxes or his rent, and through its gates, watched by the porter, passed a stream of litigants and supplicants, tenants and bailiffs, tax-collectors and messengers, intent upon their daily business. To this day there are many instances of castles, or their sites, which thus remain the centres of local government, some in consequence preserved thereby and others mutilated. There were then other miscellaneous affairs of a pious and paternal authority too, as when Henry III ordered his constable of Windsor, in 1241, 'to cause the hall of our castle of Windsor, and also the hall within the tower (i.e. the keep) of the same castle, to be filled with poor folk on Good Friday, and to feed them'.[27] We may be sure that 'the chamber of the clerks' which was built in the castle at Nottingham in 1186[28] long remained a busy place as the king's writs came in and were returned (suitably endorsed), juries were empanelled, and rolls and vouchers of dues, payments and pending cases made up.

The seat of kings, magnates and their officials, the centre of local government and affairs, the castle, by virtue of its strength, might have other more specific uses, as a treasury perhaps, or as an armoury, or, almost invariably in fact, as a prison. King John, in particular, laid his treasure up in certain of the royal castles that it might be more conveniently available as he moved indefatigably about his realm, and a royal mint (eventually *the* Royal Mint – and hence Mint Street in the outer bailey) remained in the Tower of London until the nineteenth century, when it moved to a site nearby. The Tower still houses, too, the

Queen's Armoury, and some of the monarch's armourers have been there since at least the time of Edward I (in whose reign the king's carpenters at the Tower made a model castle for the king's son, Alphonse, the which, we may be sure, was no toy fort for the nursery but a large scale model by which the arts of siege-craft and defence might be better learnt). As for the castle in its very frequent subsidiary rôle as prison, it may seem suitable to end with that, since nothing has contributed more, unjustly yet not entirely without cause, to its popular romantic notoriety and in so doing has even changed the meaning in the English language of the once honourable *donjon* to the deep, dark, dank and dismal *dungeon*. Medieval records are indeed full of references to the gaol in the castle – as Henry II, in his Assize of Clarendon in 1166 ordered every county without a gaol to have one constructed in a castle or a borough – and in places resound also with complaints, true or false, of unjust detention and improper treatment by the constable who was in charge of it. He, indeed, seems at times to have been, by modern standards, high-handed in his acts, and we read of a constable of Banbury (a castle of the bishop of Lincoln) who, pursuing an escaped prisoner, caught and executed him on the spot. He may have had provocation, for very heavy fines could be imposed on those who allowed their prisoners to escape. One would not suppose escape to have been easy, though a letter of king John in 1203 contains what seems to be a reference to a notable prison riot.[29] The king, having ordered the constable of Corfe to send him two of his prisoners, namely Savaric de Malleon and Amery de Forz, under good and sufficient escort, adds that he is to take care that a sufficient garrison remains to guard the castle and its remaining prisoners 'better than it was guarded when the aforesaid Savaric took and held the keep against us'. As for the castle prisoners themselves, they included not only local offenders and common criminals but also high-placed political prisoners and prisoners of state, and amongst the latter there were certainly some whose lot was tragic enough to justify the castle's grim reputation in this respect. The unhappy Eleanor, 'the Beauty of Brittany', sister to that Arthur of Brittany whom king John stands accused of murdering for his claims upon the English throne, was confined (albeit honourably, with her ladies in waiting and the king's gift of robes) mainly in Bristol, and sometimes Gloucester, castle for forty years until her death in 1241. All contemporary chroniclers agree that the same king caused the wife, son and daughter-in-law of his broken companion and vassal, William de Braose, to be starved to death in Windsor castle, Berkeley in Gloucestershire is stained to this day with the atrocious murder of the deposed Edward II in 1327, and Richard II died violently at Pontefract. Nevertheless, such things, though they happened, are vastly overdone by popular guides and guide books, and the modern visitor to the Tower of London might be forgiven if he supposed that the castle (though in fact by then, after five hundred years, near the end of its active history) had been built exclusively by Tudor monarchs for the sole purpose of incarcerating, racking and beheading their political opponents. In fact there is rather more to the history of castles than the prisoners inside them, not all of whom were romantic, and very few indeed of whom were to be found in 'dungeons' in the modern sense, least of all in the much maligned Middle Ages. If the ravens at the Tower were shooed away or shot, we and our medieval history would be the better served.

Chapter 9

The Castle in General

T he first five chapters of this book dealt, first, with the origin of the castle both in this country and on the Continent, a matter now very much again the focus of attention, though mainly by archaeologists, and, thereafter, dealt with the architectural history of the English castle, its development and decline. That architectural history has also received a good deal of attention during the last century or so, though it must be added that castles still lag far behind churches in the amount of study lavished upon them by professional architectural historians, and, further, like so much else in the medieval period, the later castle remains neglected by comparison with the earlier. A subsequent chapter dealt with castlebuilding, i.e. with the question of how castles were built, a subject of which very much more is known now than when this book was first planned and written over twenty years ago. Next, some attempt was made to answer the question which should matter most to historians, namely why castles were built, in terms of their function and value to contemporaries both in peace and war. On this subject it is still true to say that little work has been done, even though it ought to be self-evident that architecture cannot or should not be separated from the society which produces it and whose needs and aspirations it embodies. In this respect one may venture to suggest that the history of architecture is too important to be left to those professional architectural historians preoccupied with mere description, affinities and styles, and it would be difficult to say which is the more regrettable in the modern world of over-specialization, the divorce which tends too often to exist between ordinary and architectural historians, or that between the former and the archaeologists. Lastly, there yet remain some more general points and observations to round off this study of the castle in England and Wales, though it must be emphasized that so little work has hitherto been done upon the subject from any save the architectural and archaeological point of view that any discussion of these matters can only be both brief and tentative.

It is some indication of the state of castle studies that no bare list, even, of sites in England and Wales exists in print, nor until very recently was there any estimate of their total number, though obviously such basic facts are essential for any general study of the subject as a whole. It is also an indication of the state of unawareness even of the educated public interested in the past, that the total number of castle sites surviving in this country would come as a startling surprise if ever it were established and agreed. Thus the only printed estimate to date, based upon careful field surveys and other research, puts the total of existing castle sites in England and Wales at 1,580, of which 367 are in Wales (less Monmouthshire with fifty-four of its own).[1] If, on the one hand, these figures are too high in including certain later fortresses of dubious status, on the other, they do not include castles known to have existed but of which no visible trace remains. They certainly make it very clear that the castle is a feature of the medieval period not lightly to be passed over if we wish to understand.

Less startling estimated figures, yet equally impressive on reflection, can be obtained another way. The totals just quoted are overall totals derived chiefly from surviving remains: they seek to comprise all the castles there have ever been, and it by no means follows, of course, that all the castles thus added up were all in existence at the same time. A list of castles in England and Wales published some years ago and based upon contemporary written sources (both documents and chronicles) for the period 1154–1216, shows a total of some three hundred and fifty thus recorded as active in *c.*1200.[2] This is reasonably firm fact while what follows is informed guesswork, but making due allowance for the inevitable inadequacy of contemporary written evidence to record every castle then in existence, we may probably take four hundred as a safe notional figure for the total number of castles in use in that area at that time. And next, from the vantage point of this more or less firm ground, we can project some reasonable estimate both backwards and forwards. First, formidable though the number of four hundred castles in *c.*1200 may seem, there is no doubt that it represents a considerable reduction of the total in existence some fifty years before in *c.*1150, and indeed we may be sure that there were never more castles in England than in the first half of the twelfth century and at that date. By then, to the very large numbers of castles raised in England and Wales as part and parcel of the Norman Conquest and initial settlement,[3] there had been added others planted by later arrivals of the second generation (thus in Norfolk the family of Albini, arriving under Rufus and achieving eminence under Henry 1, had raised and abandoned Old Buckenham and built two other castles at New Buckenham and Castle Rising before 1150[4]), others which, as in the eleventh century, were the means and mark of further Norman expansion in the north and west, and the innumerable new and mainly 'adulterine' castles which are traditionally associated with the 'Anarchy' or civil wars of Stephen's time when, according to the Anglo-Saxon Chronicle, 'they filled the land full of castles'.[5] The chronicler Robert of Torigny, it will be remembered, declared that one thousand one hundred and fifteen adulterine or unlicensed castles were destroyed at the end of the wars and the succession of Henry of Anjou, son of the empress Mathilda, as Henry 11.[6] Although there is a curious precision about abbot Robert's figure, doubtless it is not to be taken literally but as a dramatic indication of the reduction of castles brought about the the advent of peace. Certainly, thereafter, the Angevin kings, Henry, Richard and John, followed a settled and successful policy of closely controlling castle-building, reasserting their right to former royal castles lost in Stephen's time, and confiscating and sometimes demolishing the castles of known rebels or, upon occasion, those merely suspected of disloyalty. By such means (obtaining our figures again exclusively from written sources) the number of baronial castles in the realm was reduced from 225 in 1154 to 179 by 1214, while the number of castles in the king's hand almost doubled during the same period. Probably more important, however, than political considerations in reducing the overall number of castles in this period is the great and mounting cost of building in stone and in the latest fashion. Castles could no longer be raised with what seems the prodigal ease of the first decades of the Norman Conquest, nor, of course, was the same compulsion any longer present, and since even to keep one's castles up to date called for a huge investment of resources, many were abandoned. Thus we come again to the estimate of some four hundred castles about the year 1200, and if we now look forward we may perhaps surmise, though with less confidence and more guesswork, that this figure remains more or less constant for the next two centuries until the declining military importance of the castle began the long and final process of ultimate reduction. Though, of course, new castles were raised in the thirteenth and fourteenth centuries and even thereafter, as we have seen, they were, as we have also seen, exceptional in being new castles on new sites when so many, probably too many, already existed, and it is at least probable that their number was balanced by the abandonment or destruction of others through war, economic circumstance or political vicissitude.

The distribution of these hundreds of castles is full of interest, though it seems likely that the several reasons for it are not all equally or generally understood. First as to the facts, the castles of England and Wales are to some extent inevitably concentrated in the frontier regions of the medieval kingdom, in the south-east towards the Continent, in the north towards Scotland, and, above all, in the wide and sprawling band of country which formed the Marches of Wales. Yet one of the most striking facts about them is that they are also found, literally, all over the place, so that there is no English county without its castles, and inland counties far removed from any external threat nevertheless have at first sight surprisingly large numbers of surviving castle sites (e.g. twenty-two in Bedfordshire, twenty-one in Buckinghamshire, twenty in Leicestershire, and twenty-nine in Northamptonshire.)[7] The basic explanation, of course, lies in the dual nature of the castle as both residence and fortress, and thus the nature of the society which produced it. To these fundamental considerations we must return, but meanwhile there are two preliminary facts to be borne in mind in seeking any explanation of the distribution of English castles. The first is that, even if we regard them exclusively from the military point of view, which is an error, we still should not imagine their overall distribution to be the result of a central and comprehensive plan imposed from above in the interest of national defence or security. Indeed it may seem unlikely that even the necessary geographical knowledge can have been available for such centralized, strategic planning even had the political, social and economic structure of the kingdom made it conceivable – and this especially perhaps in the early days of the second half of the eleventh century, which will bring us in a moment to our second introductory point. Meanwhile it is necessary to see the siting and distribution of castles as for the most part tactical rather than strategic, that is to say they are usually to be seen in a local rather than a national context, and they are where they are in most cases for local and often personal reasons. Thus even the thickly planted castles of the Welsh Marches were not units in a national plan against the long-suffering Welsh but, rather, separate strongholds set to defend and extend the particular territory of their individual lords, and where there is an element of interdependence which is real and not a pattern imposed by ingenious historians, this, too, is local and not national. The distribution of English castles (as of castles elsewhere) in any given period and not least in the beginning is chiefly the arbitrary result of innumerable local plans and *ad hoc* decisions. Secondly this overall pattern, while there will be variations of detail in subsequent periods, is overwhelmingly the result of the Norman Conquest and the Norman settlement. Castles were then a principal means whereby a new and alien military aristocracy established themselves in England and in Wales. That conquest and that settlement proved permanent, and so did the pattern of their settlement, their lordships, centred upon their castles, so that, while many were afterwards abandoned, the typical architectural history of the typical English castle – as previous chapters of this book have emphasized – is of an early foundation followed by continuous development on the same site.

The fundamental explanation of the distribution of castles is to be found in the fact that the castle was not exclusively a military fortress but a fortified residence, combined with the nature of the society which produced it. Most castles, after all, are where they are because the king or, more frequently, some other lord had lands there. Further, we are not dealing with a national monarchy or national state on the ancient, and modern, pattern, but with a feudal monarchy and a feudal state. Feudalism, properly understood, is a positive and not a negative force, cohesive and centralising: at the highest political level it adds to, and does not detract from, the power of kings and princes, and never more so than in England where William the Conqueror and his successors added the formidable powers of feudal suzerain, the lord of lords, to the already impressive power of an ancient and pre-feudal, Germanic and Carolingian monarchy, reinforced by the surviving concept of Christian kingship. Nevertheless, seen from the other way about, feudal society is characterized by a marked decentralization of power, both military and political as well as social and economic, whether we regard this as the sharing of power between the prince and his vassals, or, as kings will come to insist, the mere delegation of royal authority. The Anglo-Saxon boroughs of king Alfred and his successors can be said to have formed a national system of defence (and, in the beginning, offence) because they were evidently all royal and, so far as we know, raised as a direct exercise of royal authority, just as the

Anglo–Saxon military system of which they formed a part was a national system based upon the obligation of all free men to provide military service as subjects of the king.[8] The military system, at least for the ruling class of knights and barons, after the Conquest was different: they owed knight-service to the lord of whom they held their land as fiefs, and that lord might or might not be the king. Maitland's dictum that after the Conquest all military service is the king's appears to be a notable instance of lawyers' wishful thinking.[9] And as they held their fiefs, conditional upon fealty and service, so evidently they held their castles, though subject to even stricter conditions and control than those governing the tenure of land. In consequence, by no means all castles were in the king's hand, and, of those many which were not, not all were held directly of him (though most were). Thus in the beginning the Conqueror granted out the land of England, save that which he held himself or was held by the Church, to his great vassals to be held of him as fiefs, and they raised castles where they thought fit or he directed, as the very means of conquest and settlement, as their fortified residences, as their power bases, and as the centres and symbols of their lordship. The Norman Conquest, we may say, was an exercise in feudalism, and the keynote of both is cooperation between lord and vassal. And just as the great vassals, the tenants-in-chief of the king, in due course granted parcels of their lands to their own vassals to be held of them as fiefs, so also in some cases they allowed their own vassals thus enfiefed to have and to hold castles of them. We do not in fact know on what terms and conditions castles were held in the first generation of the Conquest, but it becomes very clear when records are more plentiful in the later twelfth century that baronial castles greatly outnumber royal ones, just as it is also clear that any feudal lord – and the king is the greatest of feudal lords, as well as enjoying ancient royal majesty and sovereignty – retained important rights and ultimate control in the castles of his vassals, being entitled to the use of them if urgent occasion required and insisting that they must be rendered to him on demand.[10]

Of the hundreds of castles of the Conquest and the first century of English feudalism, some, as we have seen, came to be abandoned at an early date, some to be demolished as an act of war or politics, and some moved their site (e.g. Old Buckenham, as it then became, to New Buckenham[11]), but very many stayed where they were as the established seats of lordship even though the circumstances had passed which brought them into being, and, of course, others – though never so many again – were added to their number as new men rose to the top or new conditions demanded. But probably not even in the beginning, in the first strenuous generation after 1066 or in the time of Stephen, and certainly not afterwards, were strictly military reasons necessarily the only, or even the paramount, motive for the foundation, still less the maintenance and development, of castles. The castle, once again, was residence as well as fortress. A recent and important paper by a French scholar[12] has shown an instance, in the district of Le Cinglais in Normandy in the eleventh century, of castles (like religious houses in some other contexts) as the instruments of colonization and cultivation, planted as the bases for the taking-in of new land, and thus the centres of new lordships in the economic as well as the political sense. In this country such studies have scarcely been attempted, and in any case such evidence is hard to come by. Motives are often difficult to establish in the Middle Ages. Yet meanwhile we may wonder what real military reasons the young William of Albini II had in the 1140s for building his two grandiose castles at (New) Buckenham and Rising (**15**) in place of his father's (Old) Buckenham, and what motives drove him on save the compulsions of status, prestige and self-assertion, the need to show in fitting manner the lofty eminence he had achieved by marrying 'Alice the queen' (as his charters call her), the widow of king Henry I, who brought him also the title of earl and the honour and castle of Arundel.[13] This is mere hypothesis, albeit not unreasonable, but what seems a positive statement of the motive for building a castle is made by a knowledgeable thirteenth-century chronicler in describing king John's new castle at Odiham in Hampshire, built between 1207 and 1212. It is, he writes, 'a castle ... set in fair meadows and close to the woods which the king had caused to be built for his sport'. The manor of Odiham certainly lay in good and therefore favoured royal hunting country, and John in choosing it as the site for his new castle was evidently moved more by the delights of the chase than by military necessity – though when the test came a few years later the castle was strong enough to be held, so Roger of Wendover tells us, for three days by a garrison of three knights and ten sergeants only.[14]

Which brings us to a point. For whatever reasons a castle was founded and maintained, it became at once a place of at least potential military value, and therefore of political importance. The control of any region depended in the last resort upon the possession of its castles. A late twelfth-century chronicler, in striking metaphor, called the royal castles 'the bones of the kingdom',[15] but, as we have seen, the majority of castles at that time were not royal. The schoolboy heresy of 'King versus Baronage' (and vice versa) as the theme of medieval political and constitutional history is not less a heresy because it has been in the past handed down by very eminent historians in very distinguished books. The obvious and clarifying retort must surely be that if all the barons had been against all the kings all the time there could not have been any kings. Barons by and large are not revolting, and, on the other side, no monarch in the Middle Ages ever conducted an anti-baronial policy, still less an anti-feudal one. The ideals of feudal society involved loyalty, cooperation and mutual obligation. Nevertheless there is political opposition in all periods, including our own, and in the earlier feudal period especially, setting aside the Church (usually in favour of kings and always in favour of order), this could only come from the baronial class, who, together with the king, monopolized political power. Further, in that age political opposition, in certain circumstances, could and did appeal to arms. Any king worth his salt, therefore, would look to the castles of his realm, look after his own, seek to ensure, by the exercise of his huge power of patronage, that as many castles as possible were in the hands of those he could trust, and seek also to contain, control, confiscate, or even demolish, the strongholds of his known or suspected political enemies. Indeed, so long as castles retained their military importance, the question of their distribution and control could be and often was the very stuff of medieval politics. In an earlier chapter the building of the castle of Orford in Suffolk (**17**) was discussed in terms of how it was done. If we now ask why it was done, the known circumstances seem to indicate a clear example of a castle founded as the result of political considerations.[16] When Henry II succeeded to the kingdom of England in 1154 there were no royal castles in Suffolk, and power in the county must have seemed dangerously concentrated in the hands of Hugh Bigod, made earl of Norfolk by Mathilda in 1141, and the lord of the three Suffolk castles of Bungay, Framlingham and Walton together with Thetford just on the Norfolk border. As early as 1157 the king, upon some pretext now unknown, was able to seize all four Bigod castles, as well as Eye in Suffolk and Norwich, the administrative centre of the two counties. Although in 1165 Henry restored Framlingham and Bungay to earl Hugh, he retained Walton and Thetford, and in the same year he began the construction of a new royal castle at Orford, on the coast and not far from Framlingham. It is possible that about the same time the earl greatly strengthened his regained castle at Bungay, since this is the date generally given to the rectangular tower keep whose ruins still remain there.[17] Orford was finished by 1173, just in time it may be said, for in that year a serious rebellion broke out in which Hugh Bigod was one of the leaders and East Anglia one of the principal theatres of action.

('Were I in my castle of Bungay,
Upon the river of Waveney,
I would ne care for the King of Cockney')

In view of this context of events there seems little doubt that Orford was raised as part of a struggle for power between king and earl in Suffolk and East Anglia, just as these same events throw light on the motives which led Hugh Bigod to rebel. The outcome was the defeat of earl Hugh and his allies, and the confiscation, and this time demolition, of his castles of Framlingham and Bungay. In twenty years therefore the political balance of power in Suffolk in terms of castles had been entirely reversed. Yet also these events are a confrontation between this king and that earl: we are not observing any manifestation of a general anti-baronial policy, nor yet of any inevitable dichotomy between an abstraction called 'the Baronage' and another called 'the Crown'. Generations, too, and with them personalities, change. After the death of both king Henry and earl Hugh, Framlingham was restored to Hugh's heir, Roger Bigod, by the next king, Richard I, and rebuilt better than before (**12**) – to become again, as it happened, a rebel stronghold against king John, who took it in 1216.

All history, it has been said, is local history. Certainly the history of individual castles can often help to explain great political events, and much of the history of medieval England, not to speak of Wales, is locked up in its castles. We have seen that their possession and control could be a burning issue, and we have discussed so far the attitude of kings. From the baronial point of view, castles it was no less desirable to have and equally essential to hold. Prestige was at stake as well as politics and power, and the castle, the symbol of lordship, was also the symbol of status, the focal point of patrimony, identity and lineage. Kings, albeit feudal suzerains, might well be ill-advised to press too hard on this. There is the ring of truth in the simple account by a Welsh chronicler[18] of the causes of the political crisis of 1215 which led to civil war against king John and so to Magna Carta. The rebels, he writes, swore they would not make peace with the king until he restored the liberties of the Church, 'and until there should be restored to each one of them their laws and their power and their castles which he had taken from them without law or truth or justice'. He was not so far out, for amongst the individual lords and barons who appealed to arms against the king on this occasion were Clinton who had lost Kenilworth, Lacy who had lost Pontefract, Stuteville who had lost Knaresborough, and fitz Walter, Mowbray and Mandeville who claimed by right the custody, allegedly withheld, respectively of Hertford, York and the Tower of London – while Magna Carta itself, the Great Charter of Liberties in English history, insisted in one of its most important clauses (*c.*52) on the restoration of castles no less than lands and liberties and rights seized arbitrarily by the king without due process of law.

The substance of much military and therefore political power, the residence of the great, the cherished symbol of status and often nobility, the hub of administration and the centre in so many ways of public and private life, affecting one way and another most ranks of society through its manifold functions and the labour and service of its maintenance – how then is the decline of the castle in the later Middle Ages to be explained? Paradoxically this, although a book on castles, is scarcely the place to attempt anything like a full explanation, which ultimately lies in the complex reasons which slowly but surely brought about a change in the whole nature of society. We have seen how the castle emerged in Western Europe in the tenth century as a manifestation and a characteristic of a new type of society, which we call feudal, then evolving. The fundamental explanation of its decline, therefore, can only be the decline of feudalism itself, and to explain that would surely require another and a different book. Yet anything less can only be summary and, to a degree, superficial. Thus it has already been emphasized that the most popular reason generally advanced for the decline of the castle, namely the introduction of gunpowder, will not begin to do as an immediate cause, for it was not before the sixteenth century, and over two hundred years after its first use in Britain, that gunpowder began to render obsolete medieval forms of fortification, and that fortresses made their appearance designed on new principles both to resist and be defended by heavy cannon. Until then, the occasional insertion of gunports into towers and walls constructed on the old and lofty pattern is the only obvious result of the new devices. Far more interesting, because more significant, to the historian is the fact that these coastal fortresses of the Tudors were exclusively military, no longer residential, and also exclusively royal or national – which things bring us back again to the changing nature of society and of the monarchy at its head. Meanwhile another feature of late medieval English monarchy, though from our point of view a superficial rather than a fundamental cause, is certainly relevant to our problem. The chronic impecuniosity of fifteenth-century Lancastrian kings contributed in practice to the decline of English castles in that it brought about the decay of so many of them in fact through sheer neglect. The king's castles were always vastly more numerous than those of any other individual lord, and they became more numerous still when, in 1399, the duchy of Lancaster was added to the royal demesne. The Crown's resources were inadequate for so much maintenance, as the many surveys of dilapidations surviving from the period make clear, and at this point it is relevant to note that, whatever the military situation may have been, the king no longer needed so many castles for his residence as of old. As the medieval period proceeds so the pace and the extent of the royal itinerary declines and the king becomes increasingly sedentary, especially in and about London.

Changes in the nature of warfare, also, have of course been put forward as a principal reason for the decline of the castle, and notably the increasing occurrence of pitched battles in the field instead of sieges as of old. Setting aside, however, the hazards of generalising about medieval warfare in this way when in reality we still know too little about it, it is obvious that to speak thus of a change in the conduct of war is simply to speak of the declining military importance of the castle in different words, though certainly that military decline is the crucial element, since the residential role of the castle continued, and indeed still exists for the fortunate few. Moreover, military organization and the conduct of war are themselves an integral part of social organization and a manifestation of its type, so that we are brought back again to the fundamental explanation which lies in the changing nature of society.

It may be that at this stage we should bring into the train of thought that well known feature of almost every historical period, and thus endlessly useful in the solution of difficult sociological problems, namely the rise of the middle classes. As the text-books make clear, the bourgeoisie, at least, do not fit comfortably into any blueprint notion of feudal society, and though in fact they were present throughout there is no doubt that they were more prominent at the end than at the beginning of the feudal period, and that not least in England. It is not true that even in the beginning the noble class and warrior aristocracy of feudal society monopolized warfare in the sense that no one else took part, nor that the contribution of others and of infantry was not valued; but they, their tactics and their specialized skills were dominant, they called, so to speak, the military tune, and they had a near-monopoly (save for the Church to which they were closely related) of political and economic power as of social eminence. That near monopoly was surely broken or much diluted towards the end, whether we think of Parliament, with the Commons within it, evolving from the old feudal 'great council' comprised of the king's vassals, or of changes in the nature of taxation which lie behind it, feudal taxes falling initially only on the tenants-in-chief giving way to the new, national, parliamentary taxes, paid not on land but personal property, and by all free men as subjects of the king. And though outstanding individual members of the prospering middle classes might rise by wealth and emulation into the ranks of the aristocracy – like the de la Poles from Hull who rose by wool to their castle of Wingfield in Suffolk, and higher yet to be earls and dukes – merchants and clothiers did not generally live in castles, nor were they bred in any military or chivalrous tradition. It is possible, though here again the hypothesis becomes superficial, hazardous, and as yet unproven, that an increasing concentration upon towns as opposed to castles, both in terms of fortification and of warfare, in the later Middle Ages may be a reflection of these social developments.

If these changes were taking place within society, and, as it were, from the bottom upwards, there were also slow, cumulative changes in its overall manifestation as the state, and in the monarchy at the top of it. The steady expansion of royal power, and with it of the function and responsibility of royal government, though by no means always the result of conscious policy, is a continuous and dominant theme of English medieval history with the exception of the fifteenth century (or, rather, a period which might be better defined as the last quarter of the fourteenth century and the first three-quarters of the fifteenth), so that the allegedly 'new monarchy' of the early Tudors is at once the revival and culmination of medieval practice. In the emergent nation state under a national monarchy – as, for that matter, *mutatis mutandis*, under the national and pre-feudal monarchy of Alfred and his successors in England before the Conquest there is less room and occasion for that fragmentation or devolution of public authority, including military power, characteristic of feudal society. Just as whole generations of history students in schools and even elsewhere have been warped in their understanding of the past by being taught that the fifteenth century is representative of the Middle Ages and feudalism, so few phrases have done more harm to history than the 'overmighty subject' which is hopelessly anachronistic if applied to earlier periods, but the fact that Fortescue could use it in the late fifteenth century may well be significant of attitudes then changed or changing. The one thing certain is that changes in the nature of society are usually, unless caused by some cataclysmic event, slow and gradual as well as continuous, held back by inheritance, custom, tradition and habit, and very difficult for the historian to pin down. It is very probable that the 'new monarchy' of the Tudors is an even bigger myth than their 'revolution in government', and there is certainly much in the attitude of Henry VIII (let alone Henry VII) that is shared by Edward I or Henry II centuries before. So doubtless it comes about that an eminent historian once declared, in a weak moment, that the baronial castle was an anachronism by the later twelfth century, while others have seen the end of English feudalism in Edward I's time and others earlier still. On the other hand we should remember, not least at the end of this book, that English castles had their Indian Summer of military importance in the mid-seventeenth-century Civil War, when to the battles of Naseby and Marston Moor are added the sieges of Corfe and Colchester, Raglan, Pembroke and Nunney, Bolton, Donnington, Newark and many others.

'And now it is all gone – like an unsubstantial pageant faded.' So wrote Froude, in a splendid passage of his History, on the passing of the Middle Ages. But in fact the Middle Ages, happily, are not gone. They live on in their institutions, Church, Monarchy, Parliament, Law Courts and Universities, in the great mass of learning, books and records they have left behind, in their artistic achievements, and most immediately of all, perhaps, in the architecture they have bequeathed us. And certainly there is nothing unsubstantial about the castle, not even usually in its ruins. Of all buildings the castle is the most characteristic of the feudal Middle Ages by belonging uniquely to them, and thus affording those who seek it direct access to a past by no means wholly vanished and still with much to give.

Notes

Chapter I

1 *Cartularium Saxonicum*, ed. W. de G. Birch, ii, 222.

2 *Annales Bertinianorum*, in Migne, *Patrologia Latina*, cxxv, 1253. *Cf.* Armitage, *op. cit.*, p. 65.

3 *Domesday Book* ('Record Commission'), i, 184*d*.

4 See the Norman *Consuetudines et Justicie* of 1091, *c*.4, printed in C.H. Haskins, *Norman Institutions* (New York, 1918), p. 282.

5 *Cf.* below, p. 159.

6 The word 'keep' itself first appears in the English language in 1586, in Sidney's *Arcadia*.

7 Below, p. 15.

8 *History of the King's Works*, ed. H.M. Colvin, *The Middle Ages* (H.M.S.O., 1963), pp. 115, 326 n. 4, 625, 741, 781.

9 For the 'shell keep', see below, pp. 58–60.

10 An alternative derivation for some early forms of the word from the Flemish *dunc, dung, dunk*, meaning an elevated place above a marsh, is much less favoured by lexicographers both French and English.

11 Leonardo Villena, 'Glosario de términos castellologicos medievales en lenguas románicas', *Castillos de España*, No. 71 (1971).

12 See the important paper by C.L.H. Coulson, 'Rendability and castellation in medieval France' in *Château-Gaillard*, vi (1972); also his unpublished thesis (Ph.D., London University, School of History).

13 See Stewart Cruden, *The Scottish Castle* (London, 1960), pp. 1–6.

14 See Mrs Armitage, *op. cit.*, pp. 324–7.

15 Below, p. 29.

16 M. de Boüard, 'Les petites enceintes circulaires d'origine médiévale en Normandie', *Château-Gaillard*, i (1962).

17 B.K. Roberts, 'Moats and Mottes', *Medieval Archaeology*, viii (1964); H.E. and J. Le Patourel, *Moated sites of Yorkshire* (Soc. Med. Arch., Monograph 5, 1973).

18 *Topographia Hibernica*, in *Geraldi Cambrensis Opera* (Rolls Series) v (1867)ed. J.F. Dimock, p. 183.

19 For what follows, see R. Allen Brown, *Origins of English Feudalism* (London, 1973), pp. 21ff .

20 R.W. Southern, *The Making of the Middle Ages* (London, 1953), p. 82.

21 *M.G.H. Capitularies*, ed. Krause, t. ii, p. 328, l.20 *et seq.*

22 Michel de Boüard, 'De l'aula au donjon. Les fouilles de la motte de La Chapelle à Doué-la-Fontaine (x^e–xie siecle)', *Archéologie Médiévale*, iii–iv (1973–4).

23 See below, pp. 135, 148.

24 For the quotation and what follows, see R.W. Southern, *op. cit.*, pp. 84ff, on the formation of the county of Anjou. For the castles see also Marcel Deyres, 'Les châteaux de Fulk Nerra', *Bulletin Monumental*, t.132 (1974).

25 For what follows see especially J. Yver, 'Les châteaux-forts en Normandie jusqu'au milieu de xiie siècle' . . ., *Bulletin Soc. des Antiquaires de Normandie*, liii (1955–6). For the great tower at Rouen see also Brown, *Château-Gaillard*, iii (1966), 13.

26 Michel Fixot, 'Les fortifications de terre et la naissance de la féodalité dans le Cinglais', *Château-Gaillard*, iii.

27 E. Zadora-Rio, 'L'enceinte fortifié du Plessis-Grimoult, résidence seigneuriale du xie siecle', *Château-Gaillard*, v (1970).

28 William of Jumièges, *Gesta Normannorum Ducum*, ed. J. Marx (Rouen and Paris, 1914), pp. 115–16, 123; *Cf.* William of Poitiers, *Histoire de Guillaume le Conquérant.* ed. R. Foreville (Paris, 1962), pp. 14–20.

29 *Gesta Regis Henrici Secundi*, ed. W. Stubbs (Rolls Series, 1867), i, 48–9.

30 *Op. cit.*, p. 78, n. i.

31 *Château-Gaillard* v, and above.

32 B.K. Davison, 'A survey of the castle of Arques-la-Bataille, Seine-Maritime', *Journal*

British Archaeological Association, (3), xxxvi (1973).

33 See e.g. B.K. Davison, 'Normandy Field Survey, 1969', *Archaeological Journal*, cxxvi (1969).

34 Deyres, *op. cit.*, pp. 8–9.

35 *Histoire de Guillaume le Conquérant, ut supra*, p. 18.

36 *The Ecclesiastical History of Orderic Vitalis*, ed. M. Chibnall, iv, 290.

37 Jordan Fantosme, *Chronique de la guerre entre les Anglois et les Ecossois*, in *Chronicles . . . of Stephen, Henry II and Richard I*, ed. R. Howlett (Rolls Series), iii (1886), p. 227.

38 *Recueil d'Annales angevines et vendomoises*, in V. Mortet, *Recueil des textes relatifs à l'histoire de l'architecture . . . en France* (Paris), i (1911), 78.

39 *Chronique de Lambert d'Ardres*, in Mortet, *Op. Cit.*, p. 182.

40 For Abinger see especially B. Hope-Taylor in *Arch. Journ.*, cvii (1950); also in *Recent Archaeological Excavations in Britain*, ed. R.L.S. Bruce-Mitford (London, 1956).

41 Armitage, *op. cit.*, p. 148, citing and translating Laurence the prior of Durham.

42 *Medieval Archaeology*, iii, 333.

43 No proper report on the excavations at South Mimms has so far been published: see meanwhile J.P.C. Kent in *Barnet and District Local History Society Bulletin*, No. 15, November 1968. For Farnham see M.W. Thompson, 'Recent excavations in the keep at Farnham castle, Surrey', *Medieval Archaeology*, iv (1960). See also M.W. Thompson, 'Motte Substructures', *Ibid.*, v (1961), 305–6.

44 *Archaeological Journal*, cvii, 42; *Château-Gaillard*, iv, 219; S.E. Rigold in *Transactions Devonshire Association*, lxxxvi (1954); D.F. Renn, *Norman Castles in Britain* (1968), p. 276.

45 *Antiquaries Journal*, xxxix (1959), 219.

46 *Medieval Archaeology*, iv (1960), 56.

47 *Medieval Archaeology*, iii (1959), 307.

48 T.C.M. and A. Brewster, 'Tote Copse Castle, Aldingbourne', *Sussex Archaeological Collections*, cvii (1969).

49 M. de Boüard, *op. cit.*, p. 93.

50 *Roman de Rou*, ed. H. Andresen (Heilbronn, 1879), ii, 178.

51 P. Siguret, 'Trois mottes de Bellême (Orne)' in *Château-Gaillard*, i, 135 and *n*.

52 See *The Bayeux Tapestry*, ed. F.M. Stenton, 2nd edition (London, 1965), and p. 81.

53 Above and *n.* 41. Translation from Mrs Armitage, *op. cit.*, p. 148 who suggests the defensive hourdes or hoarding for her galleries. But *cf.* also Dol as shown in Scene 23 of the Bayeux Tapestry, ed. F.M. Stenton.

54 *Miracula Sancti Benedicti*, L–VIII, *c.*xvi, in Mortet, *Recueil des textes*, i, 10.

55 Mortet, *op. cit.*, i, 183–5: translation (with some alterations) from Mrs Armitage, *op. cit.*, pp. 89–90.

56 See A. Herrnbrodt in *Château-Gaillard*, i; the English review of Hermbrodt's *Der Husterknupp . . .* (Cologne: Böhlau, 1958) in *Medieval Archaeology* iii (1959), 332–4; B.K. Davison in *Château-Gaillard*, iii, 42. *Cf.* W. Anderson, *Castles of Europe* (London, 1970), p. 41.

57 B.K. Davison, 'Early earthwork castles: a new model', *Château-Gaillard*, iii, 45–6.

58 Below.

59 See M. de Boüard in *Château-Gaillard*, ii (1964), pp. 25–6; A.J. Taylor, 'Three early castle sites in Sicily . . .', *Ibid.*, vii (1974).

60 Above.

61 Mortet, *Receuil des textes*, i, 78, 182 and above.

62 M. Deyres, *Bulletin Monumental*, t.132, above.

63 De Boüard, 'Quelques données françaises et normandes concernant le probleme de l'origine des mottes', *Château-Gaillard*, ii.

64 *Château-Gaillard*, iii, above.

65 Above, p. 11.

66 Below, p. 41.

67 On the whole the instance seems at least as clear as Mrs Armitage thought it (*op. cit.*, pp. 72–3) although the edition of the source she used was evidently inaccurate and the date is *c.*1030 rather than 1010. Count Fulk and his son planned a castle (*castellum*) on the western side of the hill Mont-Glonne but were dissuaded from going on with it by the monks. Instead they fortified the cemetery of the church (presumably with bank and ditch) and also raised (*erexerunt*), in sight of the monastery, *aggerem . . . cum curte lignea* (where the text reads *curte* and not *turre* as Mrs Armitage was led to believe). This sounds like a motte and bailey (we are told that the monks subsequently enclosed it with masonry), and that the *agger* was in fact a motte seems confirmed by a later charter of 1061 which refers back to Fulk and Geoffrey as having built *castellum terraeque cumulo ac ligniis magnae altitudinis asilium circa monasterium* (L. Halphen, *Le comte d'Anjou au xie siècle* (Paris, 1906), pp. 52, 155; *Historia Sancti Florentii Salmurensis*, in *Chroniques des églises d'Anjou* (ed. P. Marchegay and E. Mabille, *Soc. de*

l'histoire de France, Paris, 1869), p. 282; *Bibl. de l'Ecole des Chartes*, t.xxxvi (1875), p. 396). See also O. Guillot, *Le Comte d'Anjou et son entourage au xi siècle* (Paris, 1972), i, 230, n. 133.

Chapter II

1 The substance of this chapter is largely taken from three previous publications by the present writer – in chronological order, 'The Norman Conquest and the genesis of English castles', *Château-Gaillard* iii; 'An historian's approach to the origins of the castle in England', *Arch. Journ.*, cxxxvi (1969); and *The Origins of English Feudalism* (London, 1973).

2 Ordericus Vitalis, *The Ecclesiastical History*, ed. M. Chibnall (Oxford, 1969), ii, 218.

3 Thus Maitland, who himself saw feudalism in pre-Conquest England, was constrained to write in 1897: 'There are indeed historians who have not yet abandoned the habit of speaking of feudalism as though it were a disease of the body politic', yet, he concludes, in the sequence of historical development, 'feudalism means civilization'. For the whole passage, see F.W. Maitland, *Domesday Book and Beyond* (London, 1960), pp. 267–8. *Cf.* the quite extraordinary attitude and remarks of E.A. Freeman for whom the unhappy events of 1066 were 'only a temporary overthrow', by which England was to gain in the event 'not so much by anything which our Norman conquerors brought with them, as through our own stores which it was an indirect result of the Conquest to preserve to us', so that 'in a few generations England was England once again, and the descendants of the Norman invaders were found to be among the truest of Englishmen'. Freeman, who could scarcely bear to think of the patriotic defeat of true-born Englishmen in 1066, very nearly succeeds in making the Norman Conquest a non-event. See *The Norman Conquest*, i (2nd edition, Oxford, 1870), p. 2; v (Oxford, 1876), pp. 334, 709, 726–32 – and, indeed, passim. See also Brown, *The Normans and the Norman Conquest* (London, 1969), pp. 1–7.

4 The most useful general survey of English boroughs is by C.A. Ralegh Radford, 'The later pre-Conquest boroughs and their defences', *Medieval Archaeology*, xiv (1970). See also N. Brooks, 'The unidentified forts of the Burghal Hidage', *Ibid.*, viii (1964).

5 F.M. Stenton, *Anglo-Saxon England* (2nd ed., Oxford, 1947), p. 288.

6 A.J. Robertson, *Anglo-Saxon Charters* (1939), p. 246.

7 *Op. cit*, p. 11.

8 Above, p. 11.

9 See below and for the events, Brown, *The Normans and the Norman Conquest*, pp. 119ff.

10 *Anglo-Saxon Chronicle*, ed. D. Whitelock (London, 1961), p. 119; for the vernacular, see C. Plummer, *Two of the Saxon Chronicles Parallel* (Oxford, 1892–9), i, 173–4. The identification of this castle is uncertain: for the four or more alien castles in Herefordshire at this time, see below.

11 *Ibid.*, p. 125. In each case 'castele' in Plummer, *op. cit.*, pp. 180–1.

12 By J.H. Round in *Feudal England* (London, 1895), p. 324 and *Victoria County Histories*, Essex, i, 345.

13 *Chronicon ex Chronicis*, ed. B. Thorpe (English Historical Society, London, 1848–9), i, 209.

14 *Ibid.*, and Brown, *Normans and the Norman Conquest*, pp. 116–17.

15 Brown as above. *Pace* Stenton, *Anglo-Saxon England*, p. 554, n. 1, Hereford is not mentioned in the Anglo-Saxon Chronicle for 1055, when the 'C' version reads 'And earl Harold made a ditch about the *town* ('port') during that time' (ed. Whitelock, p. 131. *Cf.* Plummer, i, 186).

16 William of Poitiers, *Histoire de Guillaume le Conquérant*, ed. R. Foreville (Paris, 1962), pp. 102–4. *Cf.* the later writer Eadmer, *Historia Novorum in Anglia*, ed. M. Rule (Rolls Series, London, 1884), pp. 7, 8.

17 Ed. Whitelock, pp. 117–18.

18 Not, that is to say, somewhere in Herefordshire as has often been maintained (thus Plummer, *op. cit.*, ii, 237, and *cf.* Stenton, *Anglo-Saxon England*, p. 555.

19 Ed. Thorpe, i, 205–6.

20 *Histoire de Guillaume le Conquérant*, pp. 210–12 (*castellum, castrum*). *Cf. The Carmen de Hastingae Proelio*, ed. C. Morton and H. Munz (Oxford Medieval Texts, 1972), p. 38 (*castrum*).

21 It was, of course, offered first by Mrs Armitage, *op. cit.*, pp. 139 *et seq.*

22 For Dover as an Iron Age fortress, see H.M. Colvin in *Antiquity*, xxxiii (1959). *Cf.* Mrs Armitage, p. 144.

23 For Pevensey and Hastings, see A.J. Taylor, 'Evidence for a pre-Conquest origin for the chapels in Hastings and Pevensey castles', in *Château-Gaillard*, iii (1966), and *cf.* below, p. 31.

24 *Cf.* above, p. 22.
25 Ed. Whitelock, p. 118; Plummer, *op. cit.*, i, 173.
26 Ed. Whitelock, p. 118: Plummer, i, 173.
27 'Precepit Angligenis euacuare domos', *Carmen de Hastingae Proelio*, p. 38.
28 Martin Biddle in *Medieval Archaeology*, vi and vii (1962–3), 322; viii (1964), 254–5.
29 *Cf.* Mrs Armitage, *op. cit.*, p. 25. See also p. 8 above.
30 For the important study of feudal terminology, see K.J. Hollyman, *Le développement du vocabulaire féodal en France pendant le haut moyen âge* (Paris and Geneva, 1957). This work unfortunately omits *castrum* and *castellum*, and no such work at all has yet been undertaken for England.
31 See B.K. Davison, 'The Origins of the Castle in England', *Arch Journ*, cxxiv (1967), 204.
32 F. Liebermann, *Die Gesetze der Angelsachsen* (Halle, 1903–06), i, 456; translation in *English Historical Documents*, i, ed. D. Whitelock (London, 1955), p. 432. It is to be noted, however, that in the latter edition the words *burh-geat* are translated without comment as 'castle-gate'.
33 'Church and kitchen' omitted in some versions.
34 See L. Alcock, 'Castle Tower, Penmaen: a Norman Ring-work in Glamorgan', *Antiquaries Journal*, xlvi (1966).
35 F.W. Maitland, *Domesday Book and Beyond* (Fontana, 1960), p. 232 *n.*3. *Cf.* the pre-Conquest legal text. 'Thus far shall the king's peace extend from his *burh-geat* where he is sitting...' (*Ibid.*, p. 226; Liebermann, *op. cit.*, i, 390).
36 A.H. Smith, *English Place-Name Elements*, Part 1 (English Place Name Society, vol. xxv, 1956), pp. 58ff.
37 *New English Dictionary*. *Cf.* Mrs Armitage, *op. cit.*, p. 17.
38 Ine, cap. 45, in F.L. Attenborough, *Laws of the Earliest English Kings* (Cambridge, 1922), pp. 50, 51.
39 Cap. 40, in Attenborough, *op. cit.*, pp. 48, 49.
40 Cap. 40, Attenborough, pp. 82, 83.
41 *Rural Economy and Country Life in the Medieval West* (London, 1968), p. 7.
42 *Ibid.*, p.35.
43 *Ibid.*, pp. 35, 364.
44 For interim reports and comment, see B.K. Davison in *Medieval Archaeology*, v, 328; vi–vii, 333; viii, 237; xiii, 236; *Current Archaeology*, ii, 19–22; *Château-Gaillard*, ii,

45–6; *Arch. Journ.*, cxxiv, 208–9, and cxxv, 305.
45 Thus the Norman *Consuetudines et Justicie* (cap. 4) of 1091, relating the custom and rights of the duke in the Conqueror's day (printed by C.H. Haskins, *Norman Institutions*, New York, 1918, p. 282).
46 F.M. Stenton, *The First Century of English Feudalism* (Oxford, 1932) p. 197. *Cf.* p. 162 below.
47 William of Jumièges, ed. Marx, p. 134; William of Poitiers, ed. Foreville, p. 168; *Anglo-Saxon Chronicles*, ed. Whitelock, p. 143; *Bayeux Tapestry*, ed. F.M. Stenton, Pl. 51.
48 William of Poitiers, pp. 218, 236.
49 See F.M. Stenton, *Norman London* (London, Historical Association, 1938) and, for the tower of London, B.K. Davison, 'Three eleventh-century earthworks in England: their excavation and implications', *Château-Gaillard*, ii.
50 Brown, *Normans and the Norman Conquest*, pp. 185–7, and, for the debatable identification of the 'Guenta' of William of Poitiers as Norwich, note 221.
51 Ed. Foreville, pp. 236–8.
52 Ed. Whitelock, p. 145.
53 For what follows, see Brown, *Normans*, pp. 190ff. and the references there given.
54 *Anglo-Saxon Chronicle*, p. 148.
55 It is at this point in Orderic's narrative that there occurs his well-known comment on the rarity of castles in pre-Conquest England with which this chapter began.
56 Ed. Chibnall, ii, 218.
57 Ed. Whitelock, p. 156.
58 *Domesday Book*, i 336d; ii, 116.
59 *Regesta Regum Anglo-Normannorum*, i (Oxford, 1913), ed. H.W.C. Davis, No. 78.
60 Ed. Whitelock, p. 164.
61 William of Malmesbury, *De Gestis Pontificum Anglorum*, ed. N.E.S.A. Hamilton (Rolls Series, London, 1870), p. 253.
62 Above, p. 15.

Chapter III
1 For the history of the castle in Scotland, see *The Scottish Castle* by Stewart Cruden (Nelson, 1960). For the origin of castles in Scotland see also G.W.S. Barrow, 'The beginnings of feudalism in Scotland', *Bulletin Institute of Historical Research*, xxix (1956), and G. Simpson and B. Webster, 'Charter evidence and the distribution of mottes in Scotland', *Château-Gaillard*, v.
2 See D.J.C. King and Leslie Alcock, 'Ringworks of England and Wales',

Château-Gaillard, iii, and D.J.C. King, 'The field archaeology of mottes in England and Wales', *Ibid.*, v, 102. Since the authors evidently include among their 'ringworks' the even more ambiguous 'ring-mottes' (as they are elsewhere called), i.e. the smaller, inner enclosure of a castle with a larger, outer bailey, the number of simple enclosures is by that much reduced. The overlap, so to speak,between the 'ringwork' and the bailey of a castle, it may be added, is one more instance of the impossible impracticability of the term.

3 See B.K. Davison *Procs. Somerset Arch. Soc.*, cxvi (1972); *cf.* p. 19 above. The questions may be raised whether or at what stage Castle Neroche was ranked as a castle by contemporaries, for we have no written references to it.

4 B.K. Davison, *Medieval Archaeology*, xiii (1969), p. 258.

5 The point is worth emphasizing because often denied. See Brown, 'The Architecture' in *The Bayeux Tapestry*, ed. F.M. Stenton (2nd edition, London, 1965), pp. 76ff. For Hastings on the Tapestry, *see Ibid.*, Pl. 51.

6 For Hastings see P.A. Barker and K.J. Barton, 'Excavations at Hastings castle, 1968', *Arch. Journ.*, cxxv (1968), p. 303; A.J. Taylor in *Château-Gaillard*, iii, 144ff. For Richard's Castle, see P.E. Curnow and M.W. Thompson, 'Excavations at Richard's Castle, Herefordshire, 1962–4', *Journal British Arch. Assoc.*, (3) xxxii (1969). Ewyas Harold has not been archaeologically investigated.

7 Recent excavations at the Baile Hill at York, which may be the older of the two castles of the Conqueror raised in 1068 and 1069 respectively, suggest that the motte is an original feature, nor is there any evidence that the motte beneath the present Clifford's Tower of York castle is not original. See P.V. Addyman, *Arch. Journ.*, cxxv (1968), pp. 307–8 and cxxvi, 178–9; *Château-Gaillard*, v. *Cf.* Mrs Armitage, *op. cit.*, pp. 242ff.

8 S.E. Rigold, *Château-Gaillard*, iii, 128ff.

9 P.A. Barker, *Ibid.*, p. 27.

10 Above, p. 19.

11 For occasional examples of thirteenth century mottes in Wales, see King, *Château-Gaillard*, v, 108.

12 Above, p. 15.

13 *Château-Gaillard*, v, 101ff.

14 P.A. Barker, *Château-Gaillard*, iii, 27.

15 The early twelfth-century legal compilation called the *Leges Henrici Primi* lists the *castellum trium scannorum* amongst 'the rights which the king of England alone and above all men has in his land', and it has been suggested that the castle of the text is one with three banks and thus a double ditch (see Liebermann, *Die Gesetze der Angelsachsen*, i, 556; Stubbs, *Select Charters*, p. 125; *History of the King's Works*, i, 33–4).

16 *Arch. Journ.*, cvii (1950).

17 Ed. Stenton, Pls. 23–4, 26, 28, 51.

18 Above, p. 16.

19 With reference to Le Puiset castle in Suger's early twelfth-century *Life of Louis VI the Fat*; (ed. H. Waquet), p. 140; cited in Mortet, *Receuil des textes* .... i, 337, *n*. 2. *Cf.* p. 124 below.

20 Above, p. 15.

21 Above, p. 16. For the revetting see the references there given.

22 Above, p. 16 and references. The motte at Farnham is now revetted in stone but this is thought to be a later phase after the demolition of the tower: *Château-Gaillard*, ii, 103).

23 Below, p. 124.

24 Above, p. 15.

25 Above, p. 18.

26 From the Vita *Johannis episcopi Teruanensis* by Walter the archdeacon, in *Mon. Germ. histor.*, Script., xv, part 11 (1888), pp. 1146–7, and in Mortet *Receuil des Textes* ... , 1, 312–15. *Cf.* Mrs Armitage, pp. 88–9. Merchem, identified by Mortet as Merckem near Dixmude in Belgium, has also been identified as Merckerghem near Dunkirk. A certain clerical prejudice should, of course, be allowed for in the author's comments on the nobles of the district.

27 This phrase translates literally 'looking down upon or despising all things' (*omnia despiciat*) and is evidently meant to apply to the keep (*arx*).

28 Pl. 24. *Cf.* 23, 25, 28.

29 *Arch. Journ.*, cvii, 33.

30 *Château-Gaillard*, v, p. 9.

31 *Cf.* the timber gate tower at the 'ringwork' of Penmaen, *Antiquaries Journal*, xlvi (1966), reconstruction p. 186. A very early stone gate tower of *c.*1068 survives at Exeter castle (p. 42 below).

32 *Arch. Journ.*, cxxv, 303.

33 *Ibid.*

34 *Château-Gaillard*, iii, 20.

35 Above, p. 31. *Pevensey Castle* (Official Guide, H.M.S.O.). *Cf.* A.J. Taylor in *Château-Gaillard*, iii, 150–1. For the

suggestion that the ditch and bank of the Conqueror's castle ran right across the borough to the Roman north wall, see D.F. Renn in *Sussex Archaeological Collections*, cix, 55.

36 Above, p. 31. B.K. Davison in *Château-Gaillard*, ii, and Plan, p. 41.

37 *Dover Castle* (Official Guide, H.M.S.O., 2nd edition, 1974). *Cf.* p. 27 above.

38 *Old Sarum* (Official Guide, H.M.S.O.).

39 Above.

40 L. Alcock, 'Castle Tower, Penmaen: a Norman ring-work in Glamorgan', *Antiquaries Journal*, xlvi (1966).

41 *Rochester Castle* (Official Guide, H.M.S.O.). It is thought that the first Rochester castle, raised soon after 1066, was of the motte-and-bailey type and stood south of the present one on the site known as Boley Hill, just outside the line of the Roman city wall.

42 See *Framlingham Castle* (Official Guide, H.M.S.O.); D.F. Renn in *Proceedings of the Suffolk Institute of Archaeology*, xxxiii (1973).

43 Above, p. 26.

44 *History of the King's Works*, i, 29. For the Tower, see *Ibid.* and (the most detailed description), Royal Commission on Historical Monuments (England), *London*, vol. v (H.M.S.O., 1930).

45 M. de Boüard, *Archéologie Médiévale*, iii–iv, 81–2. *Cf.* p. 9 above.

46 Above and Brown in *The Bayeux Tapestry*, ed. F.M. Stenton (1965 ed.), p.81.

47 *Chepstow Castle* (Official Guide, H.M.S.O.).

48 Above, p. 8.

49 Below, p. 46.

50 See e.g. D.F. Renn, *Journal British Arch. Assoc.* (3), xxiii (1960), p. 11.

51 *Ex in form.* P.A. Faulkner.

52 *See Pevensey Castle* (Official Guide, H.M.S.O.) and D.F. Renn in *Sussex Archaeological Collections*, cix.

53 See especially *Rochester Castle* (Official Guide, H.M.S.O.).

54 Royal Commission on Historical Monuments (England), *Essex*, i (1916), pp. 53–6.

55 See *Castle Rising* (Official Guide, H.M.S.O.).

56 *Kenilworth Castle* (Official Guide, H.M.S.O.) and Brown in *Arch. Journ.*, cx.

57 *History of the King's Works*, i, 39–40; Royal Commission on Historical Monuments, *Dorset*, ii, *South East*, Part I (1970), pp. 71ff.

58 *History of the King's Works*, ii, 852; D.F. Renn in *Medieval Archaeology*, iv (1960).

59 *History of the King's Works*, i, 37.

60 *Ibid.*, ii, 578.

61 *Ibid.*, ii, 595–6.

62 *Ibid.*, i, 73.

63 Official Guide, H.M.S.O.

64 *Peveril Castle* (Official Guide, H.M.S.O., 1950 edition).

65 *Richmond Castle* (Official Guide, H.M.S.O.). For Ludlow, see especially W.H. St. John Hope in *Archaeologia*, lxi (Pt. I), pp. 304ff.

66 H. Braun, 'Some notes on Bungay Castle.' *Procs. Suffolk Institute of Archaeology*, xxii (1936).

67 *Norham Castle* (Official Guide, H.M.S.O.).

68 *Middleham Castle* (Official Guide, H.M.S.O.).

69 See André Chatelain, *Donjons romans des pays d'ouest* (Paris, 1973), and in *Château-Gaillard*, vi.

70 Below, p. 140.

71 It is possible that at Castle Rising there is the first surviving example of the architectural arrangement of 'Ladies' and 'Gentlemen' since of the pair of garderobes opening off the great chamber in the west wall one only has a urinal in the passage leading to it.

72 For many of the keeps and dates cited in this paragraph see P. Héliot, 'L'évolution du donjon dans la nord-ouest de la France et en Angleterre au xii siècle', *Bulletin Archéologique*, N.S. 5 (1969). The same author's most recent study, 'Les origins du donjon residentiel et les donjons-palais romans de France et d'Angleterre', *Cahiers de Civilisation Médiévale*, 1974, came to hand too late to be incorporated in the present book.

73 Houdan was a castle of the count of Dreux: Etampes was royal.

74 *Orford Castle* (Official Guide, H.M.S.O.).

75 *Conisborough Castle* (Official Guide, H.M.S.O.).

76 The rectangular form (so to speak) of the tower *en bec* is occasionally found in donjons, as, for example, at Prény in Lorraine, and *cf.* the triangular Beaucaire, of uncertain date, in Languedoc.

77 Below, p. 162.

78 *Rotuli de Liberate ac de Misis et Prestitis* ....ed. T.D. Hardy (Record Commission, 1844) p. 93.

79 *Rotuli Litterarum Clausarum*, ed. T.D. Hardy, i (Record Commission, 1833), p. 17.

80 A.J. Taylor, 'The date of Clifford's Tower, York', *Arch. Journ.*, cxi (1955).

81 *History of the King's Works*, i, 420.
82 The famous passage occurs in the Anglo-Saxon or 'Peterborough' Chronicle under the year 1137 (ed. Whltelock, pp. 198–200).
83 In *Chronicles of the Reigns of Stephen, Henry II and Richard I*, Rolls Series, ed. R. Howlett, iv (1889) p. 177.
84 See F.M. Stenton, *First Century of English Feudalism* (Oxford, 1932), p. 201, quoting the *Gesta Stephani* (Medieval Texts, London, 1955, ed. K.R. Potter, p. 92).
85 Listed and discussed by D.F. Renn, *Norman Castles in Britain*, pp. 46–52.
86 I am much indebted to Philip Mayes of Leeds University, the director of the still continuing excavations, for information about this important site.
87 S.E. Rigold, 'The earliest defences of Carisbrooke Castle', *Château-Gaillard*, iii.
88 For Windsor, see W. St. John Hope, *Windsor Castle, i*, 65 and below; for Builth, *History of the King's Works*, i, 296; for Pickering, M.W. Thompson, *Pickering Castle* (Official Guide, H.M.S.O.), p. 16.
89 *History of the King's Works*, ii, 561.
90 Below, p. 155.
91 Below, p. 94.
92 For Dover see R. Allen Brown, *Dover Castle* (Official Guide, H.M.S.O.); D.F. Renn, The Avranches traverse at Dover Castle', *Archaeologia Cantiana*, lxxxiv (1969). *Cf.* below, p. 83.
93 A recent study of Château-Gaillard will be found in *Château-Gaillard*, i, by P. Héliot, whose notes give references to most earlier work.

Chapter IV
 1 For Beeston, Cheshire, see especially M.H. Ridgway and D.J.C. King in *Journal Chester Arch. Soc.*, xlvi (1959); for Bolingbroke, M.W. Thompson in *Medieval Archaeology*, x (1966).
 2 C.A. Ralegh Radford, *Goodrich Castle, Herefordshire* (Official Guide, H.M.S.O., 1958); P.A. Faulkner, 'Castle Planning in the Fourteenth Century', *Arch. Journ.*, cxx (1963), p. 221ff.
 3 C.A. Ralegh Radford, *White Castle, Monmouthshire* (Official Guide, H.M.S.O., 1946); *cf.* A.J. Taylor, 'White Castle in the Thirteenth Century: a reconsideration', *Medieval Archaeology*, v (1961).
 4 *History of the King's Works*, ii, 644–5; E.W. Cox, 'Diserth Castle', *Journal Chester Arch. Soc.*, N.S. v (1895).
 5 *Dover* Castle (Official Guide, H.M.S.O.), p. 14, and *cf.* p. 83 below.

 6 D.F. Renn, 'An Angevin gatehouse at Skipton Castle', *Château-Gaillard*, vii (1974).
 7 *History of the King's Works*, ii, 720–1. *Cf.* J.H. Harvey, 'The western entrance to the Tower', *Transactions London and Middx. Arch. Soc.*, N.S. ix, pt. 1 (1944).
 8 Below, pp. 113ff.
 9 See especially A.J. Taylor, *Caernarvon Castle* (Official Guide, H.M.S.O., 1953), and in *History of the King's Works*, i, 369ff.
10 Official Guide, p. 23.
11 Hence e.g. the absence of banded masonry and mural galleries along the north front towards the town.
12 *Flores Historiarum*, ed. H.R. Luard (Rolls Series, 1890), iii, 59.
13 *The Mabinogion*, ed. T.P. Ellis and John Lloyd (Oxford, 1929), i, 133–50.
14 Thus A.J. Taylor, *History of the King's Works*, i, 370. The appreciation of the significance of Caernarvon is entirely the result of Dr Taylor's researches.
15 See A.J. Taylor, *Conway Castle and Town Walls* (Official Guide, H.M.S.O., 1956) and in *History of the King's Works*, i, 337ff.
16 Harlech Castle (Official Guide, H.M.S.O., 1964); A.J. Taylor in *History of the King's Works*, i, 357ff.
17 *Beaumaris Castle* (Official Guide, H.M.S.O., 1943); A.J. Taylor in *History of the King's Works*, i, 395ff.
18 A.J. Taylor, *Rhuddlan Castle* (Official Guide, H.M.S.O., 1955) and in *History of the King's Works*, i, 318ff.
19 *Rhuddlan Castle*, p. 17.
20 *Flint Castle* (Official Guide, H.M.S.O., 1946); A.J. Taylor in *History of the King's Works*, i, 308ff.
21 C.A. Ralegh Radford, *Kidwelly Castle* (Official Guide, H.M.S.O., 1952). *Cf. History of the King's Works*, ii, 685–7.
22 William Rees, *Caerphilly Castle: a history and description* (Cardiff, 1937), written for the Marquis of Bute who rescued and restored the castle before the last war. The Official Guide (H.M.S.O., 1958) is largely based upon this.
23 *Cf.* p. 42 above. For what follows, see B.K. Davison in *Château-Gaillard*, ii (1964), pp. 40–3; *History of the King's Works*, ii, 707ff.
24 See R.A. Brown, *Dover Castle* (Official Guide, H.M.S.O., 1974).
25 See Royal Commission on Historic Monuments, *Dorset*, ii, *South-east*, Pt. I (1970) pp 57ff; *History of the King's Works*, ii, 616ff.

26 J.C. Perks, *Chepstow Castle* (Official Guide, H.M.S.O., 1955).

27 *History of the King's Works*, i, 115–16. For York, see also A.J. Taylor. 'The date of Clifford's Tower, York', *Arch. Journ.*, cxi (1955), and for Castle Cornet, J. and J. Le Patourel, 'Castle Cornet: excavations, 1953' in *Société Guernesiase Reports and Transactions*, xv (1955).

28 *History of the King's Works*, i, 296.

29 *Ibid.*, ii, 585–6.

30 *Ibid.*, ii, 782.

31 M.W. Thompson, *Pickering Castle* (Official Guide, H.M.S.O., 1958).

32 Quoted by Stewart Cruden, *The Scottish Castle*, p. 224.

33 See P.A. Faulkner in *Arch. Journ.*, cxv (1958), pp. 154, 156.

34 J.F.A. Mason, *Stokesay Castle*.

35 C.A. Ralegh Radford, 'Acton Burnell Castle', in *Studies in Building History*, ed. E.M. Jope (1961).

36 *Ibid.*, p. 96.

Chapter V

1 See especially *History of the King's Works*, ii, 895ff, 'The King's Houses'.

2 For which sec B.H. St. J. O'Neil, *Castles and Cannon* (1960).

3 *Cf.* Lumley, Co. Durham, and see S. Toy, *Castles of Great Britain* (1953), p. 220.

4 See specially C.J. Bates, *Border Holds of Northumberland* (1891), i, 57ff.

5 A.J. Taylor, *Raglan Castle* (Official Guide, H.M.S.O., 1950).

6 See *History of the King's Works*, ii, 793ff.

7 *Ibid.*, p. 793.

8 William Anderson, *Castles of Europe* (1970), p. 177.

9 S.E. Rigold, *Nunney Castle* (Official Guide, H.M.S.O., 1956).

10 See, e.g. W. Douglas Simpson, ' "Bastard Feudalism" and the later castles', *Antiquaries Journal*, xxvi (1946), and many other places.

11 Above, pp. 85–6.

12 *History of the King's Works*, ii, 689–90. The tower, whose ruins remain, is described, with plans and sections, by G.T. Clark, *Medieval Military Architecture* (1884), ii, 171ff.

13 *History of the King's Works*, ii, 842–3; *The Itinerary of John Leland*, ed. L. Toulmin Smith (London, 1964), i, 277.

14 C.H. Hunter Blair and H.L. Honeyman, *Warkworth Castle* (Official Guide, H.M.S.O., 1954).

15 See especially M.W. Thompson, *Tattershall Castle* (National Trust, 1974).

16 H.D. Barnes and W. Douglas Simpson, 'Caister Castle', *Antiquaries Journal*, xxxii (1952).

17 T.L. Jones, *Ashby-de-la-Zouche Castle* (Official Guide, H.M.S.O., 1953).

18 At Tattershall, for example, in the building accounts – *in magna turre vocata le Dongeon*, 'in the great tower called the Dongeon' (*The Building Accounts of Tattershall Castle*, ed. W. Douglas Simpson, Lincs. Record Soc., 55, 1960, p. 36). For Dunstanburgh and Knaresborough see *History of the King's Works*, ii, 642, 691.

19 Quoted by R. Fawtier, *The Capetian Kings of France*, p. 17, from Suger, *Vie de Louis VI le Gros*, ed. and trans. H. Waquet (Paris, 1929), p. 38.

20 Quoted in *The History of the King's Works*, ii, 690.

21 *Op. cit.*, p. 16.

22 See the plan of the royal lodging in the upper bailey, in W. St. John Hope, *Windsor Castle* (1913), ii, 568.

23 For this, and what follows, see especially P.A. Faulkner, 'Castle Planning in the Fourteenth Century', *Arch. Journ.*, cxx (1963). *Cf.* p. 60 above.

24 For Sandal see Philip Mayes, 'Sandal Castle, Wakefield (Yorkshire)', forthcoming.

25 *History of the King's Works*, ii, 872ff.

26 Below, p. 120.

27 Ed. J.R. Lumby (Rolls Series), viii, 359.

28 See M.W. Thomson 'The date of "Foxe's Tower, Farnham Castle, Surrey', in *Surrey Archaeological Collections*, lvii (1960).

29 S.E. Rigold, *Baconsthorpe Castle* (Official Guide, H.M.S.O., 1966), p. 4.

30 D.J.C. King and J.C. Perks, 'Carew Castle, Pembrokeshire', *Arch. Journ.*, cxix (1964), p. 304.

Chapter VI

1 E.g. John Harvey, *English Mediaeval Architects, a Biographical Dictionary down to 1550* (London, 1954).

2 William of Poitiers, *Histoire de Guillaume le Conquérant*, ed. R. Foreville, p. 212; Orderic Vitalis, *Ecclesiastical History*, ed. M. Chibnall, ii (1969), p.222.

3 *Anglo-Saxon Chronicle*, ed. D. Whiteioek (London, 1965), pp. 164, 199.

4 See R. Allen Brown, 'Royal castle building in England, 1154–1216', *English Historical Review*, lxx (1955); *History of the King's Works*, i, 64ff.

5 S. Painter, *Studies in the history of the English feudal barony* (Baltimore, 1943), pp. 170–1.

6 See *Orford Castle* (Official Guide,

H.M.S.O.); *History of the King's Works*, ii, 769ff. *Cf.* above, p. 53.

7 See *Dover Castle* (Official Guide, H.M.S.O.); *History of the King's Works*, ii, 629ff. *Cf.* above, p. 61.

8 See F.M. Powicke, *The Loss of Normandy* (Manchester University Press, 1913), pp. 282ff., 303–5; T. Stapleton, *Magni Rotuli Scaccarii Normanniae*, ii (1844), p. 309.

9 For what follows, see especially *History of the King's Works*, i, 293ff.

10 *Ibid.*, i, 157.

11 *Ibid.*, i, 310.

12 *Ibid.*, i, 417.

13 H.D. Barnes and W. Douglas Simpson, 'The building accounts of Caister Castle, A.D. 1432–1435', *Norfolk Archaeology*, xxx (1952).

14 *The Building Accounts of Tattershall Castle, 1434–1472*, ed. W. Douglas Simpson (Lincoln Record Society 55, 1960).

15 A. Hamilton Thompson, 'The building accounts of Kirby Muxloe castle, 1480–1484', *Transactions Leicestershire Archaeological Society*, xi (1913–20). *Cf.* Sir Charles Peers, *Kirby Muxloe Castle* (Official Guide, H.M.S.O., 1957).

16 *History of the Kings Works*, ii, 872ff. For all things pertaining to Windsor see also the magnificent two volumes of W. St. John Hope, *Windsor Castle* (1913).

17 *Polychronicon*, ed. J.R. Lumby (Rolls Series), viii, 359.

Chapter VII

1 Suger, ed. and trans. H. Waquet, *Vie de Louis VI le Gros* (Paris, 1929), pp. 130; 136–40. A plan of the castle is given in William Anderson, *Castles of Europe*, p. 83. For the range of castles, see also p. 148 below.

2 *The Legend of Fulk fitz Warin*, printed in Ralph of Coggeshall, *Chronicon Anglicanum*, ed. J. Stevenson (Rolls Series, 1875), p. 315.

3 *in mota scilicet turre lignea superiori se recepit.* *Cf.* p. 38 above.

4 C. Appel, *Bertran de Born* (Halle, 1931), No. 40. Translation from Marc Bloch, *Feudal Society* (trans. L.A. Manyon), p. 293.

5 *Pipe Roll 6 Richard I* (Pipe Roll Society, New Series v), p. 175; *History of the King's Works*, i, 418.

6 *Ibid.*, and n. 6.

7 'The King, more curious than became him, did stand near the gunners when the artillery discharged; his thigh-bone was dung in two with the piece of a misformed gun that brake in shooting, by which he was stricken to the ground and died hastily'.

Thus Pitscottie: see Stuart Cruden, *The Scottish Castle*, p. 205.

8 *Ibid.*, p. 204.

9 *Ibid.*, p. 207.

10 *Itinerarium . . . Regis Ricardi*, ed. W. Stubbs (Rolls Series, 1864), p. 225.

11 R. Allen Brown, *The Normans and the Norman Conquest*, p. 191.

12 *Rotuli Litterarum Clausarum*, ed. T.D. Hardy (Record Commission, 1833), i, 238b.

13 Roger of Wendover, *Flores Historiarum*, ed. H.O. Coxe (London, Society of Antiquaries, 1842), iv, 96–7.

14 *Cf.* P.A. Faulkner, *Arch. Journ.*, cxx (1963), p. 235.

15 E.g. Walter of Coventry, ed. W. Stubbs (Rolls Series), ii (1873), p. 226; Roger of Wendover, *ut supra*, iii, 330.

16 *Ibid.*, ii, 380.

17 *Ibid.*, iii, 371.

18 *Pipe Roll 20 Henry II* (Pipe Roll Soc., xxi), pp. 37, 105.

19 *Pipe Roll 5 Richard I* (Pipe Roll Soc., New Series, iii), pp. 13, 165.

20 *Rotuli Litterarum Clausarum*, i, 254b.–255; *Rotuli Litterarum Patentium*, ed. T.D. Hardy (Record Commission, 1835), i, 171.

21 *Pipe Roll 22 Henry II* (Pipe Roll Soc. xxv), pp. 119–20.

22 *Itinerarium . . . Regis Ricardi*, ed. Stubbs, p. 217.

23 Walter of Coventry, ed. Stubbs, ii, 227.

24 *Pipe Roll 17 John* (Pipe Roll Soc., N.S. xxxvii), p. 56.

25 See further, R. Allen Brown, *Rochester Castle* (Official Guide, H.M.S.O.).

26 Walter of Coventry, ii, 227.

27 *Ibid.*

28 See further, R. Allen Brown, *Dover Castle* (Official Guide, H.M.S.O.).

29 See especially G.H. Fowler, in *Beds. Historical Record Soc.*, v, 117–32. See also *Victoria County History*, *Bedfordshire*, iii, 10.

30 Annals of Dunstable in *Annales Monastici*, ed. H.A. Luard (Rolls Series), iii (1866), p. 87.

31 *Chronicon Anglicanum*, ed. J. Stevenson (Rolls Series, 1875), p. 206.

32 For recent excavations on the site, see D. Baker in *Château-Gaillard*, vi.

33 *op. cit.*, pp. 87–8.

34 For the siege of Kenilworth there is no equivalent of Fowler's splendid article on Bedford. See V.C.H., *Warwickshire*, ii, 429–30.

35 Jordan Fantosme, *Chronique de la guerre entre les Anglois et les Ecossois*, in *Chronicles . . . of*

Stephen, Henry II and Richard I, iii, ed. R. Howlett (Rolls Series, 1886).

36 For the later Middle Ages, however, see M.H. Keen, *The Laws of War in the later Middle Ages* (1965), some of which, in the absence of anything comparable for the earlier period, can with due care be read back.

37 See Sir John Hackett in William Anderson, *Castles of Europe*, p. 13, and *cf.* the remark in Suger's *Life of Louis VI* about the range of Le Puiset cited above, p. 124.

38 *Gesta Regis Henrici Secundi*, ed. W. Stubbs (Rolls Series), i (1867), p. 68. The distance from Leicester to Northampton is thirty-two miles.

39 *Rotuli Litterarum Patentium*, i, 159b.

40 Wendover, ed. Coxe, iii, 349.

41 *Ibid.*, p. 379.

42 *Ibid.*, p. 381.

43 *Rotuli Litterarum Patentium*, i, 194b.

Chapter VIII

1 See especially P.A. Faulkner, 'Castle planning in the fourteenth century', *Arch. Journ.*, cxx.

2 Giraldus Cambrensis, *Itinerarium Kambriae*, in *Geraldi Cambrensis Opera* (*Rolls* Series), vi (ed. J.F. Dimock, 1868), p. 92; translation in *The Itinerary through Wales and the Description of Wales by Geraldus Cambrensis* (1908), pp. 84–5.

3 For what follows see W.H. St. John Hope, *Windsor Castle*, pp. 15ff., 568; *History of the King's Works*, ii, 865.

4 *Cf. History of the King's Works*, ii, 855–7.

5 *Ibid.*, p. 756.

6 *Ibid.*, p. 554 n. 3.

7 *Rot. Litt. Claus.* (Record Commission), i, 52b.

8 *King's Works*, ii, 617; Royal Commission on Historic Monuments, *Dorset*, vol. ii, *South East*, Pt. 1 (1970), pp. 74–7.

9 Printed in calendar form to 1272 in *Calendar of the Liberate Rolls preserved in the Public Record Office* (H.M.S.O., 1916–64), 6 vols.

10 *Cal. Liberate Rolls*, 1245–51, p. 325.

11 *King's Works*, ii, 858–9, 860.

12 *Ibid.*, p. 861.

13 Hope, *Windsor Castle*, pp. 31ff.; *King's Works*, ii, 866–9.

14 *Cal. Liberate Rolls, 1240–45*, p. 234; *Cf. King's Works*, ii, 730.

15 *Cal. Liberate Rolls, 1240–45*, p. 64; *Cf. King's Works*, ii, 736.

16 *King's Works*, ii, 854.

17 *King's Works*, ii, 837.

18 *Ibid.*, p. 827.

19 Hope, *Windsor Castle*, pp. 57, 69.

20 Above, p. 120; Hope, *Windsor Castle*, pp. 128ff.; *King's Words*, ii, 870ff.

21 R. Allen Brown, 'King Edward's Clocks', *Antiquaries Journal*, xxxix (1959). For the slightly later clock at Queenborough, see p. 95 above.

22 R. Allen Brown, *Dover Castle* (Official Guide, H.M.S.O.).

23 Quoted by A.J. Taylor, *Raglan Castle* (Official Guide, H.M.S.O.), p. 11.

24 *King's Works*, i, 338.

25 *Rot. Litt. Claus.*, i, 75.

26 Joinville's *Memoirs of St. Louis*, translated in *Chronicles of the Crusades* (London, Bohn, 1848), p. 382.

27 *Cal. Liberate Rolls, 1240–45*, p. 37.

28 *Kings Works*, ii, 756.

29 *Rot. Litt. Pat.*, i, 33b.

Chapter IX

1 See Table 11, pp. 124–5 to D.J.C. King and L. Alcock, 'Ringworks of England and Wales' (*Château-Gaillard*, iii, 1966) which gives overall and county totals of castle sites of all kinds now surviving in England and Wales.

2 R. Allen Brown, 'A List of Castles, 1154–1216', *English Historical Review*, lxxiv (1959).

3 Above, pp. 30–2.

4 R. Allen Brown, *Castle Rising* (Official Guide, H.M.S.O., forthcoming).

5 *Anglo-Saxon Chronicle*, ed. D. Whitelock and others, p. 199. *Cf.* pp. 11, 55 above.

6 Above, p. 55.

7 King and Alcock, *op. cit.*

8 Above, pp. 22–3.

9 F. Pollock and F.W. Maitland, *History of English Law* (1895), i, 243. *Cf.* Brown, *Origins of English Feudalism*, p. 59.

10 C. Coulson, 'Rendability and castellation in medieval France', in *Château-Gaillard*, vi. A comparable study of this subject for England and Wales is very badly needed.

11 For Buckenham, see Brown, *Castle Rising* (Official Guide, as above); for the movement of castle sites in general, see D.F. Renn, 'Mottes: a classification', *Antiquity*, xxxiii (1959).

12 M. Fixot, 'Les fortifications de terre et la naissance de la féodalité dans le Cinglais', *Châteaux-Gaillard*, iii. *Cf.* p. 10 above.

13 Brown, *Castle Rising* (forthcoming).

14 *Histoire des ducs de Normandie* .... ed. F. Michel (Soc. de l'histoire de France, Paris,

1840), p. 174; Wendover, *Flores Historiarum*,
ed. Coxe, iii, 371 .

15 William of Newburgh, in *Chronicles* of . . .
Stephen, Henry II and Richard I, ed. R.
Howlett (Rolls Series), i, 331.

16 See R. Allen Brown, 'Framlingham Castle
and Bigod', *Procs. Suffolk Institute of
Archaeology*, xxv (1951); *Orford Castle*
(Official Guide, H.M.S.O.). *Cf.* p. 110
above.

17 H. Braun, 'Some notes on Bungay castle',
Procs. Suffolk Institute of Archaeology, xxii
(1936).

18 *Brut y Tywysogion*, ed. T. Jones (Board of
Celtic Studies, 1952), p. 89.

Guide to Further Reading

Further Reading
For comprehensive bibliographies see J. R. Kenyon, *Castles, Town Defences, and Artillery Fortifications in Britain and Ireland: A Bibliography* Vol. *i* (London, 1978); *ii* (London, 1983); *iii* (London, 1990). The Castle Studies Group publishes annual bibliographies: details can be found at www.castlestudiesgroup.org.uk. For a detailed account of recent historiographical trends see C. Coulson, 'Cultural Realities and Reappraisals in English Castle-Study', *Journal of Medieval History* xxii (1996), pp. 171–207.

Gazetteer
King, D. J. C., *Castellarium Anglicanum* (New York, 1983)
Pettifer, A., *English Castles: a Guide by Counties* (Woodbridge, 1995).
———— *Welsh Castles: a Guide by Counties* (Woodbridge, 2000).

Historical Background
Bates, D., *Normandy Before 1066* (London, 1982).
Brown, R. A., *The Normans and the Norman Conquest* (Woodbridge, 1985).
Carpenter, D. A., *The Struggle for Mastery: Britain, 1066–1284* (London, 2003).
Clanchy, M. T., *England and its Rulers, 1066–1272* (Oxford, 1998)
Davies, R. R., *The Age of Conquest: Wales 1063–1415* (Oxford, 1991).
Williams, A., *The English and the Norman Conquest* (Woodbridge, 1995).

General Works
Brown, R. A., Colvin, H., and Taylor, A., *The History of the King's Works*, 2 vols. (HMSO, 1963).
Coulson, C. L. H., *Castles in Medieval Society* (Oxford, 2003).
Creighton, O. H., *Castles and Landscapes* (London, 2002).
———— and Higham, R., *Medieval Castles* (Princes Risborough, 2003)
Kennedy, H., *Crusader Castles* (Cambridge, 1994).
Kenyon, J. R., *Medieval Fortifications* (Leicester, 1990).
———— (ed.), *Castles in Wales and the Marches: Essays in Honour of D. J. Cathcart King* (Cardiff, 1987).

King, D. J. C., *The Castle in England and Wales: An Interpretative History* (London, 1988).

McNeill, T., *Castles* (London, 1992).

———— *Castles in Ireland: Feudal Power in a Gaelic World* (London, 1997).

Morris, M., *Castle* (London, 2003).

Platt, C., *The Medieval Castle in England and Wales* (London, 1982).

Pounds, N. J. G., *The Medieval Castle in England and Wales: A Social and Political History* (Cambridge, 1990).

Tabraham, C., *Scottish Castles and Fortifications* (Edinburgh, 1986).

Thompson, M. W., *The Rise of the Castle* (Cambridge, 1991).

Early Works

Armitage, E. S., *The Early Norman Castles of the British Isles* (London, 1912).

Clark, G. T., *Mediaeval Military Architecture in England*, 2 vols. (London, 1884).

Hamilton Thompson, A., *Military Architecture in England During the Middle Ages* (Oxford, 1912).

The Norman Conquest and Anglo-Norman Castles

Baylé M. (ed.), *L'architecture Normande au Moyen Âge*, 2 vols (Caen, 1997).

Coulson, C., 'Peaceable Power in Norman Castles', *Anglo-Norman Studies* 23 (2001), pp. 69–95.

Fernie, E., *The Architecture of Norman England* (Oxford, 2000).

Higham, R. and Barker, P., *Timber Castles* (London, 1992).

———— *Hen Domen, Montgomery. A Timber Castle on the English-Welsh Border: A Final Report* (Exeter, 2000).

Liddiard, R. (ed.), *Anglo-Norman Castles* (Woodbridge, 2003).

Meirion-Jones, G. Impey, E. and Jones, M. (eds.), *The Seigneurial Residence in Western Europe AD c800–1600* (BAR International Series 1088, 2002).

Mesqui, J., *Châteaux et Enceintes de la France Médiévale*, 2 vols (Paris, 1991;1993).

Renn, D., *Norman Castles in Britain* (London, 1968).

———— 'Burhgeat and Gonfanon: Two Sidelights from the Bayeux Tapestry', *Anglo-Norman Studies* 16 (1994), pp. 178–98 (reprinted in Liddiard, *Anglo-Norman Castles*).

Williams, A., 'A Bell-House and a Burh-Geat: Lordly Residences in England before the Conquest', in C. Harper-Bill and R. Harvey (eds.), *Medieval Knighthood* 4 (Woodbridge, 1992), pp. 221–40 (reprinted in Liddiard, *Anglo-Norman Castles*).

Yver, J., 'Les Châteaux-forts en Normandie jusqu'au Milieu de XIIe Siècle', *Bulletin de la Société des Antiquaires de Normandie* liii (1955–6), pp. 28–115.

Warfare

Bradbury, J., *The Medieval Siege* (Woodbridge, 1992).

France, F., *Western Warfare in the Age of the Crusades, 1000–1300* (London, 1999).

Keen, M. (ed.), *Medieval Warfare: A History* (Oxford, 1999).
Prestwich, M., *Armies and Warfare in the Middle Ages: The English Experience* (New Haven, 1996).
Rogers, R., *Latin Siege Warfare in the Twelfth Century* (Oxford, 1992).
Strickland, M. (ed.), *Anglo-Norman Warfare* (Woodbridge, 1992).
———— *War and Chivalry: the Conduct and Perception of War in England and Normandy, 1066–1217* (Cambridge, 1996).
Smail, R. C., *Crusading Warfare (1097–1193)*, 2nd edn., intr. C. Marshall (Cambridge 1995).

Edwardian Castles

Coldstream, N., 'Architects, Advisors and Design at Edward I's Castles in Wales', *Architectural History* 46 (2003), pp. 19–35.
Mathieu, J. R., 'New Methods on Old Castles: Generating New Ways of Seeing', *Medieval Archaeology* 43 (1999), pp. 115–42.
Morris, R. K., 'The Architecture of Arthurian Enthusiasm: Castle Symbolism in the Reigns of Edward I and his Successors', in M. Strickland (ed.), *Armies, Chivalry and Warfare in Medieval England and France* (Stamford, 1998), pp. 63–81.
Taylor, A. J., *The Welsh Castles of Edward I* (London, 1984).

Later Medieval Castles

Coulson, C., 'Structural Symbolism in Medieval Castle Architecture', *Journal of the British Archaeological Association* 132 (1979), pp. 73–90.
———— 'Fourteenth-Century Castles in Context: Apotheosis or Decline?', in N. Saul (ed.), *Fourteenth Century England* I (Woodbridge, 2000), pp. 133–51.
Emery, A., *Greater Medieval Houses of England and Wales Vol. 1: Northern England* (Cambridge, 1996)
———— *Greater Medieval Houses of England and Wales Vol. 2: Midlands, East Anglia and Wales* (Cambridge, 2000).
Johnson, M., *Behind the Castle Gate: From Medieval to Renaissance* (London, 2002).
Thompson, M.W., *The Decline of the Castle* (Cambridge, 1987).

Index

Place-names indicate castles unless otherwise stated. References in bold indicate illustrations.

Aberystwyth, Cardig., 68, 162.
  fortified town, 68
  works, 114
Abinger, Surr., 15, 38-9, 41
Acre, siege of, 130, 132, 138, 146.
Acton Burnell, Salop., 88; **30**
Adulterine castle. *See* Castle.
Agger, 11, 20, 41.
Aigues-Mortes, Gard, *tour de Constance*, 76.
Albini, family of, 45, 53 156 162.
  earls of Arundel or Sussex, 46, 166.
  of Belvoir, 139.
Aldingbourne, Suss., 16 38.
Aldingham, Lancs., 36.
Alfred, king of Wessex, 2, 22 23 29 164 170.
Alice, queen, widow of Henry I, 46, 166.
Almonry, 152.
Alnoth, master, 'engineer' and mason, 111.
Alnwick, Northumb., 60, 90, 121.
  siege of, 144-5.
Anderida. *See* Pevensey.
Anglesey, Isle of, 70, 72.
Anjou, county of, 9, 10.
  counts of. *See* Fulk Nerra; Geoffrey; Henry II; John; Richard I.
Annapes (Flanders), 30.
Antioch, siege of, 146.
Appleby, Westm., 50, 136.
  siege of, 145-6.
Aquitaine, dukes of, 34.
Archers. *See* Bow.
Ardres, Pas-de-Calais, 15, 18, 19, 40, 107, 151.
  Arnold, lord of, 15, 18, 19.
  Lambert of, 18.
Armitage, Mrs E.S., 1, 21, 22, 23.
Arques-la-Bataille, Seine-Maritime, 14, 53.
  siege of, 12.
Arundel, Suss., 38, 39, 41, 153 166.
  earl of, *See* Albini.
Ascot Doilly, Oxon., 16.
Ashby-de-la-Zouche, Leics., 97, 98.

Baconsthorpe, Norf., 102, 104.
Ballista. See Engine.
Bamburgh, Northumb., 47, 90.
  seige of, 129.
Bampton, Oxon., 55.

Banbury, Oxon., 159.
Bank, rampart, 3, 12, 13, 14, 22, 30, 41, 42, 74, 124, 125.
Barbican, 60, 61, 68, 71, 82, 85, 87, 94, 104, 141.
Barmkin, 91.
Barnard Castle, Durh., 53, 54.
Bastion, 81, 138.
Bastle, 91.
Battlements. *See* Crenellation
Baugé, Maine-et-Loire, 9.
Bayeux, Calvados, 9, 14, 15, 17, 38, 40, 41; **6**.
  bishop of, 11.
  Tapestry, 15, 18, 31, 36, 37, 38, 40, 41, 107, 124.
Baynard's Castle, London, 31.
Beaucaire, Gard, 54*n*. 76.
Beaumaris, Anglesey, 14, 64, 68, 72-4, 76, 80, 99, 155, 156; **XVI, 24**.
  gatehouses, 66-7, 72-3, 139.
  works, 113-14.
Bedford, siege of, 131, 139, 140-3, 147, 149.
Bedingfield, family of, 102.
Beeston, Ches., 64, 67.
Belfry. *See* Siege-tower.
Bellême, Orne, family of, 10.
Belsay, Northumb., 91.
Berkeley, Glos., 58, 159.
Berkhamstead, Herts., 38, 58, 59, 60, 87; **18**.
Berry Pomeroy, Devon, 105.
Bigod, family, earls of Norfolk, 43, 47, 85, 167.
Blois, counts of, county of, 8, 9, 10, 15, 39.
  Henry of, bishop of Winchester, 61.
Bodiam, Suss., 99, 130, 156, 157; **XXVI, 35**.
Bolingbroke, Lincs., 64.
Bolton-in-Wensleydale, Yorks., 99; **XXV**.
  siege of, 171.
Bore, 130, 131-2.
Born, Bertran de, 124, 145.
Borough, *burge, burgh, burh*, 2, 5, 22, 26-30,42, 61, 83, 111, 164.
  burg-bot, 29.
  burg-bryce, 29.
  burh-geat, 28 and *n*. 32, 30.
  Burghal Hidage, 22.
  burgh-work, 108.

Bow, 138.
  bowmen, 136, 138.
  crossbow, 126, 138, 141.
  crossbowmen, 131, 136, 138, 141, 143.
  longbow, 138.
  Cf. Loops.
Bowes, Yorks., 47, 111.
Bramber, Suss., 38.
Brattices, 110.
Bréauté, Fawkes de, 141, 143, 148.
Brick, 97, 99, 102, 104, 118, 119, 120.
Bridge, 41, 132.
  draw-bridge, 67, 68, 69, 81, 92, 93, 104, 132.
  turning-bridge, 132.
Bridgenorth, Salop., 47, 49.
Brionne, Eure, 14.
  siege of, 12, 14.
Bristol, Glos., 47, 57, 159.
Brittany, Eleanor of, 159.
Brix, Manche, 9.
Broch, 5.
Bronllys, Brec., 53.
Brough, Westm., siege of, 145, 146, 147.
Buckenham, New, Norf., 53, 54, 55, 162, 165, 166.
Buckenham, Old, Norf., 162, 165, 166.
Builth, Brec., 59, 68, 86.
  works, 114.
Bungay, Suff., 47, 49, 50, 167.
Burgh. *See* Borough.
Burgh Castle, Suff., fortress, 1.
Burgh, Hubert de, 131, 136, 140.
Burnell, Robert, 88.
Bywell, Northumb., 90.

Cadbury, South, Som., fortress of, 22.
Caen, Calvados, 9, 53, 110.
  fortified town, 9.
  stone, 46, 49, 111.
Caernarvon, 14, 30, 38, 42, 62, 64, 65, 68-71, 72, 80, 81, 87, 106, 155, 157; **XIII, 21**.
  fortified town, 38, 68.
  Eagle Tower, 69, 70.
  King's Gate, 69.
  Queen's Gate, 69.
  works, 69-71, 113-14.
Caerphilly, Glam., 64, 78, 80-1, 85, 87,

99, 106, 121, 130, 151, 155, 156,
157; **XX, 26**.
gatehouses, 66, 67, 68, 139.
screen wall, 80-1.
Caister-by-Yarmouth, Norf., 92, 97,
99; **33**.
works, 117-18.
Caldicot, Mon., 54.
Camber, Suss., coastal fort, 1, 89.
Cambridge, 32, 86, 96.
Cannon. *See* Gun.
Canterbury, Kent, 45, 47, 136.
Carcassonne, Aude, fortified city, 3.
Cardigan, 86.
Carew, Pembs., 105; **38**.
Carisbrooke, Isle of Wight, 36, 37, 41,
58, 60.
Carlisle, Cumb., 47, 57, 90, 153.
siege of, 145.
Castel del Monte, S. Italy, 78, 94.
Castle:
adulterine, 55, 162.
as armoury, 123, 149.
as centre of colonization, 10-11,
165-6.
as centre of local government, 123,
158.
as prison, 123, 158-60.
as treasury, 123, 158.
baronial, 10, 78-81, 117-20, 121,
156, 158, 163, 165, 170.
concentric, 62, 64, 72, 73-4, 75, 78,
80, 82, 94, 99.
demolition, slighting, 55, 94, 105,
143, 163, 165, 167.
earthwork and timber, 12-13, 30,
35-6, 55, 57-8, 107-8, 124.
enclosure type, 12-14, 15, 19-20, 28,
30, 36, 42-3, 55, 60, 64, 65, 69,
71, 95, 96, 119.
timber replaced by stone, 55-7, 109,
163. *See also* Bank; Castle, motte-
and-bailey; Ditch; Tower;
Palisade.
Cf. Castle, concentric; Castle,
quadrangular; Keep; Tower,
great.
episcopal, 8, 121, 159.
in England before Conquest, 24-30.
military rôle, 1, 9, 11-12, 123ff., 135,
148, 166.
model, 159.
motte-and-bailey, 15-20, 36-42, 55,
57, 60, 75, 87, 92, 103, 107, 124.
Cf. Motte.
movement of sites, 165.
nomenclature: *castele, castelle*, 24, 25,
27; *castellum*, 8, 21, 24, 27; *castrum*,
8, 25, 27, 41; *château*, 1, 21, 89;
firmamentum, 8, 31; *firmitas*, 8;
municipium, 8, 41; *munitio*, 8, 21,
31, 41; *oppidum*, 8
numbers and distribution, 5ff., 31,
55, 108, 161ff.
political importance, 166-8.
quadrangular, 98-9, 105.
range, 124, 148-9.
residential rôle, 1ff., 39-41, 46, 48-9,
50-2, 59, 60, 87, 87-90, 95, 98-9,
103, 105, 150ff., 165-6, 168.
rock sites, 62, 64, 66, 69, 72, 113,
130, 132.
symbolism, 70, 97, 107, 135, 150,
155-6, 165, 168.
tenure, 165.

time taken to build, 107-8, 110-11,
112-13, 114.
water defences, 64, 81, 99, 104, 130,
131, 143.
Cf. Moat.
Castle Acre, Norf., 37, 38, 45, 59; **10**.
fortified town, 38.
Castle Cornet, Guernsey, 86.
Castle-guard, 133.
Castle Hedingham, Essex, 46, 50, 57,
156.
Castle Neroche, Som., 19, 36.
Castle Rising, Norf., 14, 45, 46, 49, 50,
52 and *n.* 71, 55, 57, 156, 162, 166;
15.
Chambers, 12, 18, 47, 48, 50, 54, 60,
71, 94, 99, 121, 151, 152-6 *passim*,
158.
chamber block, 58, 88.
Chancery, records and rolls, 47, 114,
131, 136, 148, 157.
Liberate Rolls, 153-4.
Chapel, 12, 18, 41-2, 44, 46, 49, 50, 52,
58, 60, 71, 88, 94, 99, 103, 118, 121,
151, 152, 153, 154, 155.
Chaplain, 110, 135, 136, 153.
Chartly, Staffs., 54.
Châteaudun, Eure-et-Loir, 53.
Château-Gaillard, Eure, 62, 64, 81,
106, 121; **XII, 20**.
keep, 47, 50, 54, 62, 65; **XII**.
siege, 139.
works, 112-13, 114.
Château-Gontier, Mayenne, 9.
Château-sur-Epte, Eure, 53.
Chaumont-sur-Loire, arr. Blois, 9.
Chaworth, Payn de, 78.
Chepstow, Mon., 3, 45, 50, 85;
XXIII, 28.
Cherbourg, Manche, 9.
Cherrueix, Ille-et-Vilaine, 9.
Chester, Ches., 68.
earl of, 64, 70, 109.
Chilham, Kent, 47, 53, 54; **XI**.
Chinon, Indre-et-Loire, 3, 53, 110.
Chipchase, Northumb., 91.
Chirk, Denb., 68.
Christchurch, Hants., 60.
Cinglais, le (district of Normandy), 10-
11, 19, 165.
Clare, Suff., family of, 67, 78.
Clavering, Essex, 24, 25.
Clifford, Heref., 60.
Clinton, family of, 47, 168.
Clocks, 95, 156.
Cloisters, 154, 157.
Clun, Salop., 17, 59.
Colchester, Essex, 44, 45, 46, 48, 50;
13.
siege, 171.
Conches, Eure, 53.
Conisborough, Yorks., 53, 54; **X, 16**.
Constable, custodian, 31, 110, 135,
136, 142, 144-5, 148, 159.
Consuetudines et Justicie (1091), 3n. 4,
30n. 45.
Conway, Caerns., 38, 42, 62, 64, 68,
69, 71-2, 74, 130, 157; **XIV, 22**.
fortified town,38, 68.
gateways, 66, 71.
works, 114-15.
Corbridge, Northumb., Vicar's Pele,
91.
Corfe, Dors., 47, 84-5, 87, 143, 149,
151, 159.

'Gloriette', 61, 98, 153.
siege, 171.
Corse Castle, Aberdeenshire, 87.
Cour Marigny, La, Loiret, 17.
Crenellation, 3, 38, 59, 69, 71, 89, 90,
91, 104, 132, 157; **XXX**.
false, 88, 102, 104.
licence to crenellate, 3, 90, 95, 99.
Cricklade, Wilts., Anglo-Saxon
borough, 22.
Crossbow. *See* Bow.
Crusade, crusaders, 2, 5, 19, 62.
Curtain-wall. *See* Wall.

Deal, Kent, coastal fort, 1, 89.
Dean, Forest of, 142.
Denbigh, 68.
Dilapidations, surveys of, 169.
Dinan, C.-du-Nord, 15, 17, 38, 39, 41;
5.
siege, 124.
Ditch, moat, 3, 12, 13, 14, 15, 22, 30,
37, 38, 42, 43, 68, 69, 73, 74, 75, 82,
89, 94, 96, 98, 99, 102, 110, 119,
124, 125, 131, 132, 142.
double, 38.
rock-cut, 62, 72.
Ditchers, 115.
Dol, Ille-et-Vilaine, 15, 17 and *n.* 53,
38, 41.
Domfront, Orne, 45, 53.
siege, 12.
Donjon, 3-4, 9, 12, 14, 15, 17, 18, 31,
40, 42, 45, 46, 48, 53, 54, 59, 65, 69,
76, 85, 94, 95, 97, 118, 159.
Cf. Keep.
Donnington, Berks., siege, 171.
Doué-la-Fontaine, Maine-et-Loire, 8,
9, 14, 16, 19, 44; **3**.
Dourdan, Seine-et-Oise, 53, 76.
Dovecotes, 154, 157.
Dover, Kent, 3, 25-7, 31, 42, 43, 44,
54, 61-2, 64, 65, 66-7, 68, 83-4, 86,
107, 110, 113, 121, 133, 139, 156; **I**.
Anglo-Saxon borough, 26-7; **I**.
Avranches Tower, 43, 61.
gateways, 61, 66, 83-4, 140.
Iron Age fortress, 2, 22, 27; **I**.
keep, 17, 47, 48-9, 50, 52, 53, 61,
86, 111-12; **VIII, I**.
siege, 132, 136, 139, 140, 148.
works, 111-12.
Drawbridge. *See* Bridge.
Dudley, Worcs., 95, 96, 97, 105.
Dunstanburgh, Northumb., 66, 97.
Dunster, Som., 39.
Durham, 16, 17, 32, 42, 59, 60, 90,
104, 121.
bishop of, 47, 49, 104.
Laurence, prior of, 17.
Durtal, Maine-et-Loire, 9.
Dyserth, Flints., 65.

Edlingham, Northumb., 91.
Edward I, 13, 34, 55, 59, 62, 64-88
passim, 90, 113-15 *passim*, 121, 126,
127, 138, 139, 143, 148.
Edward II, 71, 87, 96, 98, 159.
Edward III, 59, 60, 94-5, 103, 104,
106, 114, 120-1, 127, 155-6.
Edward IV, 49, 92, 120, 156.
Eleanor, queen of Edward I, 71, 157.
Engineers, 136. *See* Alnoth; Maurice;
St George.

Engine, siege, 72, 95, 125-7, 128, 130, 131, 138, 140, 141, 142, 144.
  ballista, 126-7, 138.
  mangon, mangonel, 126, 138, 141, 142.
  petraria, 126, 131, 132, 138, 141, 142.
  springald, 126.
  trebuchet, 95, 126, 127, 138, 141; **XXVIII, XXIX**.
  See also Bore; Gun; Ram.
Escalade, 65, 131.
Etal, Northumb., 90.
Etampes, Seine-et-Oise, 53 and *n.*, 54, 86.
Ewyas Harold, Heref., 24, 25, 36, 39.
Exchequer, records and rolls, 157.
  Pipe Rolls, 47, 53, 59, 109, 110-11, 112, 113, 114, 126, 136, 153.
  works accounts, 112, 113, 114, 117-20.
  'particulars' of, 114, 119.
Exeter, Devon, 32, 42, 153.
  Anglo-Saxon borough, 22.
  fortified city, 42.
  gatetower, 42, 61, 66.
  siege, 130.
Eye, Suff., 167.

Falaise, Calvados, 9, 14, 17, 45, 47, 53.
Falcons, 152.
Fantosme, Jordan, 144-6, 147.
Farnham, Surr., 16, 39, 50, 59, 104, 120, 121; **8**.
Faye-la-Vineuse, Indre-et-Loire, 9.
Ferté-en-Bray, La, Seine-Maritime, 19.
Feudalism, 2, 4, 5-8, 10, 17, 19, 21 and *n.* 3, 22-3, 27, 28, 31, 32, 78, 89, 133, 135, 150, 156, 158, 163-71 *passim*.
  'Bastard', 96.
Feudal service, 147, 165.
  See also Castle-guard.
Fief, 6, 7, 10, 31, 133, 165.
Fire, 126, 131.
  Greek, 126.
Fire-places, 18, 44, 49, 52, 97, 155, 156.
Fish-ponds, 152.
Flanders, count of, county of, 10, 18, 145.
Flint, 68, 74, 76-8, 86, 96.
  fortified town, 68.
  works, 114-15.
Fortifications other than castles:
  Anglo-Saxon. *See* Borough.
  Carolingian, 2, 5.
  fortified towns and cities, 3, 4, 12, 22, 33, 38, 42, 43, 62, 68-78 *passim*, 114, 170.
  Iron Age, 2, 4, 22, 26, 27, 42, 61, 83, 111.
  modern, 1, 2, 4, 89, 168.
    Tudor coastal forts, 89, 138, 168.
  Roman, 1, 2, 4, 22, 42, 43, 58.
  Viking, 2, 4, 13.
  Cf. Broch; Fortified manor; Rath.
Fortified manor, 3, 87-8, 90, 102, 118, 119.
  domus defensabiles, 3, 87.
Framlingham, Suff., 42, 43, 65, 110, 167; **12**.
  siege, 136.
Fréteval, Loir-et-Cher, 53.

Fulk Nerra, count of Anjou, 8, 9, 10, 14, 20.

Gaillefontaine, Seine-Maritime, 19.
Garden, 118, 152, 153, 154, 157.
Garderobes, 44, 47, 52 and *n.* 71, 96.
Garrison, 124, 133-8, 140, 141, 142, 143.
  hanged, 142, 147.
  mounted, 135, 136, 138, 148.
Gate, gatehouse, gatetower, 14, 41, 42, 43, 49, 55, 58, 60, 61, 64, 66-8, 69-85 *passim*, 88, 91, 92, 94, 97, 99, 102, 103, 104, 105, 111, 119, 124, 132, 139, 140, 144.
  postern, 72, 94, 99, 138.
  sally-port, 76.
  water-gate, 69, 71, 75-6, 80, 81-2, 83, 103.
  Cf. Portcullis.
Geoffrey, count of Anjou, 34.
Gisors, Eure, 53, 59.
Glacis, 54.
Gleaston, Lancs., 91.
Gloucester, 47, 159.
Goodrich, Heref., 64, 66, 68, 130.
Guildford, Surr., 17, 47, 59.
Gun, 95, 97, 127-9, 138, 168; **40**.
  hand, 128.
  Cf. Engine.
Gunports, 92, 93, 98, 129, 138, 168.
  Cf. Loops.
Gunpowder, 90, 125, 127-9, 130, 138, 168.

Hadleigh, Essex, 95.
Hall, 12, 14, 42, 45, 47, 50, 58, 71, 72, 78, 80, 92, 94, 99, 103, 104, 121, 152-8 *passim*.
  hall and chamber block, 88.
Harlech, Merion., 64, 68, 72, 74, 76, 87, 130, 138, 155; **XV, 23**.
  gatehouse, 66, 67, 72, 73.
  works, 113-15.
Hastings, Suss., 17, 26, 31, 36, 37, 38; **7**.
  works, 107.
Haughley, Suff., 39.
Hawarden, Flints., 68.
Helmingham Hall, Suff., 102.
Hen Domen, Montgom., 36, 37, 38, 41, 43, 58; **IV**.
Henry I, king of England, duke of Normandy, 14, 34, 45, 46, 47, 53, 59, 78, 96, 162, 166.
Henry II, king of England, duke of Normandy, count of Anjou, 11, 17, 34, 43, 47, 48, 49, 52, 53, 55, 59, 61, 62, 83, 96, 98, 108-12, 121, 136, 144, 152-3, 159, 162, 167, 170.
Henry III, king of England, 65, 81-6 *passim*, 114, 121, 152, 153, 154, 157, 158.
Henry the Fowler, 2.
Hereford, 25 and *n.*
Herstmonceux, Suss., 102.
Hertford, 168.
Hever, Kent., 102.
Hoarding, 17*n.* 53, 50, 59, 66, 71, 86, 132; **XXXI**.
  Cf. Machicolation.
Holt, Denbighs., 68.
Homestead, homestead moats, 5, 29.
Homme, Le (l'Isle Marie), Calvados, 9.
Honour and *caput* of, 11, 33, 158, 166.

Hopton, Salop., 87.
Houdan, Seine-et-Oise, 53 and *n.* 81.
Household, 4-5, 7, 12, 18, 50, 69, 99, 103, 114, 135, 151.
  Cf. Itinerary.
  'Houses in the castle', 60, 98-9.
  See Chambers; Chapel; Hall; Kitchens.
Hoverburg, the, *nr.* Cologne, 16.
Huntingdon, 32.
Husterknupp, the, *nr.* Frimmersdorf, 19.

Isle Marie. *See* Homme.
Issoudun, Indre, 55.
Itinerary, 151, 169.
  Cf. Houshold.
Ivry-la-Bataille, Eure, 9, 10, 14.

John, king of England, duke of Normandy, count of Anjou, 34, 46, 47, 53, 54, 55, 61, 109, 111, 130, 132, 136, 138, 139, 140, 141, 142, 147, 148, 153, 154, 157, 158, 162, 166, 167, 168.

Kaersgärd, Denmark, 16.
Keep, 3 and *n.* 6, 41.
  shell, 4, 15, 16, 17, 41, 49, 58-60, 87, 121, 152, 156.
  tower, great tower, 3, 4, 8-9, 12-13, 15-18, 19, 32, 35, 36, 38-9, 40-1, 43-55, 57, 60, 61, 62, 64-5, 76-8, 83, 85-6, 91, 92, 94, 95-8, 105, 107, 110, 111-12, 117, 118, 130, 132, 140, 142, 144, 156, 158, 167.
  Cf. Donjon; Motte; Pele.
Kenilworth, Warw., 47, 50, 64, 81, 104, 121, 130, 156, 168.
  siege, 132, 138, 139, 143, 147.
Kidwelly, Carms., 66, 78, 81, 87, 121; **XIX, 25**.
Kirby Muxloe, Leics., 102.
  works, 117, 118-20.
Kitchens, 18, 28, 47, 52, 58, 60, 78, 80, 93, 99, 104, 152, 153, 154, 155.
Knaresborough, Yorks., 96, 97, 168.
Knights, 6, 7, 8, 11, 31, 110, 124-5, 133, 135, 136, 139, 141, 145, 146, 148, 153, 165, 166.

Lacy, families of, 49, 68, 87, 109, 168.
Lancaster, 104, 139.
  duchy of, 169.
Langeais, Indre-et-Loire, 8, 14, 45; **2**.
Launceston, Corn., 53, 59, 60; **19**.
Layer Marney, Essex, gatehouse, 102.
Leeds, Kent, 64, 66, 81, 130.
Leicester, 148.
Lewes, Suss., 38, 59, 60, 104; **VI**.
Lillebonne, Seine-Maritime, 53.
Lincoln, 32, 38, 148.
Llantilio. *See* White Castle.
London, three castles in, 30, 31.
  Tower of, 15, 31, 42, 68, 73, 81-3, 84, 87, 95, 138, 139, 143, 149, 158-9, 160, 168; **XXI, 27**.
  White Tower in, 15, 31, 42, 44, 46, 48, 50, 52, 65, 81, 86, 97, 155; **XXI, 27**.
  works, 108, 121.
Longford, Wilts., 'castle', 102.
Longtown, Heref., 53, 54,
Loops, 69, 71, 76, 93, 132, 157.
Lordship, 2-7 *passim*, 9, 10-11, 15, 17,

22-3, 32, 97-8, 99, 150-1, 158, 164, 165, 166.
Loudun, Vienne, 15.
Ludgershall, Wilts., 153, 154.
Ludlow, Salop., 42, 43, 49, 97; **II**.
chapel, 42, 60.
Lumley, Northumb., 99.
Lydford, Devon, 16, 22, 50.
Anglo-Saxon borough, 22.

Machicolation, 50, 54, 66, 67, 71, 90, 91, 92, 95, 97, 98, 104, 132; **XXXII**.
false, 102, 104.
Magna Carta, 168.
Maiden's Castle, Dors., fortress, 1.
Maine, county of, 10.
Mandeville, family of, 33, 168.
Manéhouville, Seine-Maritime, 19.
Mangonel. *See* Engine.
Manorbier, Pembs., 151-2, 156.
Mans, Le, Sarthe, fortified city, 2
Manse, 5, 29.
Marches, 10.
of Scotland, 90.
of Wales, 52, 53, 68, 81, 90, 92, 115, 155, 163, 164.
Markenfield, Yorks., fortified manor, 87.
Marlborough, Wilts., 153, 154.
Mateflon, arr. Angers, 9.
Maulévrier, Seine-Maritime, 9.
Maurice 'the engineer', 48, 112.
Maxstoke, Warw., 99.
'Merchem', 20, 40-1 and *n*. 26.
Meurtrières, 67, 69, 104, 132.
Middleham, Yorks., 47, 49, 50, 86.
Mills, 139.
Mine, miners, 83, 86, 113, 130-1, 140, 141, 142.
Mirebeau, Vienne, 9.
Mitford, Northumb., 59.
Moat. *See* Ditch; Homestead.
Moncontour, Vienne, 9.
Mondoubleau, Loir-et-Cher, 14.
Montbazon, Indre-et-Loire, 9, 14.
Montfichet, London, 31.
Montlhéry, Seine-et-Oise, 98.
Montrésor, Indre-et-Loire, 9.
Montreuil-Bellay, Maine-et-Loire, 9.
Montrichard, Loire-et-Cher, 9.
Motte, 3, 12, 13, 15-20, 35-42 *passim*, 45, 53, 55, 57-60, 69, 70, 86, 92, 96, 97, 104, 107, 121, 124, 141, 151, 152, 156.
Motte-Montboyau, La, Indre-et-Loire, 9, 15, 19.

Naworth, Cumb., 91.
Newark, Notts., 121, 148.
siege, 171.
Newcastle-upon-Tyne, Northumb., 47-9, 50, 90, 111, 112.
Black Gate, 84.
siege, 144.
Niort, Deux Sèvres, 50, 54.
Nogent-le-Rotrou, Orne, 14.
Norham, Northumb., 47, 49, 50, 59, 129.
Norman Conquest, 5, 19, 21ff., 55, 57, 108, 124, 162-5 *passim*.
Normandy, duchy of, 5, 9-14 *passim*, 19, 20.
dukes of. *See* Henry; John; Richard; Robert; William.

Norwich, Norf., 14, 31, 32, 37, 39, 45, 46, 52, 136, 156, 167.
Nottingham, 32, 126, 148, 152-3, 158.
Nunney, Som., 92, 93, 95, 96, 98; **32**.
siege, 96, 171.

Oakham, Rutland, 42, 60.
Odiham, Hants., 47, 54, 55, 166; **XI**.
siege, 136.
works, 111.
Of People's Ranks and Laws, 27-8.
Old Sarum, Wilts., 22, 42, 61, 98, 155.
Anglo-Saxon borough, 22, 42.
Iron Age fortress, 2, 3, 13, 42.
Old Wardour, Wilts., 97.
Ongar, Essex, 39.
Orford, Suff., 43, 47, 52, 53, 54, 55, 136, 167; **IX, 17**.
works, 110-11.
Oxburgh Hall, Norf., 102.

Palisade, 3, 12, 13, 14, 15, 16, 22, 29, 30, 37, 38, 41, 43, 55, 58, 59, 74, 110, 124, 125.
Cf. Pele.
Paris, Bastille in, 95.
Park, 153, 154, 156, 157.
Passavant, Maine-et-Loire, 9.
Peak, the, in Castleton, Derbs., 15, 43, 47, 49, 50, 52.
Peckforton, Ches., 'castle', 102.
Pele, 55, 91, 97.
Pembroke, 53, 54.
siege, 171.
Penmaen, Glam., 28, 42; **III**.
Penthouse, 131.
Penwortham, Lancs., 39.
Perche, counts of, 10.
Petraria. See Engine.
Pevensey, Suss., 26, 31, 35, 42, 46.
Roman fortress, 42.
Philip II, Augustus, king of France, 44, 53, 54, 113, 138.
Philippa of Hainault, queen of Edward III, 95.
Pickering, Yorks., 59, 60, 65, 87.
Pierrefonds, Oise, 95.
Playford Hall, Suff., 102.
Pleshey, Essex, 33, 37, 38; **V, 9**.
fortified town, 33, 38.
Plessis Grimoult, Le, Calvados, 11, 13-14.
Plinth, batter, spur, 50, 65-6, 71, 78, 104, 105, 132.
See also Glacis.
Pontefract, Yorks., 96, 159, 168.
Portchester, Hants., 3, 22, 42, 47.
Anglo-Saxon borough, 3, 22, 42.
Roman fort, 3, 22, 42, 65.
Portcullis, 67, 69, 92, 104, 132.
Porter, 110, 135, 136.
Postern. *See* Gate.
Prudhoe, Northumb., siege of, 145.
Puiset, Le, Eure-et-Loire, 38*n*. 19., 124, 125, 138, 144.
Purveyance, *See* Works.

Queenborough, Sheppey, Kent, 60, 78, 93-5, 99; **XXIV**.

Raby, Durh., 99.
Raglan, Mon., 65, 92-3, 96, 97; **31**.
siege, 92, 171.
Ram, battering, 130, 131-2.
Rampart. *See* Bank.

Rath, 5, 13.
Rendability, 4, 165 and *n*. 10.
Rennes, Ille-et-Vilaine, 15, 17, 38, 41; **4**.
Restormel, Corn., 59, 60, 94.
Revetment, 22, 39 and *n*. 58, 75, 81, 142.
Rhineland, 5, 6, 16, 19, 20, 97.
Rhuddlan, Flints., 68, 74-6; **XVII**.
fortified town, 68.
works, 114-17.
Richard I, duke of Normandy (942-96),9, 10, 44.
Richard II, duke of Normandy (996-1026), 9.
Richard III, duke of Normandy (1026-7), 9.
Richard I, king of England, duke of Normandy, count of Anjou, etc., 34, 50, 54, 62, 65, 81, 106, 109, 112-13, 121, 126, 130, 136, 138, 162, 167.
Richard's Castle, Heref., 24-5, 36; **II**.
Richmond, Yorks., 42, 43, 47, 49, 60, 97, 133, 145, 157.
'Ring-work', 13, 28, 30, 36, 65.
Robert the Magnificent, duke of Normandy, 9, 11.
Roche-Guyon, La, Seine-et-Oise, 54-5.
Rochester, Kent, 43, 46, 49, 50, 52, 86, 107, 156; **VII, 14, 39**.
siege, 130, 132, 136, 139, 140, 144, 148.
Rockingham, Northants., 67.
Rouen, Seine-Maritime, 9, 14, 17, 24, 44, 53.

St Briavel's, Glos., 67, 68, 142.
St-Florent-le-Vieil, Maine-et-Loire, 9, 20.
St George, master James of, engineer, mason, master of the king's works in Wales, 73, 117.
St Mawes, Corn., coastal fort, 89.
St Peter Port, Guernsey, 86.
Ste-Maure, Maine-et-Loire, 9.
Salvin, Anthony, 102.
Sandal, Yorks., 58, 60, 103.
Scarborough, Yorks., 47, 49, 111.
Schloss Kempen, 97.
Seals, 150.
Shaftesbury, Dors., Anglo-Saxon borough, 22.
Sherborne, Dors., 60, 98.
Sheriff Hutton, Yorks., 99.
Shirburn, Oxon., 99.
Sieges, 12, 39, 46, 83, 90, 92, 96, 97, 105, 113, 123ff., 169, 171.
siege-tower, belfry, 131, 132, 138, 141.
Cf. Bore; Engine; Escalade; Gun; Mine; Penthouse; Ram.
Sizergh, Westm., 91.
Skenfrith, Mon., 53, 54, 155.
Skipton, Yorks., 67.
Solar, 78. *Cf*. Chambers.
Sortie, 84, 124, 138.
South Mimms, Herts., 16, 17, 39, 40, 57, 58.
Southampton, 96, 97.
Springald. *See* Engine.
Spur. *See* Plinth.
Stables, 60,154.

Stephen, king of England, 11, 34, 35, 47, 55, 108, 162-3, 165.
Stirling, siege of, 126, 127.
Stockade. *See* Palisade.
Stokesay, Salop., 87-8; **29**.
Sulgrave, Northants., 30, 42.

Tamworth, Staffs., 22, 59, 60.
Anglo-Saxon borough, 22.
Tarascon, Bouches-du-Rhône, 95.
Tattershall, Lincs., 52, 96, 97-8, 102; **34**.
works, 118.
Thetford, Norf., 39, 167.
Thornbury, Glos., 120.
Tickhill, Yorks., 39, 47, 54; **X**.
Tillières, Eure, 9.
Tomb, 150
Tonbridge, Kent, 38, 60, 66-7.
fortified town, 38.
siege, 148.
Totnes, Devon, 16, 39.
Tours, Indre-et-Loire, fortified city, 2.
Tower
great tower. *See* Keep.
mural, flanking, tower, 14, 41, 42, 43, 54, 58, 60-1 *passim,* 64, 65-7, 69-85 *passim,* 88, 92, 94, 95, 97, 98, 99, 102, 104, 105, 110, 111, 119, 132, 152.
See also Gatetower; Siege-tower.
'Tower-house', 96-7.
Trebuchet. *See* Engine.
Trelleborg, Zealand, Viking fortress, 2, 13.

Trematon, Corn., 59.
Très Riches Heures, 58, 103, 150.
Tretower, Brec., 53, 59.
Trèves, Maine-et-Loire, 9.
Truce, 143, 144, 145-6.

Verneuil-sur-Avre, Eure, 53.
Vincennes, Seine, 52.
Vineyard, 152, 156, 157.

Wages. *See* Works.
Wall, curtain. *See* Castle.
enclosure type; Towers, mural.
mantlet, 60, 93.
screen, 81.
wing, 59.
Wallingford, Berks., 22, 57.
Anglo-Saxon borough, 22
Walmer, Kent, coastal fort, 1, 89.
Walton, Suff., 167.
Wareham, Dors., 16, 47, 50.
Anglo-Saxon borough, 22.
Wark, Northumb., 136.
siege, 144-5, 146.
Warkworth, Northumb., 97, 98.
siege, 144.
Warwick, 32, 103-4, 121, 156; **37**.
Wasserburgen, 97.
Watchmen, 18, 110, 135, 136.
Well, 94, 139.
Wenham, Little, Suff., 87.
White Castle, Llantilio, Mon., 65, 155.
William I, the Conqueror, duke of Normandy, king of England, 9, 11, 12, 14, 15, 17, 20, 23, 25-7, 30-2, 34,

42, 44, 81, 82, 83, 96, 107-8, 110, 130, 156, 164, 165.
William II, Rufus, king of England, 34, 43, 162.
Winchester, Hants., 30, 86, 152, 153-4, 157.
Anglo-Saxon borough, 22.
Roman fortified town, 22.
Windsor, Berks., 17, 38, 57, 59, 61, 95, 98, 103, 106, 133, 142, 152, 154, 155-6, 158, 159; **36**.
siege, 148.
works, 104, 120-1, 155-6.
Wingfield, Derbs., 102.
Wingfield, Suff., 99, 102, 170.
Wolvesey, Hants., palace, 61.
Worcester, 32, 55.
Anglo-Saxon borough, 2.
Works, 106ff.
labour, impressment, 108, 115, 120; **XXVII**.
strike, 115.
purveyance, 120.
seasonal, 110-11, 114, 119.
services and taxes, 108.
wages, 114, 115, 118, 119.
See also St George, master James of.

York, two castles, 30, 32, 36 and *n.* 7, 37, 41, 107, 110, 168.
Clifford's Tower, 36*n.* 7, 54, 55, 86, 96.
Yverdon, Switzerland, 76.